Monographs in Computer Science

T0191554

Editors

David Gries
Fred B. Schneider

Springer
New York
Berlin
Heidelberg
Barcelona
Hong Kong
London
Milan
Paris
Singapore
Tokyo

Monographs in Computer Science

W.H.J. Feijen
A.J.M. van Gasteren

On a Method of Multiprogramming

Foreword by David Gries

Springer

W.H.J. Feijen
A.J.M. van Gasteren
Department of Computing Science
Eindhoven University of Technology
5600 MB Eindhoven
The Netherlands

Series Editors

David Gries
Department of Computer Science
Cornell University
Upson Hall
Ithaca, NY 14853-7501
USA

Fred B. Schneider
Department of Computer Science
Cornell University
Upson Hall
Ithaca, NY 14853-7501
USA

ISBN 978-1-4419-3179-5

Library of Congress Cataloging-in-Publication Data
Feijen, W. H. J.
    On a method of multiprogramming / W.H.J. Feijen, A.J.M. Van
Gasteren.
        p.   cm. — (Monographs in computer science)
    Includes index and bibliographical references.

    1. Multiprogramming (Electronic computers)   I. Van Gasteren,
A.J.M.   II. Title.   III. Series.
QA76.6.F43   1999
005.4´34—dc21   99-15370

Printed on acid-free paper.

To Edsger W. Dijkstra

and

Ria Dijkstra-Debets

Foreword

Just over 25 years ago, Susan Owicki started working on the problem of proving the correctness of concurrent programs (called multiprograms in this book) for her Ph.D. thesis. At the time, there was little work on the subject, and my attempts to teach that little work in a summer course had led to dissatisfaction and to my asking her to work on the topic. Susan did a great job, coming up with the idea of interference freeness, which, in one form or another, is at the core of most work on correctness of concurrent programs. Interference freeness is quite simple to state.

> Consider two processes P and Q, which communicate using shared variables. If execution of P doesn't interfere with the proof of correctness of Q, and if execution of Q doesn't interfere with the proof of correctness of P, then P and Q can be executed properly together —their correctness proofs are consistent with their concurrent execution. P and Q are said to be interference free.

Thus was born the first complete programming logic for partial correctness of multiprograms, now called the "Owicki/Gries Theory". By concentrating on a process not interfering with the proof of another process, instead of with execution of that other process, the task of proving correctness of multiprograms became tractable.

But it is difficult to prove a program correct after it has been written. It is far easier to develop the proof and program hand in hand —with the proof ideas leading the way. A methodology for developing programs, which is based on a theory of correctness, is quite necessary.

In 1969, Tony Hoare gave us the first partial correctness logic for sequential programs in his famous paper "On an axiomatic basis for computer programming". It took five more years for Edsger W. Dijkstra to present us with a methodology for developing programs, in his 1974 paper "Guarded commands, nondeterminacy and formal derivation of programs" and his 1976 book "A Discipline of Programming".

However, a useful methodology for developing multiprograms has eluded us. There have been attempts in the past 25 years, but, as far as I can see, nothing emerged that was really simple, teachable, usable. Until this book!

Wim Feijen and Netty van Gasteren have done a marvelous job of discussing the formal development of multiprograms. First, they keep the core theory simple, allowing one to focus on the problem instead of the tool being used to solve it. So much in the literature is encumbered by awkward, complex theory!

Second, they develop just a few manageable techniques for reducing the workload required for proving correctness, like orthogonality, system invariants, mutual exclusion, exploitation of symmetry, the construction of a body of useful theorems, and abstraction.

Third, they create a nice notation for remembering what remains to be accomplished in developing a proof and program. In science and engineering, so much depends on the notations we use!

Fourth, they carefully craft strategies and principles to be used in guiding the development of a multiprogram, keeping them to a manageable few. So much depends on the guidelines we can give others and the way they are presented, and Wim and Netty have done a superb job in this regard.

Fifth, they illustrate their methodology on many real multiprograms — from concurrent vector writing to the safe sluice to Peterson's mutual exclusion example to handshaking protocols. The reader has no choice but to be convinced that the ideas in this book are useful!

Finally, the writing is impeccable! Simple. Clear. Economical. Terse, but not to a fault. The care that went into writing this book exudes from every page.

The formal development of programs has not caught on in the world of computer science as much as some of us had expected it would. Not that every program should be constructed formally —but the ideas should filter into one's everyday programming. For example, it just made sense, we thought, for every beginning programming course to teach about loop invariants when discussing loops. And yet, today, in most computing departments, majors can go through four years of study without learning these basic concepts!

The reason for this may lie in the fact that teaching a methodology implies teaching people how to think, and most people have an aversion to changing how they think. Their motto might be, "We know how to think; just give us the facts." All of us have this tendency in us to some degree, as we can see from Mark Twain's, "Nothing needs changing so much as the habits of others."

Therefore, this fine book that Wim and Netty have produced may not have the impact that it could (or should). But those who revel in economy of thought, who delight in seeing how powerful clear thought can be, who like to see guiding principles and strategies at work, who are interested in clarifying their own thought processes concerning the development of multiprograms —all these people are in for a treat when they pick up this book.

David Gries
William L. Lewis Professor Of Engineering and
Cornell Weiss Presidential Fellow
Computer Science Department
Cornell University
3 February 1999

Preface

It was around 1960 that parallel processing became an economic necessity and — fortunately — a technically feasible option as well. Ever since, interest in this field of computing has been booming. By now, thousands of papers and hundreds of books inform us about a huge variety of topics related to parallelism, such as operating systems, machine architectures, communication networks, circuit design, synchrony and asynchrony, systolics, protocols for communication and synchronization, distributed algorithms, massive parallelism, logics for concurrency, automatic verification, model checking, and so on, and so forth. So why add yet another book to the field? The answer is simple: something is missing.

Among all the interests in parallelism, there is an essential and fundamental one that has remained largely unexplored, namely the question of *how* to design parallel programs from their specification. And that is what this book is about. It proposes a method for the formal development of parallel programs — *multiprograms* as we have preferred to call them — , and it does so with a minimum of formal gear, viz. with the predicate calculus and with the meanwhile well-established theory of Owicki and Gries. The fact that one can get away with just this theory will probably not convey anything to the uninitiated, but it may all the more come as a surprise to those who were exposed earlier to correctness of multiprograms. Contrary to common belief, the Owicki/Gries theory can indeed be effectively put to work for the formal development of multiprograms, regardless of whether these algorithms are distributed or not. That is what we intend to exemplify with this book.

We wish to state, right at the start, that the uninitiated reader may have an advantage in coming to grips with our text. He has no choice but to read from Chapter 1 onwards, chapter after chapter, and that is precisely what we would like *every* reader to do. The more experienced reader may perhaps start browsing, recognizing all sorts of familiar things, and then conceive them in the way he is used to. For instance, he may dive into Chapter 8 where the guarded skip is discussed, and then conclude that it is nothing but the usual await-statement. But then he is on the verge of missing our point.

We understand and construct our multiprograms in a purely static way, i.e. without recourse to any form of understanding of what may possibly happen during execution. Indeed, we deal with them via the relationship between the program text and the corresponding proof obligations. When developing multiprograms we will always be guided by the specification and by the proof rules of Owicki and Gries, which then lead the way in how to proceed with the design. So, readers who are inclined to hold an operational view of multiprograms will most likely have to make a U-turn in their appreciation of the subject matter. In our writing, we have anticipated this, and we have tried to implant this different feel for the subject in a stepwise fashion, building up our concepts and nomenclature, chapter after chapter, at a leisurely pace.

However, it is not true that we can dispense with the computational model entirely, because there are a few occasions where we need it for arguing about progress or "liveness" properties. Since our method is driven solely by the requirement of partial correctness, be it enhanced with a number of strategic rules to not exclude progress beforehand, each of our developments will, by necessity, end with the obligation to demonstrate progress for each of the components of the multiprogram. Because we will not introduce a formalism for dealing with progress, we will every now and then have to resort to the operational interpretation of our program texts. We say "every now and then" because there is a huge class of algorithms that run under control of what we have called a *multibound*, and for such algorithms progress for the individual components follows from the absence of total system deadlock. And demonstrating the latter is completely within the scope of the Owicki/Gries theory.

*   *

*

We now briefly sketch the structure of the book and the prerequisites for reading it.

For just *reading* it, not much is required: a passive familiarity with the predicate calculus suffices, and prior exposure to Hoare-triple-like semantics of (sequential) programming is an advantage. However, for an *active partaking* in the development of multiprograms, well-versedness in the predicate calculus is indispensable; but what is more, it requires a nearly undefinable mathematical discipline, aiming at simplicity and at not taking premature or hasty design decisions. The reader who embarks on the exercises will definitely notice this. So although technically speaking, the material can be taught to freshmen, it factually belongs to the computing major and to graduate studies, in which we have given classes on it for many years.

The book consists essentially of two parts, separated by Chapter 12 — the Yellow Pages, which contain a summary of the foregoing. The first part sets out the ingredients, vocabulary, techniques and attitudes to be used in the second part. In particular, Chapter 10 explains our mode of derivation of multiprograms in all relevant detail. The second part contains the true subject matter: it presents a long series of examples of program derivation. In the first half of this series — say up to and including Chapter 21 — , general strategies, heuristics and rules of thumb guiding the design process are discussed along with the examples. Thereupon, they are freely used in the second half of the series. The last technical chapter — Chapter 31 — signals a fundamental shortcoming of our method — one that is related to progress issues — and it provides a constructive proposal for how to overcome it.

The book was written as a research monograph, not as a textbook. On urgent request of David Gries we included a collection of exercises, which can be found in the Yellow Pages. Other exercises are scattered through the text, and they can be traced via the index.

Finally we wish to confess that, no matter how cumbersome the process of publication is, we are glad to have undertaken it. Through the composition of this text we have gained a much better understanding of parallel programming, and we hope that our readers can now have a share in this experience.

*   *
*

In a research project like this, many people get involved, some a little more and some a little less, some consciously and some without knowing it. And therefore here is the place where it is our pleasure to give credit where credit is due.

The last two people who got involved were Michael Streichsbier (CS-major at the Technical University of Munich), who — on our behalf — had to fight the LaTeX-standards, and Dr. William R. Sanders (Sr Editor Computer Science, Springer-Verlag, California), who conducted the publication process. We very much appreciate their help.

Among the first people involved were Krzysztof R. Apt and Ernst-Rüdiger Olderog, without them knowing it. Their monograph [AO91] taught us that what we were doing was not essentially wrong, which was a reassuring observation.

Then, when we had almost finished our text, Fred B. Schneider's textbook [Sch97] was published, and that was exactly what we needed. In it, one can find, through his Proof Outline Logic, the mathematical and logical underpinning of the kind of objects that we are dealing with here. We are glad that next to our engineering-flavoured approach to multiprogramming, he managed to present a more fundamental study on the subject.

Next we wish to thank our colleague Rob R. Hoogerwoord, who eagerly followed and supported our experiments. He also made a number of technical contributions, some of which we were happy to record in this book.

The ETAC (Eindhoven Tuesday Afternoon Club) — with Lex Bijlsma, Ronald W. Bulterman, Carel S. Scholten, and Frans W. van der Sommen as the (other) core members over the last five years — had an enormous influence on our thinking, not just on multiprogramming but on mathematical design in general. It is hard to envision our own scientific development without this forum and its members.

When at some point, due to a number of local circumstances, our project had gone into a dip, two very devoted students applied for doing their master's with us. They were Perry. D. Moerland and Frans W. van der Sommen. Their dedication to the subject was so heartwarming and their results were so respectable that we soon got out of our dip. Without them, we would never have written this book, and they will recognize their contributions and influence all over the place.

Another student, Dana S. Buhăceanu, taught us about distributed barrier synchronization [BF96], of which Chapter 27 is a variation. We are very grateful for her lessons.

Once we had decided to embark on our monograph, we felt the need and obligation to have the outcome judged by people with different educational and cultural backgrounds. We then asked four colleagues, each of them active computing scientists, whether they would be willing to do this for us; they were Lex Bijlsma (Dutch, Eindhoven University of Technology), Carroll C. Morgan (Australian/British, Oxford University, UK), Greg Nelson (American, Digital Equipment Corporation, now Compaq, Palo Alto), and Birgit Schieder (German, Technical University of Munich), and they all agreed. Sadly enough, Greg Nelson had to give up, due to serious health problems. We thank him for his willingness to participate. The others gave us their comments and criticisms and they did so in an impeccable way, going far beyond what we could reasonably expect from any of them. We have been happy to incorporate their many suggestions.

Then there is a man who calls himself "the Gries". Of course, we realize that our manuscript is entirely based on the theory of Susan S. Owicki and David Gries, a theory for which they both deserve our greatest respect, but there is more to the man whom by now we have known for twenty years. He was and still is our American teacher (sometimes pretending to be our pupil!), our advisor and collaborator in many enterprises, scientific and otherwise, and ... he is a friend. We owe him a lot.

And finally, there is Edsger W. Dijkstra, who guided our first steps into the discipline of programming and who has been teaching us, up to this very day, what computing and mathematics are really about. To him, and to Mrs. M.C. Dijkstra-Debets — who always took care of all the rest! — we express our warmest gratitude. Without them, we would never have developed into what we are now, and it is to both of them that we dedicate this monograph.

W.H.J. Feijen
A.J.M. van Gasteren
Eindhoven, The Netherlands
24 February 1999

Contents

1

On Our Computational Model

In this monograph we investigate sets of sequential programs that are executed concurrently. Therefore we shall start with an elaboration of the two key elements in this description of our subject, viz. "execution of a sequential program" and "concurrent execution (of programs)".

Of these two notions, we first investigate the one of a sequential program and its execution, because it is the simplest and most familiar one. A sequential program is a recipe under control of which some mechanism, e.g. an automatic computer, generates a sequential process, that is: a sequence of primitive actions — to be called actions, for short. The precise details of these actions do not concern us now, but it is important to know that they take place one after another. That is to say, an action does not begin until the preceding one has ended.

There are two fundamental constraints, however, that we wish to impose on the sequential processes to be considered. These are

- any constituent action will take a finite period of time;
- if upon termination of an action the recipe — the program — prescribes a next action to take place, then this next action will begin within a finite period of time after the preceding action has terminated.

To put it differently, we will confine our attention to recipes and execution mechanisms that can only produce sequences of terminating actions with terminating pauses in between the actions. Such sequences can be finite or infinite. The only way in which a sequence can be finite is because the recipe demands it, and not because there is an eternal last action or pause. In short, the show goes on as long as necessary.

Here is an example. Consider sequential program

|[**var** $x : int$;
  $x := 0$
; **do** $true \rightarrow x := x+1$ **od**
]| ,

with the usual interpretation of the statements. Our constraints now imply that the value of x will eventually exceed any natural number. So execution mechanisms that at some moment can halt indefinitely, for instance because being irreparably out-of-order, fall outside the scope of our current interest.

Also, if some mechanism has been designated to execute the above program and, in addition to that, program

|[**var** $y : int$;
  $y := 0$
; **do** $true \rightarrow y := y+1$ **od**
]| ,

our constraints imply that the values of both x and y will eventually exceed any natural number. More specifically, if a number of sequential programs are, for instance, to be run "simultaneously" on a one-processor installation, the underlying scheduling mechanism for granting computation time to the various programs has to be designed in such a way that our "progress" constraints are met.

The usual jargon would say that, by our constraints, we have adopted a "weak fairness" regime for our system. True as this may be, however, we have ample reason to avoid the notion "fairness", one reason being that it tends to invite overwhelming complexity — see, for instance, [Fra86].

*   *
*

Now we turn our attention to the *concurrent* execution of sequential programs. By concurrent execution we just mean that the various sequential processes take place simultaneously. But what if two actions of different processes overlap each other in time? Usually, actions change the state of affairs, so the critical question now is what happens if the two overlapping actions change the same state of affairs in a conflicting manner.

Consider, for instance, the "simultaneous" activities of putting a high voltage level on a wire and putting a low voltage level on that same wire. It is very likely then, that neither of the two activities will have the intended effect. Short circuit could be the result, or worse. If we really want the two activities to yield their intended effect, the only safe way out seems to be to see to it that these conflicting actions do not overlap but take place one after the other: they have to mutually exclude each other in time.

Many mechanisms provide protection against unwanted interference. Most toilet pots can, by construction, be used by only one person at a time, and most cars have only one steering wheel. On many a computer installation simultaneous access to one and the same memory location is impossible. The presence of some of such built-in, indivisible, non-interferable activities — to be called atomic activities — is vital for the organization of concurrently executed sequential programs.

So our concept of sequential processes now needs to be constrained one further step, to the extent that in our computational model all primitive actions will be considered atomic. This means that if our programs are to be run by a particular mechanism, it had better provide "atomic implementations" of these actions. And if it does, conflicting actions no longer are a problem: if, in the concurrent execution of a number of sequential programs, an attempt is made to execute two conflicting activities simultaneously, the result will be as if the two activities take place in some order.

What about the concurrent execution of two non-conflicting actions? There is nothing wrong if at one and the same time one flip-flop is forced to become flip and a different flip-flop is forced to become flop; simultaneity is harmless in such cases. But we can still *think* of the result as if the two non-conflicting activities take place in some order, and for reasons of homogeneity we shall do so.

As a result, our final understanding of the concurrent execution of a number of sequential programs is that the execution mechanism generates, under control of the various programs, a huge sequence of atomic actions that is an interleaving of the individual sequential processes.

Note that time plays no rôle in our understanding of sequential processes and concurrency. Nothing is known about the relative speeds of processes, and as far as we are concerned, the duration of atomic actions can be anything, as long as it is finite. The only thing that matters is the *order* of the atomic actions in the interleaving.

*   *

*

As far as the description of our computational model is concerned, we could leave it at this. It is quite instructive, however, to illustrate some of the many phenomena that concurrency can lead to. Here is an example that we learned from [Sne93].

Consider the statements $x := 1$ and $x := 2$, taken from two different sequential programs. If the execution mechanism provides an atomic implementation of such assignments, the concurrent execution of $x := 1$ and $x := 2$ yields $x = 1 \lor x = 2$. But suppose that we have a different organization. Suppose that $x := 1$ is implemented by writing bit string $(0, 1)$ into a two-bit memory location, bit by bit and from left to right, and that, similarly, $x := 2$ is implemented by writing $(1, 0)$ into that same memory location. Now even if writing a single bit is atomic, the composite result of the concurrent execution of $x := 1$ and $x := 2$ can yield any of the final values 0, 1, 2 or 3 for x, rather than the values 1 and 2 only. This is due to the six interleavings, i.e. orderings, in which $2 + 2$ individual bit assignments can take place. If, with such an organization, we nevertheless wish to achieve $x = 1 \lor x = 2$, we have to do something about it. What we have to do is to superimpose, on the bit string writing, an additional algorithm that precludes the generation of the faulty answers 0 and 3, and we shall do so in a later chapter. One of the conclusions to be drawn from this example is that our programming task essentially depends on which statements are considered atomic.

Here is another example of what concurrency has in store for us. Consider the following very simple, meaningless program

$$x := y + 1$$
$$; \ x := y^2$$
$$; \ x := x - y \quad .$$

It consists of just three assignment statements, each of which we consider atomic. Now if we start it in an initial state such that $x = 7 \land y = 3$, it will deliver $x = 6 \land y = 3$ as a final answer.

Also consider the equally simple and meaningless program

$$y := x + 1$$
$$; \ y := x^2$$
$$; \ y := y - x \quad .$$

When started in the same initial state $x = 7 \land y = 3$,
it yields $x = 7 \land y = 42$.

Now let us run these programs concurrently. Our advice to the reader is not to waste time on finding out what the result is. The possible final values for x and y are listed below.

x	y
−4032	8128
−3968	4032
−600	1225
−575	600
−72	153
−63	72
−1	2
2	−1
6	30
20	380
56	3080
132	12
240	−224
496	−240
1722	42
2352	−2303
4753	−2352
5112	72
6480	−6399
13041	−6480

The moral of the story of course is, that while each of the individual programs is of an extreme simplicity, their parallel composition has become a horrendous beast.

2

Our Program Notation and Its Semantics

Since in this monograph we will be studying the design of concurrently executed sequential programs, we need a notation for sequential programs in the first place. At this point we have made a very traditional choice by adopting Dijkstra's Guarded Command Language, which was first defined in [Dij76]. Its distinguishing features are notational and mathematical austerity, and the incorporation of nondeterminacy in sequential programs. In our study of multiprogramming, nondeterminacy will hardly play a rôle, but mathematical austerity will do so all the more. We will briefly describe this program notation, which we expect to offer no problem to anyone familiar with ALGOL60, Pascal, or even C. We will discuss its semantics in more detail, anticipating in our discussion that in later chapters sequential programs will be considered in cooperation with other ones rather than in isolation.

2.0 The notation

The elementary statements are

- *skip*   % which does nothing

and

- $x := E$ % which evaluates expression E and then assigns its value to variable x.

The first statement is just called "the skip", and the second is "an assignment (statement)". Assignment statements can also take the form of so-called "multiple assignments"

- $x, y := E, F$ % which evaluates E and F and then assigns their values to x and y respectively.

Out of existing statements, one can construct new statements. The Guarded Command Language provides three possibilities for construction. They are — with S_0 and S_1 existing statements —

- $S_0 ; S_1$ % first S_0 is executed, and then S_1.

  This is the so-called "sequential composition (of S_0 and S_1)".

- **if** $B_0 \to S_0$ % executes S_0 if B_0 evaluates to *true*, or
     $\| \ B_1 \to S_1$ S_1 if B_1 evaluates to *true*, and otherwise
     fi   we don't know yet — see much later.

  This is the so-called "Alternative Construct". It consists of the two guarded commands $B_0 \to S_0$ and $B_1 \to S_1$. An alternative construct may consist of any number of guarded commands, even zero. The B's are called "the guards" and the S's are the "guarded statements".

- **do** $B_0 \to S_0$ % this is just a loop, which keeps executing
     $\| \ B_1 \to S_1$ S_0 or S_1 as long as the corresponding
     od   guard evaluates to *true*. When both guards
             are *false* the loop terminates.

  This is the so-called "Repetitive Construct" or the "Loop". Like the alternative construct, it may contain any number of guarded commands.

So much for our notation.

2.1 Hoare-triples and the *wlp*

In view of the operational complexity that we are faced with when sequential programs evolve concurrently, the operational description given of the semantics of our program notation is all but completely useless. Instead, we will resort to a formalism that not only precisely describes what we can expect of a program when it is executed on a machine, but — most importantly — departs from computational associations as rigorously as possible. The formalism that we have chosen is the so-called "predicate transformer semantics", and more in particular the predicate transformer semantics as given by "the weakest liberal precondition", *wlp* for short.

The first stepping stone towards explaining the *wlp*-semantics is the notion of a "Hoare-triple", so named in honour of C.A.R. Hoare. A Hoare-triple [Hoa69] consists of a pair of predicates — P, Q — and a statement — S. It is denoted

$$\{P\}\, S\, \{Q\}$$

Its operational interpretation is as follows:

> $\{P\}\, S\, \{Q\}$ is a boolean that has the value *true* if and only if *each terminating* execution of S that starts from an initial state satisfying P is guaranteed to end up in a final state satisfying Q.

So if $\{P\}\, S\, \{Q\}$ holds and S is started in a state satisfying P, we can be sure that S either terminates in a state satisfying Q or does not terminate at all. We wish to draw attention to the fact that nonterminating executions are considered as well. The jargon therefore says that $\{P\}\, S\, \{Q\}$ only models "partial correctness", or that $\{P\}\, S\, \{Q\}$ is just a "safety property" or expresses — as Leslie Lamport once phrased it — that "no bad thing can happen".

Remark In many texts on sequential programming, $\{P\}\, S\, \{Q\}$ denotes the stronger property that S when started in P is guaranteed to terminate in Q. The semantics corresponding to this notion is the predicate transformer semantics that is based on weakest preconditions (*wp*'s) rather than weakest liberal preconditions (*wlp*'s). It requires what is called "total correctness" instead of just "partial correctness". This *wp*-semantics is okay for sequential programs in isolation, but far too demanding for handling sequential programs in cooperation.
End of Remark.

Now we can explain the notion of "weakest liberal precondition". For statement S and predicate Q, $wlp.S.Q$ is the weakest precondition P such that

$$\{P\} \, S \, \{Q\}$$

holds. This state of affairs is covered quite succinctly by what, by postulate, will be the relationship between Hoare-triples and wlp's:

(0) $\{P\} \, S \, \{Q\} \equiv [\, P \Rightarrow wlp.S.Q \,]$.

   (The square brackets are a shorthand for "for all states" [DS90].)

In words, $wlp.S.Q$ is a predicate that is *true* in precisely those states — i.e. no more and no fewer — from which each terminating execution of S is guaranteed to end up in a final state satisfying Q.

2.2   Properties of Hoare-triples and the wlp

We shall define predicate transformer $wlp.S$ for each statement S of our program notation. It so happens that all the $wlp.S$'s so obtained share the mathematical property of being "universally conjunctive", i.e. for X ranging over an arbitrary set of predicates, they all satisfy (see [DS90])

(1) $[\, wlp.S.\langle\, \forall X :: X \,\rangle \equiv \langle\, \forall X :: wlp.S.X \,\rangle \,]$.

From (1) we can derive — proofs omitted — that

- $wlp.S$ is "finitely conjunctive", i.e.

(2) $[\, wlp.S.(X \wedge Y) \equiv wlp.S.X \wedge wlp.S.Y \,]$ for all X, Y

- $wlp.S$ is "monotonic", i.e.

(3) $[\, X \Rightarrow Y \,] \Rightarrow [\, wlp.S.X \Rightarrow wlp.S.Y \,]$ for all X, Y

- $wlp.S$ is "top-strict", i.e.

(4) $[\, wlp.S.true \equiv true \,]$.

From these properties of wlp combined with (0), we can derive a wealth of properties of Hoare-triples. (In his seminal paper [Hoa69], C.A.R. Hoare has cast these properties in the form of inference rules, but now, a quarter of a century later, we have come to prefer algebraic calculation to logical reasoning.) Here, we list some of them

- $\{P\} S \{Q\}$ is universally conjunctive in Q, i.e.

(5) $\{P\} S \{\langle \forall X :: X \rangle\} \equiv \langle \forall X :: \{P\} S \{X\} \rangle$

- $\{P\} S \{Q\}$ is finitely conjunctive in Q, i.e.

(6) $\{P\} S \{X \wedge Y\} \equiv \{P\} S \{X\} \wedge \{P\} S \{Y\}$

- $\{P\} S \{Q\}$ is monotonic in Q, i.e.

(7) $[X \Rightarrow Y] \Rightarrow (\{P\} S \{X\} \Rightarrow \{P\} S \{Y\})$

  "one can always weaken a postcondition without falsifying an established Hoare-triple", or in a formulation geared to program construction rather than verification: "one can always establish a Hoare-triple by establishing a Hoare-triple with a stronger postcondition — and the same precondition".

- The anonymous property

(8) $\{X \vee Y\} S \{Q\} \equiv \{X\} S \{Q\} \wedge \{Y\} S \{Q\}$

- $\{P\} S \{Q\}$ is antimonotonic in P, i.e.

(9) $[X \Rightarrow Y] \Rightarrow (\{X\} S \{Q\} \Leftarrow \{Y\} S \{Q\})$

  "one can always strengthen a precondition without falsifying an established Hoare-triple", or formulated constructively: "one can always establish a Hoare-triple by establishing a Hoare-triple with a weaker precondition — and the same postcondition".

- And finally

(10) $\{P\} S \{true\}$.

2.3   Definition of the *wlp*'s

Now the moment has come to define the *wlp* for each statement of our program notation. This we do by defining *wlp* first for the elementary ones directly, and then for the composites in terms of their components.

2.3.0   The skip, the assignment, and the composition

The skip

By definition,

$$[\, wlp.skip.R \,\equiv\, R\,]\qquad \text{for all } R\,.$$

There is little useful to be said about this. The most prominent use that we make of this definition of *skip* is that we have

$$\{P\}\, skip\, \{Q\} \,\equiv\, [\,P \Rightarrow Q\,]\qquad.$$

The assignment

By definition,

$$[\, wlp.(x := E).R \,\equiv\, (x := E).R\,]\qquad;$$

here $(x := E).R$ stands for a textual copy of expression R in which each free occurrence of x is replaced with E.

For the multiple assignment we have, by definition,

$$[\, wlp.(x, y := E, F).R \,\equiv\, (x, y := E, F).R\,]\qquad;$$

here $(x, y := E, F).R$ stands for a textual copy of expression R in which all free occurrences of x and y are replaced with E and F respectively.

In what follows, we refer to this definition of the assignment by phrases like "rule of assignment", "axiom of assignment", or "substitution".

We will not elaborate the axiom of assignment here, because nowadays it is widely known, accepted, and appreciated by the scientific-programming community.

The most prominent use that we make of this definition of the assignment is that we now have

$$\{P\}\, x := E\, \{Q\} \,\equiv\, [\,P \Rightarrow (x := E).Q\,]\qquad.$$

The sequential composition

For statements S_0 and S_1 we have, by definition,

$$[\, wlp.(S_0\,;\, S_1).R \,\equiv\, wlp.S_0.(wlp.S_1.R)\,]\qquad.$$

From this, one can easily prove that semi ";" is associative. We shall grate-
fully use this fact by omitting parentheses in program fragments like

$S_0 \; ; \; S_1 \; ; \; S_2$.

There is a little theorem on sequential composition that we heavily rely
on in practice. It reads: for any Q

$\{P\}\, S_0 \; ; \; S_1 \,\{R\}$

$\Leftarrow$

$\{P\}\, S_0 \,\{Q\} \,\wedge\, \{Q\}\, S_1 \,\{R\}$.

Here is a proof:

$\{P\}\, S_0 \; ; \; S_1 \,\{R\}$

$\equiv$ {definition of Hoare-triples}

$[\; P \;\Rightarrow\; wlp.(S_0 \; ; \; S_1).R \;]$

$\equiv$ {definition of sequential composition}

$[\; P \;\Rightarrow\; wlp.S_0.(wlp.S_1.R) \;]$

$\Leftarrow$ {$wlp.S_0$ is monotonic}

$[\; P \Rightarrow wlp.S_0.Q \;] \,\wedge\, [\; Q \Rightarrow wlp.S_1.R \;]$

$\equiv$ {definition of Hoare-triples}

$\{P\}\, S_0 \,\{Q\} \,\wedge\, \{Q\}\, S_1 \,\{R\}$.

The typical way in which we use this theorem is by explicitly including the
intermediate condition Q in the program text, in the following way:

$\{P\}$

S_0

$; \{Q,$ see Note 1$\}$

S_1

$\{R,$ see Note 0$\}$.

Here Note 0 is supposed to contain a proof of correctness for Hoare-triple
$\{Q\}\, S_1 \,\{R\}$, and Note 1 for $\{P\}\, S_0 \,\{Q\}$. In such a way our programs
will, on-the-fly, become fully documented. Which is nice.

When we are looking for a correctness proof of $\{P\}\, S_0; S_1 \,\{R\}$ or designing a program of the form $S_0; S_1$ that should establish R , the question is: what intermediate assertion Q should we choose? The recom-
mendation almost always is to choose $wlp.S_1.R$ for Q . This choice has
multiple advantages. One advantage is that now $\{Q\}\, S_1 \,\{R\}$ holds by
definition. And secondly, because $wlp.S_1.R$ is the *weakest* possible choice

for Q, it generates the *weakest* possible proof obligation $\{P\} S_0 \{Q\}$ — thanks to the monotonicity of Hoare-triples in their second argument. Here we see a clear-cut advantage of having a notion like the *weakest* (liberal) precondition at our disposal. This is just one advantage, however, out of many more.

Finally we mention that conditions between braces, as they occur in our program texts, are, in this context, called "assertions" , and programs that contain assertions are said to be "annotated" (with these assertions).

2.3.1   The alternative construct

For statements S_0 and S_1, boolean expressions B_0 and B_1, and *IF* short for

> **if** $B_0 \rightarrow S_0$
> **‖** $B_1 \rightarrow S_1$
> **fi**   ,

we have, by definition,

$$[\, wlp.IF.R \;\equiv\; (B_0 \Rightarrow wlp.S_0.R) \,\wedge\, (B_1 \Rightarrow wlp.S_1.R)\,] \quad .$$

Because conjunction is symmetric, we see from this that the order in which the guarded commands occur in an alternative construct is of no significance.

Here also, there is a little theorem concerning if-statements (i.e. alternative constructs) that is of great practical value. It reads (simple proof omitted)

> $\{P\}\, IF\, \{R\}$
> $\equiv$
> $\{P \wedge B_0\}\, S_0\, \{R\} \;\wedge\; \{P \wedge B_1\}\, S_1\, \{R\}$.

We typically use the theorem by annotating an if-statement as follows

> $\{P\}$
> **if** $B_0 \rightarrow S_0\{R,$ see Note 0$\}$
> **‖** $B_1 \rightarrow S_1\{R,$ see Note 1$\}$
> **fi**
> $\{R\}$.

Here Note 0 is supposed to contain a proof of $\{P \wedge B_0\}\, S_0\, \{R\}$, and Note 1 of $\{P \wedge B_1\}\, S_1\, \{R\}$.

*   *

*

We have to spend some words on the operational interpretation of an if-statement. In a state in which B_0 holds, IF can establish R via S_0, if $wlp.S_0.R$ holds in that state — see definition of IF. Likewise, if B_1 holds, S_1 can establish R. And if both B_0 and B_1 hold, either of S_0 and S_1 can be selected to establish R; which of the two will be chosen (by an implementation) is entirely beyond our influence, and we couldn't care less, our only care being that R be established.

It is the alternative construct that introduces nondeterminacy into sequential programs. This introduction has been a giant leap forward in the study of the semantics of programs and of the behaviour of systems. However, as alluded to before, nondeterminacy will hardly play a rôle for our subject of study, which is program construction. And indeed, if we take a closer look at how to handle the "nondeterministic" if-statement, we see that it faces us with just a number of independent proof obligations — $\{P \wedge B_0\} S_0 \{R\}$ and $\{P \wedge B_1\} S_1 \{R\}$ in the above —, and that's it. Nondeterminacy has faded and theorem proving is left. Nondeterminacy has become a phenomenon that only pops up in relation to executions. It has become an artefact of a particular implementation chosen, and it does not belong to the world of program construction. Because in this monograph we will be concerned with the formal design of programs, not with their implementation, we will, therefore, never be bothered by the potential complications caused by nondeterminacy (which has always been considered the main source of complexity in handling multiprograms).

Not all has been said yet about our operational interpretation of the if-statement. For instance, what about a state in which both B_0 and B_1 are *false*? In such a state each of the alternatives S_0 and S_1 may fail to establish the desired postcondition R. So neither S_0 nor S_1 can be selected for execution, and in one way or another the execution of IF gets stuck. But now recall our operational interpretation of wlp's, which tells us that the execution of a statement should either terminate in a state satisfying R or not terminate at all. So a very viable implementation of IF in case both guards are *false* is "wait" (i.e. keep evaluating the guards) until one of them becomes *true*. For a sequential process in isolation this boils down to waiting forever, i.e. to nontermination, and that was one of the options. This implementation — to which we shall stick — does not make much sense for a program in isolation, but it does make a lot of sense for a program cooperating with other programs, because through the activities of these other programs the *false* guards may very well become *true*, in which case continuation of the "delayed" IF may again become possible.

In our description of the computational model we have promised to see to it that the execution of a sequential program should result in a sequence of *finite* atomic actions. For the finite atomic actions that result from an execution of the *IF* we propose

- the evaluation of a guard to *false*

- the evaluation of a guard to *true* followed by the execution of the corresponding guarded statement. This guarded statement, however, has to be such that it is guaranteed to terminate in isolation, i.e. without interference from outside [†].

Finally, it goes without saying that during the process of evaluating the guards it should not be the case that one of the alternatives is ignored forever: the evaluation of the guards ought to take place on a fair basis.

$$*$$
$$*   *$$

The above choice for an implementation of the if-statement has a number of severe consequences for what is called "progress", or "liveness", or the circumstance — as Leslie Lamport once phrased it — "that eventually some good thing will happen". We illustrate this by a number of examples.

Because

$$wlp.(\textbf{if } B \vee C \rightarrow S \textbf{ fi}).R$$

$\equiv$ {definition wlp **if**}

$$B \vee C \Rightarrow wlp.S.R$$

$\equiv$ {predicate calculus}

$$(B \Rightarrow wlp.S.R) \wedge (C \Rightarrow wlp.S.R)$$

$\equiv$ {definition wlp **if**}

$$wlp.(\textbf{if } B \rightarrow S \parallel C \rightarrow S \textbf{ fi}).R   ,$$

the two program fragments

$$\textbf{if } B \vee C \rightarrow S \textbf{ fi}$$

and

$$\textbf{if } B \rightarrow S \parallel C \rightarrow S \textbf{ fi}$$

[†]Because of this constraint, having a different notation for the if-statement would be preferable, since we do not want to impose such a constraint on the regular alternative construct as used in sequential programs. However, in this text no confusion will arise.

cannot be distinguished by looking at their *wlp*'s. This is only to be expected, because *wlp*'s address partial correctness only. However, if it comes to termination, the two program fragments may very well differ in their behaviours, in particular so when run concurrently with other programs. Consider, for instance, a second program that all the time changes B and C, but does so in such a way that it maintains $C \equiv \neg B$. In that case fragment

   if $B \lor C \to S$ **fi**

is guaranteed to terminate, because the atomic evaluation of guard $B \lor C$ will yield the value *true*. However, for fragment

   if $B \to S \parallel C \to S$ **fi**

each evaluation of B and each evaluation of C may yield the value *false*, because such an atomic evaluation may always take place in a state where the other guard happens to be *true*.

Since in this text we will hardly offer a formalism for discussing progress, the incorporation of if-statements with more than one alternative would present us with severe additional problems in arguing about progress. This is one of our most compelling reasons for sticking to if-statements with just one guarded command. Fortunately, we can travel a long, long way with these.

There is one case, however, in which we can live with the above two program fragments alike. That is the case where one of the expressions B or C is stable under the operations of the rest of the system (stable means: cannot be falsified). Once the stable expression has become *true* — if it does so at all —, both program fragments can and will terminate, thanks to our postulate that no guard remains unevaluated forever.

*   *
*

We conclude this discussion of the alternative construct with a special instance, which will be used very frequently. It is

   if $B \to skip$ **fi**   ,

which we call the *guarded skip*. One of its possible implementations is

   do $\neg B \to skip$ **od**   .

The semantics of the guarded skip is given by

   $[\, wlp.(\mathbf{if}\ B \to skip\ \mathbf{fi}).R \equiv B \Rightarrow R\,]$,

or by Hoare-triple

   $\{B \Rightarrow R\}\ \mathbf{if}\ B \to skip\ \mathbf{fi}\ \{R\}$.

2.3.2   The repetitive construct

It is possible to give a definition of the *wlp* of the repetitive construct, viz. as the weakest solution of a fixpoint equation — see [DS90]. Beautiful, however, as such a definition may be, it is of little or no relevance to the construction of programs. Instead, we shall come to grips with the repetition via the so-called *Invariance Theorem for Repetitive Constructs*. It reads as follows. For statements S_0 and S_1, boolean expressions B_0 and B_1, and DO short for

$$\textbf{do } B_0 \rightarrow S_0 \ \| \ B_1 \rightarrow S_1 \textbf{ od} \quad ,$$

we have, for any P,

$$\{P\}\, DO\, \{P \wedge \neg B_0 \wedge \neg B_1\}$$
$$\Leftarrow$$
$$\{P \wedge B_0\}\, S_0\, \{P\} \ \wedge \ \{P \wedge B_1\}\, S_1\, \{P\} \quad .$$

A relation P satisfying the antecedent is called an "invariant of the repetition". This theorem, which is sometimes called the "Main Theorem of Computing Science", was first formulated by C.A.R. Hoare in [Hoa69]. Thanks to its simplicity and its utmost usefulness, it has attained a worldwide reputation. More about this later.

In order to get an operational appreciation of the repetitive construct (or "loop"), consider a state satisfying condition P. According to the consequent of the invariance theorem, an implementation can only terminate the execution of DO in a state in which P holds and both guards B_0 and B_1 are *false*. This implies that in states where at least one of the guards equals *true*, the show should go on. If B_0 is *true*, S_0 can maintain P — and will, if it terminates —, and if B_1 is *true*, S_1 can do the job. If both B_0 and B_1 are *true*, either of S_0 and S_1 can be selected for execution. In any of these cases the selected guarded statement will end up, if it terminates at all, in a state satisfying P, bringing us back to the beginning, from which the story can be repeated.

In states where both guards are *false*, the implementation not only has the permission to terminate the execution of DO, it even has the obligation to do so, since the antecedent of the invariance theorem offers no opportunity to maintain P in case the guard is *false*. Thus, the invariance theorem acts as a very compelling specification towards an implementor.

Finally, we postulate which of the actions generated by the execution of a repetitive construct are to be considered atomic. These are just the evaluations of the individual guards. In case of a *true* guard, the subsequent guarded statement to be executed is *not* a part of the atomic activity of evaluating the guard to *true*.

In what follows we will almost exclusively use repetitive constructs with just one guard:

do $B \rightarrow S$ **od** ,

in which case the invariance theorem reads

$$\{P\} \textbf{ do } B \rightarrow S \textbf{ od } \{P \wedge \neg B\}$$
$$\Leftarrow$$
$$\{P \wedge B\} S \{P\}$$

(Isn't this impressively simple?)
The typical way in which we annotate this program fragment is

$\{\text{Inv} : P\}$
  do $B \rightarrow \{P \wedge B\} S \{P, \text{see Note}\}$ **od**
$\{P \wedge \neg B\}$,

where the Note is supposed to contain a proof of $\{P \wedge B\} S \{P\}$.

An even more special instance of the repetitive construct is

do $true \rightarrow S$ **od** .

It is the prototype of a so-called *cyclic program*, and it will crop up so frequently that we introduce a special notation for it, viz.

$* [S]$.

So much for the repetitive construct.

2.4   On our choice of formalism

We conclude this chapter with some remarks on what we consider the great merits of predicate transformer semantics and Hoare-triples for the construction of and the reasoning about programs, be they sequential or concurrent.

One very important advantage of the predicate transformer semantics — if not the most important one — is that it does away with operational reasoning.

Operational reasoning refers to understanding a program by taking into account the individual computations — *all* computations — that can be evoked under control of the program. In order to illustrate what this can lead to, we consider the following example.

An operationalist needs at least three steps to check program fragment

$$\{P\}\, S_0\, ;\, S_1\, \{R\} \qquad :$$

first he executes S_0, second he retains the result, and, third, uses this to execute S_1. (We have not counted that he should check that the answer satisfies R.)

Given our semantics for the semicolon, we have to do three things as well, viz. formulate an intermediate assertion Q and then prove $\{P\}\, S_0\, \{Q\}$ and $\{Q\}\, S_1\, \{R\}$.

Next let us consider an alternative construct IF_p with p alternatives. The operationalist has to do at least p things in order to check $\{P\}\, IF_p\, \{Q\}$, viz. execute all alternatives. Given our semantics for the if-statement, we have to do p things as well, viz. fulfil the proof obligation for each alternative.

But now consider

$$\{P\}\, IF_p\, ;\, IF_q\, \{R\} \qquad .$$

Here, for each alternative of IF_p the operationalist has to execute it, retain the result, and then consider all q continuations of it as provided by IF_q. Hence his total amount of work adds up to at least

$$p \cdot (1 + 1 + q) \qquad .$$

Given our semantics, proving $\{P\}\, IF_p\, ;\, IF_q\, \{R\}$ means that we are *forced* to come up with an intermediate state Q in the first place — this is one step — and then we prove $\{P\}\, IF_p\, \{Q\}$ and $\{Q\}\, IF_q\, \{R\}$. This adds up to a total amount of work

$$p + 1 + q \qquad .$$

The difference has become dramatic (except for $p = 1 \wedge q = 1$). How come?

It is the intermediate state Q, which we were forced to introduce, that accounts for the difference. The operational interpretation of such an assertion Q is that when "program execution has reached that assertion", the state satisfies Q. Thanks to the validity, in our example, of $\{Q\}\, IF_q\, \{R\}$, execution of IF_q can do the job and establish R. But for this purpose it is absolutely irrelevant *how* the preceding computation has reached a state satisfying Q, be it via an extremely simple or a terribly complicated computational history. Thus, the intermediate assertion is a very effective *history disposal*; it erases everything that is irrelevant for the future and retains just what does matter, viz. that the state satisfies Q.

The difference with operational reasoning becomes highly dramatic in the case of the repetitive construct, which is the main producer of computational history — and which, for this very reason, is indispensable for the exploitation of the speed of electronic computers. A program like

do $B \rightarrow IF_2$ **od**

can, with just 100 iterations, generate over 2^{100} different computations. Here, the operationalist is definitely losing the game. With our semantics for the repetitive construct, we only need to do three things, viz. come up with an invariant P and prove $\{P \wedge B\}\, IF_2\, \{P\}$. Here we see in a nutshell how important the Theorem of Invariance is for coming to grips with sequential programs and why calling it "The Main Theorem [of Computing Science]" is not without justification.

So much for the quality of predicate transformer semantics in its capacity of providing us with a water-tight protection against operational reasoning.

There is one more point regarding our semantics that we would like to discuss. By definition we have

$$\{P\}\, S\, \{Q\} \;\equiv\; [\, P \Rightarrow wlp.S.Q\,] \quad .$$

The question then arises, why we retain two different concepts, viz. Hoare-triples and wlp's for expressing the same thing. We have good reasons for doing so, however.

As we have alluded to before, it is a good habit to annotate programs so that the annotation exactly reflects the proof obligations as originating from the proof rules. In such a way programs become fully documented on-the-fly. But the way we annotate programs is by the Hoare-triple notation, and that is one reason why we retain the latter.

Besides documenting a completed program, annotation also is a good thing to have for programs under construction. Halfway through its development, a program for printing the cubes of the first hundred natural numbers will, typically, have the shape

$$n := 0; \; x := 0$$
$$; \{\text{Inv} : x = n^3\}$$
$$\textbf{do } n \neq 100 \rightarrow$$
$$\quad print(x)$$
$$; \{x = n^3 \wedge n \neq 100\}$$
$$\quad W$$
$$; \{x = (n+1)^3\}$$
$$\quad n := n+1$$
$$\quad \{x = n^3\}$$
$$\textbf{od} \quad .$$

Now the annotation provides a complete specification of what remains to be done, viz. designing program fragment W so that

$$\{x = n^3 \land n \neq 100\} \; W \; \{x = (n+1)^3\} \quad .$$

In what follows we shall heavily exploit this specification potential of annotated programs.

Why do we retain wlp's? The reason is that expression $[\,P \Rightarrow wlp.S.Q\,]$ contains subexpression $wlp.S.Q$, an expression that by no means can be found in $\{P\}\,S\,\{Q\}$. Moreover, $wlp.S.Q$ is an expression that we can calculate with for each particular S. What is more, $wlp.S.Q$ is a subexpression of a predicate, so that in dealing with $[\,P \Rightarrow wlp.S.Q\,]$ we have, at one fell swoop, the full-fledged predicate calculus at our disposal. Thus, expression $[\,P \Rightarrow wlp.S.Q\,]$ offers far more manipulative freedom than its equivalent $\{P\}\,S\,\{Q\}$. The embedding of the Hoare-triple into an algebraic framework like the predicate calculus has been a major breakthrough in our potential for formal program derivation — see [Dij76] and [Gri81].

Finally, we wish to emphasize that, by the above, program correctness can now be handled by just the predicate calculus. And this is an additional advantage, because the predicate calculus is a universal tool for the compact and very precise rendering of mathematical reasoning in general — which should, therefore, be mastered anyway, by anyone who takes mathematical thought seriously.

*   *

*

This concludes our treatment of the notation for sequential programs and of their semantics when they are executed in isolation. In our operational descriptions of the various program constructs we have already anticipated the circumstance that in the subsequent chapters sequential programs will no longer be considered in isolation but in cooperation (concurrent execution) with other programs.

3

The Core of the Owicki/Gries Theory

In the previous chapter, the notion of an assertion in a sequential program has been introduced, and we have seen how sequential programs can be annotated with assertions in such a way that the annotation precisely reflects our proof obligations. We have also seen how this effectively protects us against operational reasoning, and how it aids in coming to firm grips with sequential programs. All these virtues become even more important now that we are on the verge of taking multiprograms into account, i.e. entire sets of cooperating sequential programs to be executed simultaneously.

In this chapter we shall create the basis for coming to firm, nonoperational grips with multiprograms as well. The theory employed for that purpose is the theory of Owicki and Gries, which was launched by Susan Speer Owicki and David Gries — see [OG76], but also [Dij82]. One of the nice things about this theory is that it introduces no new concepts for handling multiprograms, i.e. we can come away with just Hoare-triples and *wlp*-semantics, which have proven to be so useful for handling sequential programs in isolation. And as a result we stay within the realm of just the predicate calculus. As will become apparent in the rest of this text, the simple formal entourage of the predicate calculus and the Owicki/Gries theory will allow us to travel a long, long way into the battlefield of multiprogramming. This need not amaze us, because it is the very simplicity of the formalism that accounts for it.

3.0   Annotating a multiprogram

A multiprogram consists of a bunch of ordinary sequential programs, to which we will usually refer as the *components* of the multiprogram. Before we dive into the Owicki/Gries theory, we briefly recall the computational model that we have in mind for the simultaneous execution of such a bunch of components. Each individual component will, under control of its program text and under control of the state, evoke a sequence of terminating atomic actions. If such a component evolves in isolation, nothing happens between two successive actions. However, if other components are executed simultaneously, an arbitrary but finite number of atomic actions of these other components can take place in between. The net effect is that the execution of a multiprogram generates an unknown (but fair) interleaving of the sequences generated by the individual components.

In order to demonstrate, in a nutshell, what this brings about, we consider the following mini-example. Suppose one component contains program fragment

$$\ldots \ x := 0 \ \{0 \leq x\}; \ \ldots \qquad ,$$

in which $x := 0$ is considered atomic. Were this component to be run in isolation, we could safely assert $0 \leq x$ between the completion of atomic statement $x := 0$ and the beginning of the component's next atomic statement. In the presence of other components, however, assertion $0 \leq x$ need no longer be correct: due to the interleaving, such other components may, in between, change the value of x, for instance by statements like $x := x - 1$, and thus may violate $0 \leq x$. It seems as if we have to abandon our earlier interpretation and appreciation of assertions, which was that the state of the computation satisfies the assertion when execution of a component has reached that assertion. But we don't want to do so, and fortunately we don't have to either, as we shall explain next.

We don't want to abandon our interpretation of assertions first of all, because we badly need it for the purpose of specification. For instance, when a consumer is about to consume a portion from a buffer, the buffer had better contain at least 1 portion. We formally specify this by demanding the correctness of assertion "buffer nonempty" as a pre-assertion of the consumption.

Second, we wish to retain the assertion in its capacity of effective history-disposal, even more so in the case of multiprograms: while a component resides at an assertion Q, lots of computations can take place due to the activities of the other components, but we can ignore them all, if we can insist that the state of the system as a whole will always satisfy Q. Thus we would eliminate all interest in individual computations.

Fortunately we don't have to abandon our interpretation of assertions. To see why, let us return to our mini-example. By requiring the correctness of $0 \leq x$ in

$$\ldots \ x := 0 \ \{0 \leq x\}; \ \ldots \qquad ,$$

we demand that the other components do not violate the assertion. If, for instance, a different component contains a statement $x := x - 1$, the situation would be safe if this statement were equipped with — correct! — pre-assertion $1 \leq x$:

$$\ldots \ ; \{1 \leq x\} \ x := x - 1 \ \ldots \qquad .$$

We could then argue as follows. If the original component is at assertion $0 \leq x$, and the other component is about to execute $x := x - 1$, then — by our appreciation of the correctness of assertions — the state of the system satisfies both $0 \leq x$ and $1 \leq x$, i.e. $1 \leq x$. In this state execution of $x := x - 1$ is harmless to the validity of our target assertion $0 \leq x$. We phrase this as "$0 \leq x$ is *globally correct* under $\{1 \leq x\} \ x := x - 1$".

The moral of the above story is that in dealing with the global correctness of an assertion — $0 \leq x$ in our example — we will usually need to take other assertions into account — $1 \leq x$ in our example. That is, the price to be paid is that now we also have to take care of the correctness of these other assertions. The general state of affairs that we must be willing to consider is that a multiprogram ought to be annotated in such a way that *each* atomic statement in *each* of the components carries a pre-assertion. Then we can formulate the

Rule of Global Correctness

> Assertion P in a component is globally correct whenever for each $\{Q\} \ S$ — i.e. for each atomic statement S with pre-assertion Q — taken from a different component,
>
> $$\{P \wedge Q\} \ S \ \{P\}$$
>
> is a correct Hoare-triple.

End of Rule of Global Correctness.

Note that with the above convention for the annotation , i.e. each atomic statement carrying a pre-assertion, we created a one-to-one correspondence between atomic statements and assertions: from the given annotation we can conclude what the atomic statements are and from the choice of atomic statements we know where to plug in the assertions.

Intermission As an illustration, let us calculate the weakest Q such that assertion $0 \leq x$ is globally correct under $\{Q\}\ x := x - 1$. To that end, we have to calculate the weakest Q such that

$$\{0 \leq x \wedge Q\}\ x := x - 1\ \{0 \leq x\}$$

is a correct Hoare-triple. In *wlp*-notation this is

$$[\ 0 \leq x \wedge Q\ \Rightarrow\ (x := x - 1).(0 \leq x)\ ]\qquad,$$

or — equivalently —

$$[\ Q\ \Rightarrow\ (0 \leq x\ \Rightarrow\ (x := x - 1).(0 \leq x))\ ]\qquad,$$

and from the latter expression we see that the weakest Q is $0 \leq x\ \Rightarrow\ (x := x - 1).(0 \leq x)$. Let us simplify it:

$$0 \leq x\ \Rightarrow\ (x := x - 1).(0 \leq x)$$

$\equiv\qquad$ {substitution}

$$0 \leq x\ \Rightarrow\ 0 \leq x - 1$$

$\equiv\qquad$ {predicate calculus and arithmetic}

$$x < 0\ \vee\ 1 \leq x$$

$\equiv\qquad$ {x is integer}

$$x \neq 0\qquad.$$

So $0 \leq x$ is globally correct under $\{x \neq 0\}\ x := x - 1$.

Earlier we launched $1 \leq x$ as a pre-assertion to $x := x - 1$, which by being stronger than the $x \neq 0$ calculated above is an adequate pre-assertion indeed. As will become apparent in the rest of this monograph, the weaker $x \neq 0$ is, in general, to be preferred to the stronger $1 \leq x$, because — in view of our operational appreciation of an assertion — the stronger an assertion is, the less manoeuvring space the system has. The moral of this intermission is, that careful calculation, rather than "intelligent guessing", will be indispensable for the art of constructing multiprograms.
End of Intermission.

$$*\qquad\qquad*$$
$$*$$

The global correctness of an assertion P in a component tells us that the rest of the system, does not falsify P , i.e. does not flip the state of the system from P to $\neg P$. (We find this property commonly phrased as "P is stable".) But we want more than just P's stability. We want the state of the system to actually satisfy P . This, now, will be the task of the component in which assertion P occurs. In our mini-example

$$\ldots \; x := 0 \; \{0 \le x\} \; \ldots \qquad ,$$

assertion $0 \le x$ is clearly established by the preceding atomic statement $x := 0$. But if the preceding atomic statement were $x := y$, say, it would require a pre-assertion, for instance $0 \le y$:

$$\ldots ; \; \{0 \le y\} \; x := y \; \{0 \le x\} \; \ldots \qquad .$$

With this pre-assertion for $x := y$, assertion $0 \le x$ has become what we phrase *locally correct*.

As a result, dealing with the local correctness of an assertion — here $0 \le x$ — will usually require one other assertion — here $0 \le y$. For the benefit of locally establishing a component's initial assertion , i.e. the assertion without preceding statement, we equip the multiprogram as a whole with a precondition (which characterizes the initial state from which the execution of the multiprogram starts). We can now formulate the

Rule of Local Correctness

For the local correctness of an assertion P in a component, we distinguish two cases.

- If P is the (one and only) initial assertion of the component, it is locally correct whenever it is implied by the precondition of the multiprogram as a whole.
- If P is textually preceded by $\{Q\} \, S$, i.e. by atomic statement S with pre-assertion Q, it is locally correct whenever

$$\{Q\} \, S \, \{P\}$$

is a correct Hoare-triple.

End of Rule of Local Correctness.

Thus, checking the local correctness of annotation is just what we are used to for stand-alone sequential programs. We emphasize that the annotation should be such that it is always clear which is the textually preceding atomic statement of an assertion. The standard annotation schemes for the composition, the alternative construct, and the repetition have been designed the way they are for this purpose. (For repetitions, the evaluation of the guard counts as an atomic statement.) We will return to this issue at a later stage.

$$* \qquad *$$
$$*$$

Now we are ready to formulate what we call the *Core* of the Owicki/Gries theory. We consider a multiprogram annotated in such a way that the annotation provides a precondition for the multiprogram as a whole and a pre-assertion for each atomic statement in each individual component. Then, by Owicki and Gries, this annotation is *correct* whenever each individual assertion is *correct*, i.e.

- locally correct according to the Rule of Local Correctness, and

- globally correct according to the Rule of Global Correctness.

This is the Core of the Owicki/Gries theory. It can be summarized and memorized quite succinctly by

> the annotation of a multiprogram is correct
> $\equiv$
> each assertion is established by the component in which it occurs and it is maintained by all atomic statements of all other components

The reason why we are calling it the Core is, that later on we will have to face a distressing relaxation.

3.1 Two examples

Now the time has come to consider some examples.

Example 0   We consider the following annotated two-component multi-program

Pre : $x = 0$	
A: $\{x = 0 \lor x = 2\}$	B: $\{x = 0 \lor x = 1\}$
$x := x + 1$	$x := x + 2$
$\{x = 1 \lor x = 3\}$	$\{x = 2 \lor x = 3\}$

Component A consists of just one statement, viz. $x := x + 1$, and component B of just $x := x + 2$. Both statements are considered atomic, and both are equipped with a pre-assertion — as required. In this example, each of the components has a post-assertion as well. We now show that the annotation provided is correct. We do so for the assertions in A.

We first consider $x=0 \lor x=2$. Because this is A's initial assertion, its local correctness should follow from the precondition of the multiprogram as a whole. And indeed we have

$$x=0 \lor x=2 \Leftarrow x=0 \quad .$$

As for its global correctness, we have to show that it is not falsified by

$$\{x=0 \lor x=1\} \; x:=x+2$$

of component B. That is, we have to show the correctness of Hoare-triple

$$\{(x=0 \lor x=2) \land (x=0 \lor x=1)\}$$
$$x:=x+2$$
$$\{x=0 \lor x=2\}$$

— the Rule of Global Correctness with $x=0 \lor x=2$ for P, $x=0 \lor x=1$ for Q, and $x:=x+2$ for S.

Rendered in wlp-nomenclature, this Hoare-triple reads

$$(x=0 \lor x=2) \land (x=0 \lor x=1) \; \Rightarrow \; (x:=x+2).(x=0 \lor x=2) \quad ,$$

or — simplifying the antecedent —

$$x=0 \; \Rightarrow \; (x:=x+2).(x=0 \lor x=2) \quad ,$$

and the validity of this follows from the following little calculation

$$(x:=x+2).(x=0 \lor x=2)$$

$\equiv \qquad \{\text{substitution}\}$

$$x+2=0 \lor x+2=2$$

$\Leftarrow \qquad \{\text{arithmetic and predicate calculus}\}$

$$x=0 \quad .$$

Next we consider A's assertion $x=1 \lor x=3$. Because it is textually preceded by

$$\{x=0 \lor x=2\} \; x:=x+1 \quad ,$$

its local correctness ought to follow from

$$\{x=0 \lor x=2\}$$
$$x := x+1$$
$$\{x=1 \lor x=3\} \quad ,$$

which — by the axiom of assignment — it does.
For the global correctness of $x=1 \lor x=3$ we have to prove — in wlp-nomenclature at once —

$$(x=1 \lor x=3) \land (x=0 \lor x=1) \; \Rightarrow \; (x:=x+2).(x=1 \lor x=3)$$

or — simplifying the antecedent —

$$x=1 \; \Rightarrow \; (x:=x+2).(x=1 \lor x=3) \quad ,$$

and by a similar little calculation as before, this is correct as well.
End of Example 0.

Because the above reasoning pattern — demonstrating the local and global correctness of assertions — is, by definition, so intrinsically related to the proof obligations of the Owicki/Gries theory, we wish to give it a more conspicuous shape when rendered on paper. When dealing with an assertion P, we will supply it with a reference to a Note, like this

    ... $\{P, \text{Note}\}$ ...   ,

and the Note will get the shape

Note "P"

L: explaining why P is locally correct

G: explaining why P is globally correct.

End of Note.

Observe that the header of the Note repeats P.

Small Intermezzo The above convention may come across as a naive clerical device. However, in our experience, it is much more than that. Some of our readers will meanwhile have surmised that the Owicki/Gries theory will potentially saddle us with a prohibitively large number of proof obligations. And, indeed: taking care of the global correctness of one single assertion forces us to "visit" *all* atomic statements of *all* components. (To reassure the reader: the situation will improve in the next chapters.) In the presence of such a multitude of obligations, a clear-cut organization of the bookkeeping is a prime prerequisite, lest chaos result.
When, in one of our classes, we introduced the regime with the Notes, students started to perform significantly better.
End of Small Intermezzo.

Whereas Example 0 was purely an exercise in verification, the next example already has a more constructive flavour.

Example 1 Consider the following two-component multiprogram — comments below —:

Pre :	*true*
A: $* [\, x := E.x \,]$	B: $* [\, y := x$
	$; z := x$
	$\{?\ y \leq z,\ \text{Note } 0\}$
	$]$

where $E.x$ is an integer expression that may depend on integer x, but not on integers y and z.

First we observe that the precondition of the multiprogram is just *true* — some would say: it has no precondition! —By this we mean that the initial values of variables x, y, and z can by anything. Secondly we observe that the components' annotation is far from complete; so what are the atomic statements? Let us assume that the individual assignments are atomic. Now we can meaningfully ask the following question:

On what condition is queried assertion $y \leq z$ correct?

In order to investigate this, we address the correctness of $y \leq z$ in Note 0, as already announced in the text of component B.

Note 0 " $y \leq z$ "

L: The textually preceding atomic statement of $y \leq z$ is $z := x$, and it had better have

$$wlp.(z := x).(y \leq z)   ,$$

i.e. $y \leq x$,
as a correct pre-assertion.
We shall insert this in B's program text as a new assertion, to be dealt with later on.

G: $\{y \leq z\}\ x := E.x\ \{y \leq z\}$ is a correct Hoare-triple, and vacuously so: $y \leq z$ does not depend on x. We will return to this phenomenon in a next chapter under the heading "Orthogonality".

End of Note 0.

By the above findings, component B now has obtained the following annotated shape

B: $* [\ y := x$

   $;\ \{?\ y \leq x,\ \text{Note 1}\}$

   $z := x$

   $\{y \leq z\}$

   $]$,

and what remains is to investigate queried assertion $y \leq x$:

Note 1 " $y \leq x$ "

L: The local correctness is immediate from the preceding assignment $y := x$.

G: We have to investigate $y \leq x$ under A's statement $x := E.x$. We calculate

$$y \leq x \;\Rightarrow\; (x := E.x).(y \leq x)$$

$\equiv$ {substitution}

$$y \leq x \;\Rightarrow\; y \leq E.x$$

$\Leftarrow$ {transitivity of $\leq$}

$$x \leq E.x \;,$$

and as a result the global correctness of $y \leq x$ follows whenever we choose E such that $x \leq E.x$.

End of Note 1.

This completes the example. We suppose that someone who had an operational flirt with the original component B, will probably have guessed the answer: x is not allowed to decrease. Indeed, if the first inspection of x's value — y — is to be at most the (later) second inspection — z —, then x had better *never* be decreased in between.

End of Example 1.

3.2   Postconditions

Before we can conclude this chapter, there is one more issue to be dealt with, namely the "terminating multiprogram". In most examples that we will encounter, the components will be cyclic programs, i.e. programs of the form $*[\,S\,]$. But sometimes we will also have to address multiprograms in which all components terminate or ought to terminate, so as to establish a desired postcondition. In those cases, the multiprogram as a whole not only has a precondition but it also has a postcondition. For the correctness of the latter we have the

Rule of the Postcondition

Postcondition R of a multiprogram is correct whenever

  – all components are guaranteed to terminate, and
  – R is implied by the conjunction of the post-assertions of the individual components.

End of Rule of the Postcondition.

As an example of a terminating multiprogram, reconsider the multiprogram in Example 0, with components

  A: $x := x + 1 \;\{x = 1 \,\vee\, x = 3\}$
  B: $x := x + 2 \;\{x = 2 \,\vee\, x = 3\}$.

Both components surely terminate, and therefore they establish

$$(x=1 \lor x=3) \land (x=2 \lor x=3) \quad ,$$

i.e. $x=3$, as a postcondition of the multiprogram as a whole.

$$* \qquad *$$
$$*$$

Herewith we conclude our explanation of the Core of the Owicki/Gries theory. There is, however, more to it, because with the rules given so far, we are unable to prove that the little terminating multiprogram

Pre: $x=0$

A: $x:=x+1$

B: $x:=x+1$

establishes postcondition $x=2$. The reader might care to give it a try.

4

Two Disturbing Divergences

At the end of the previous chapter, we charged the reader with an impossible task, viz. to prove, with the Core rules of the Owicki/Gries theory, that the little multiprogram

Pre: $x = 0$

A: $x := x + 1$

B: $x := x + 1$

establishes postcondition $x = 2$. This impossibility, which we shall prove in a moment, is really disturbing, first, because from an operational point of view it is absolutely obvious that the final state satisfies $x = 2$, and, second, because it makes us wonder how many other surprises there are in store for us. (To reassure the reader, things will turn out reasonably well.)

Remark A phenomenon like the above may raise one's interest in the logic and nature of proof systems, for instance to find out their potential and their limitations. Valid and useful as, we think, such theoretical, indepth investigations are, we ourselves are rather more interested in methods for constructing multiprograms, but we are glad to observe that others are more inclined to address more fundamental issues — such as, for instance, Krzysztof R. Apt and Ernst-Rüdiger Olderog in their monograph [AO91]. **End** of Remark.

We now prove that with the Core rules of the Owicki/Gries theory we cannot possibly demonstrate the correctness of postcondition $x = 2$ in our little culprit program. We annotate it as follows

Pre : $x = 0$	
A: $\{P\}$	B: $\{P\}$
$x := x + 1$	$x := x + 1$
$\{Q\}$	$\{Q\}$
Post : R	

Because of the symmetry in the components we can, without loss of generality, confine our attention to a symmetric annotation. In order to find out what postconditions we can conclude, we calculate the strongest R that can possibly follow from the Core.

According to the Core rules, the correctness of the above annotation means

(0) $[\, x = 0 \;\Rightarrow\; P \,]$ for the local correctness
     of the two assertions P

(1) $[\, P \;\Rightarrow\; (x := x + 1).P \,]$ for the global correctness
     of the two assertions P

(2) $[\, P \;\Rightarrow\; (x := x + 1).Q \,]$ for the local correctness
     of the two assertions Q

(3) $[\, P \wedge Q \;\Rightarrow\; (x := x + 1).Q \,]$ for the global correctness
     of the two assertions Q

(4) $[\, Q \;\Rightarrow\; R \,]$ for the correctness
     of postcondition R.

First observe that (3) is implied by (2), so that we can forget about (3). Secondly, observe from (4) that the strongest R equivales the strongest Q. And thus we are left with finding the strongest Q that is admitted by (0), (1), and (2).

Since Q now only occurs in (2), the strongest Q equivales the strongest $(x := x - 1).P$ — for a detailed proof see the Appendix of this chapter. We leave it to the reader to prove, by mathematical induction, that the strongest $(x := x - 1).P$ with P satisfying (0) and (1) equivales $1 \leq x$. As a result, the strongest R that we can conclude from the Core of Owicki and Gries is

   $1 \leq x$

(which is definitely weaker than the intended $x = 2$).

Acknowledgement   We owe the above proof to our colleague Rob R. Hoogerwoord.
End of Acknowledgement.

As will become apparent later, it is not the Core that is to be blamed, but the fact that in the above example the value of x — which is the only variable in the game — cannot fully describe the states that the system can reside in. The remedy will be the introduction of auxiliary variables — not an uncommon phenomenon in proving mathematical theorems. We relegate this subject to the next chapter.

* * *

A second disturbing observation is exemplified by the following. In the previous chapter we have shown the correctness of the annotation in

Pre : $x = 0$	
A: $\{x = 0 \lor x = 2\}$	B: $\{x = 0 \lor x = 1\}$
$x := x + 1$	$x := x + 2$
$\{x = 1 \lor x = 3\}$	$\{x = 2 \lor x = 3\}$

Let us recall our interpretation and appreciation of a correct assertion P. It says that the state of the system satisfies P whenever execution of a component has reached that assertion. But then we must be willing to accept that an assertion weaker than P is correct as well, because the state of the system also satisfies this weaker assertion.

This means, for instance, that we must be willing to accept that the annotation in

Pre : $x = 0$	
A: $\{x \leq 2\}$	B: $\{x \leq 1\}$
$x := x + 1$	$x := x + 2$
$\{x \leq 3\}$	$\{x \leq 3\}$

is correct: each assertion in it is a weakening of the corresponding assertion in the earlier program. However, the problem is that we can no longer show the correctness of this annotation using just the Core. For instance, the global correctness of $x \leq 1$ in B would require a proof of

$$[\, x \leq 1 \wedge x \leq 2 \;\; \Rightarrow \;\; (x := x+1).(x \leq 1)\,]\qquad,$$

i.e. of $\;[\, x \leq 1 \;\Rightarrow\; x \leq 0\,]\,$,
which just isn't a theorem.

The result is that we will have to loosen the reins and face a relaxation of our conception of correct annotation. We do so by adding to the Core of the Owicki/Gries theory the postulate of

Weakening the Annotation

> Correct annotation remains correct by weakening an assertion
> or weakening the postcondition.

End of Weakening the Annotation.

This addendum to the rules is annoying indeed, in fact almost frightening, because the question now has become how to proceed in proving the correctness of annotation. Somehow we have to invent, find, or construct, perhaps with the aid of auxiliary variables, a *stronger* annotation, viz. one that is correct on account of the Core rules. Then the correctness of the original — weaker — annotation follows from the postulate of "Weakening the Annotation". Finding such a stronger annotation is, in general, quite a nasty task and will often require a firm operational understanding of the multiprogram. Or, to quote Leslie Lamport in [Lam88]: "Finding the proper annotation to prove a property of a concurrent program is a difficult art; anything that makes the task easier should be welcome.".

*   *
*

However annoying the observations in this chapter may seem, we need not be too pessimistic, because there is a way to avoid the problem: we shall be *developing* correct programs rather than inventing a-posteriori proofs for programs that to all intents and purposes could just have appeared out of thin air. And from sequential programming we know — paraphrasing Dijkstra [Dij76] — that the development of a program and its correctness proof — i.e. the appropriate annotation — go hand in hand, with the correctness proof being slightly ahead. Thus the development of programs and of correctness proofs have become two activities of a kind, and as we shall see this will hold for multiprograms as well.

Appendix

In this appendix we prove that $(x := x - 1).P$ is the strongest solution of
the equation in Q

$$Q: \quad [\, P \;\Rightarrow\; (x := x + 1).Q \,] \qquad :$$

$$[\, P \;\Rightarrow\; (x := x + 1).Q \,]$$

$\equiv \qquad \{\text{substitution } x := x - 1 \text{ is monotonic and invertible}\}$

$$[\, (x := x - 1).P \;\Rightarrow\; (x := x - 1).((x := x + 1).Q) \,]$$

$\equiv \qquad \{x := x - 1 \text{ and } x := x + 1 \text{ are inverses}\}$

$$[\, (x := x - 1).P \;\Rightarrow\; Q \,] \qquad .$$

And this completes our proof.

5

Bridling the Complexity

Let us consider a multiprogram with N components, each containing M atomic statements and, hence, M assertions, and let us count how much work is involved in proving the correctness of the annotation of such a multiprogram. First of all, there are $M \times N$ assertions in the game. Secondly, for each individual assertion we have to check its local correctness — counting for 1 — and its global correctness — counting for $M \times (N-1)$. As a result, the total amount of proof obligations to be fulfilled equals

$$M \times N \times (1 + M \times (N-1)) \quad ,$$

which is quadratic in the size — i.e. the number of atomic statements — of the multiprogram. Even for a modestly sized program with $M = 7$ and $N = 5$, the workload already consists of

> 1.015

proofs to be carried out. This is definitely far beyond what can be expected from a human being. Even an automatic proof system would quickly be defeated by such a quadratic explosion. The main cause of this explosion is the necessity to prove the global correctness of assertions.

Remark Nevertheless, we once more would like to point out how much has been gained by the Owicki/Gries theory. For our modestly sized multiprogram with $M = 7$ and $N = 5$, the number of possible interleavings, i.e. the number of different computations that can be generated by it, is closer to infinity than to 1.015, viz. it is

3.177.459.078.523.411.968.000[†]   .

End of Remark.

Because the main purpose of this monograph is to investigate how multiprograms can be formally derived, we *must* find out how the complexity of this gigantic proof load can be effectively bridled, lest we have to give up the whole enterprise. The main means towards that end comprise "orthogonality", the use of "system invariants", the technique of "mutual exclusion", exploitation of symmetry, the construction of a body of useful theorems, and abstraction. In this chapter we will discuss the first three issues, largely leaving the others for later. Each of the techniques discussed will, in its own way, reduce the workload, and in particular the proof load required for global correctness.

5.0   Private variables and orthogonality

Most multiprograms are constructed with the aim that the components cooperate on a common, global task. For proper cooperation, information exchange will be necessary. We wish to abstract from the various technologies for information exchange, choosing as our "communication medium" the rather neutral, unbiased universe of common variables.

Remark   This does *not* mean that we have adopted the traditional architecture of a physical common store. Of course it is a possible implementation for keeping the values of common variables, but it isn't the only one. In this text we shall hardly deal with the question of how the information as carried by the common variables is to be represented on actual physical machinery, because for the purpose of our investigations this would be too specific a concern.
End of Remark.

Highly typical of a variable is that its value gets changed. We distinguish two cases

- a variable that is changed by just one component; this we call a *private variable* of that component

- a variable that is changed by more than one component; this we call a *shared variable* of the system.

[†]This is $(7 \times 5)!/(7!)^5$, courtesy Tom Verhoeff and Mathematica.

Of course the values of common variables, whether private or shared, can in principle be inspected by all components.

It is by an adequate use of private variables that we may considerably tame the proof load, viz. we have the

Rule of Private Variables

> For an assertion in a component that depends on private variables of that component only, it suffices to prove local correctness, because its global correctness comes for free.

End of Rule of Private Variables.

Indeed, the global correctness of such an assertion comes for free, because, by the definition of private variables, the variables in the assertion are not changed by the other components.

Example 0 Consider the following two-component multiprogram

Pre : $x=0 \ \wedge \ a=0 \ \wedge \ b=0$	
A: $\{a=0\}$	B: $\{b=0\}$
$x,a := x+1, a+1$	$x,b := x+1, b+1$
$\{a=1\}$	$\{b=1\}$
Post : $a+b=2$	

Variable a is private to component A, and variable b is private to component B. Therefore, it suffices to check the local correctness of the given assertions, which is an elementary exercise of sequential programming. If, in the sequel, we address an assertion like $a=1$ above in a Note, we will do so quite synoptically, for instance like

Note "$a=1$"
    Private variable
End of Note.

In passing we observe that the given postcondition — $a+b=2$ — is obviously correct.

End of Example 0.

Example 1 We consider a multiprogram with many components. Variable d_i is private to component i.

$$
\begin{array}{|l|}
\hline
\text{Pre}: \quad x = 0 \,\wedge\, \langle\, \forall j :: d_j = 0 \,\rangle \\
\hline
\text{Comp}.i: \quad * \,[\; \{d_i = 0\} \\
\qquad\qquad x, d_i := x + 1, 1 + d_i \\
\qquad\quad ;\, \{d_i = 1\} \\
\qquad\qquad x, d_i := x - 1, -1 + d_i \\
\qquad\quad \{d_i = 0\} \\
\qquad\quad] \\
\hline
\end{array}
$$

Again, the annotation is obviously correct, thanks to the fact that d_i is private to Comp.i. Observe that $d_i = 0$ is an invariant of the *loop* of Comp.i.

End of Example 1.

In distributed systems, i.e. usually large and sparse networks of components or bunches of components, direct communication between components is physically restricted to communication between neighbouring nodes of the network. In such systems, the use of private variables tends to abound, with potentially enhanced simplicity — or rather: reduced complexity — as a result. This may offer one explanation for the popularity of distributed programs. However, the other side of the coin is that this very lack of communication facilities creates its own problems.

*   *

*

Even though the global correctness proof of an assertion in principle requires us to consider *all* atomic statements in all other components, in practice the number of actual, non-vacuous proof obligations is usually fairly limited, because the number of distinct variables occurring in an assertion is usually quite small and because we have the

Rule of Orthogonality

An assertion is maintained by *all* assignments to variables not occurring in it.

End of Rule of Orthogonality.

The proof of this rule is simple: if x does not occur in predicate P, then $\{P\}\ x := E\ \{P\}$ is a correct Hoare-triple.

In what follows, we will hardly ever mention the Rule of Orthogonality explicitly, but we will exploit it extensively in our global correctness proofs: when dealing with the global correctness of an assertion P, we will silently ignore *all* assignments — in other components — to variables that do not occur in P, and focus on just those assignments that may affect P.

Note that the Rule of Private Variables given earlier is subsumed by the Rule of Orthogonality: in fact, it describes the extreme case of orthogonality where *no* assignment in another component can affect the assertion in question. Nevertheless the Rule of Private Variables has a right of existence of its own, for the following reason. In general, when dealing with the global correctness of an assertion, we *have to* scan all other components for assignments that may affect it; however simple and quick this task may be, it cannot be ignored. If, however, the assertion depends on private variables of its component only, we know that the whole scan is superfluous.

5.1   System Invariants

More than by any other means, it is through the use of so-called system invariants that we can achieve a huge reduction of the proof load. By definition, a relation P is a *system invariant* whenever

(i) it holds initially, i.e. is implied by the precondition of the multiprogram as a whole

(ii) it is maintained by each individual atomic statement $\{Q\}\ S$ of each individual component, i.e. whenever for each such $\{Q\}\ S$

$$\{P \wedge Q\}\ S\ \{P\}$$

is a correct Hoare-triple.

From this definition we see, for instance, that *true* is a system invariant for every multiprogram, thanks to the topstrictness of $wlp.S$ for any S.

Note that the number of proof obligations to be fulfilled with respect to a system invariant is linear in the size of the multiprogram. For instance, for our program in the beginning of this chapter, the one with N components each containing M atomic statements, we have to fulfill

$$1 + M \times N$$

proof obligations for a relation to be a system invariant. This proof load is comparable to the proof load for a single assertion, but the big difference is that for a system invariant we have the beautiful property that

> a system invariant can be added as a conjunct
> to each assertion with impunity, i.e. without
> any further, additional proof obligations.

This can be proved as follows. Let P be a system invariant and R an arbitrary assertion. What we have to prove is that $R \wedge P$ is both locally and globally correct, if R is. We distinguish two cases:

- If R is the initial assertion of a component and our concern is *local* correctness, we observe that — by (i) — $R \wedge P$ is locally correct if R is.

- In *all* other cases, the original proof obligation has the shape $\{X \wedge Q\} \, S \, \{R\}$, where Q is the pre-assertion of S: if it is a global correctness obligation, X is R and if it is a local correctness obligation, X is just *true*.

What we now have to prove is
$$\{X \wedge Q \wedge P\} \, S \, \{R \wedge P\} \qquad ,$$
or — because Hoare-triples are finitely conjunctive in the postcondition —

$$\{X \wedge Q \wedge P\} \, S \, \{R\} \qquad \text{and}$$
$$\{X \wedge Q \wedge P\} \, S \, \{P\} \qquad .$$

The first of these Hoare-triples follows — by "strengthening the precondition" — from the original proof obligation $\{X \wedge Q\} \, S \, \{R\}$, and the second one follows — by the same rule — from the fact that P is a system invariant, more precisely it follows from (ii).

This completes our proof.

So the great merit of a system invariant is that we can assert it everywhere in our program text, at the expense of only a linear amount of work. But this brings about another great merit, viz.

> because a system invariant can be added as a
> conjunct to each assertion, we have the free-
> dom of not writing it anywhere in our anno-
> tation.

And this is what we shall do. Although merely clerical, this rule is very important for the clarity and economy of exposition, for writer and reader and for student and teacher alike.

A consequence, however, is that by following the rule we may break the one-to-one correspondence between assertions and atomic statements. As a result we can no longer syntactically infer from the annotated program what the atomic statements are. Therefore, we shall always obey the following rule:

> be explicit about which statements are atomic.

Example 2   We copy the annotated program of Example 0, while adding a system invariant:

Pre : $x = 0 \land a = 0 \land b = 0$	

A: $\{a = 0\}$
    $x, a := x + 1, a + 1$
    $\{a = 1\}$
	B: $\{b = 0\}$
	    $x, b := x + 1, b + 1$
	    $\{b = 1\}$

Inv : P : $\quad x = a + b$	
Post : $\quad a + b = 2$	

The invariance of P in the above is obvious.

Furthermore, we observe that — by invariant P — the postcondition of the multiprogram implies $x = 2$. If we now erase all references to the variables a and b, we have established that in multiprogram

Pre : $x = 0$	
A: $x := x + 1$	B: $x := x + 1$
Post : $x = 2$	

postcondition $x = 2$ is correct. And here we have obtained the result that previously we proved unattainable from just the Core rules of the Owicki/Gries theory (see Chapter 4). This time we succeeded, thanks to the presence of the — auxiliary — variables a and b.

Finally, observe that by erasing all references to a and b, we have weakened the annotation, because the assertions about a and b in the components have been replaced by the weaker (and invisible) assertions "*true*". Proving, from scratch, the correctness of postcondition $x = 2$ in the "stripped" program, would require us to invert the process, i.e. to invent adequate auxiliary variables and adequate auxiliary assertions, which is a kind of exercise that is not too palatable, in general.

End of Example 2.

Example 3   We copy the annotated program of Example 1, while adding two system invariants:

Pre : $x = 0 \;\wedge\; \langle\, \forall j :: d_j = 0 \,\rangle$

Comp.i: $* \,[\; \{d_i = 0\}$
     $\quad\quad x, d_i \;:=\; x + 1, \, 1 + d_i$
     $\quad ; \{d_i = 1\} \; \{1 \leq x, \text{see comments below}\}$
     $\quad\quad x, d_i \;:=\; x - 1, \, -1 + d_i$
     $\quad\quad \{d_i = 0\}$
     $\quad]$

Inv : $P_0 :$ $\langle\, \forall j :: 0 \leq d_j \,\rangle$ $P_1 :$ $x = \langle\, \sum j :: d_j \,\rangle$

In the above annotation we added assertion $1 \leq x$ by juxtaposing it to $d_i = 1$. Such juxtaposition of assertions stands for their conjunction, and it forms a notational technique that has proven to come in handy in the design of multiprograms and their correctness proofs. We will return to this in later chapters. Assertions $d_i = 1$ and $1 \leq x$ are called "co-assertions" of each other.

We are indeed entitled to add $1 \leq x$ as a conjunct to $d_i = 1$, because from P_0 and P_1 — recall: invisible co-assertions of $d_i = 1$ — we conclude

$$d_i = 1 \;\Rightarrow\; 1 \leq x$$

or, equivalently,

$$d_i = 1 \;\equiv\; d_i = 1 \,\wedge\, 1 \leq x \quad .$$

Again, the invariance of P_0 and P_1 is obvious, from techniques of sequential programming only. There is one additional phenomenon, though, that deserves our attention. It goes under the name "symmetry". If the, say, N components in the above multiprogram, each containing 2 atomic statements, are to maintain a system invariant, we have to carry out $2 \times N$ proofs. However, in the current example symmetries abound. First of all, all components are alike: component j is just component i with i replaced by j. Secondly, our current system invariants are symmetric in the components: by interchanging the names of two arbitrary components, the invariants do not change.

As a result of the symmetries in the components and in the invariants, it suffices to consider one — arbitrary — component and show that it maintains the invariants. Thus the proof burden is reduced from $2 \times N$ to just 2 per invariant!

We conclude with the observation that invariants P_0 and P_1 together imply the invariance of

$$0 \leq x \quad .$$

a result to be used below.

End of Example 3.

*   *
*

The multiprogram in the above example gives rise to a useful theorem: from weakening the annotation through removal of all references to the variables d, we obtain the

First Topology Lemma

The following multiprogram — with arbitrary number of components — is correctly annotated

Pre : $x = 0$
Comp.i: $*\,[\ x := x + 1$
$;\ \{1 \leq x\}$
$x := x - 1$
$]$
Inv : $0 \leq x$

End of First Topology Lemma.

Each component first increments x and then decrements it. In between, the value of x exceeds its initial value, irrespective of what the other components have done to x. Such a configuration pops up every so often, and having a theorem about it has proven to be worthwhile. It is the "topographic" positioning of the assignments to x that accounts for the theorem's name.

5.2   Mutual Exclusion

Most machine architectures provide only a limited repertoire of statements that can be considered atomic. Many programming problems, however, demand system invariants that cannot be maintained by just the atomic statements provided by the machinery. For example, if the machinery only supplies atomic increments or decrements of single variables, it will be hard to maintain an invariant like

$$x + y = z   :$$

a program fragment like

$$x := x + 1$$
$$; z := z + 1$$

will, during execution, create an intermediate state where x has been increased already, but z hasn't. In that intermediate state the invariant no longer holds, and all sorts of nasty and unintended things could happen due to the activities of other components. However, if in one way or another we could see to it that, during the intermediate state, variables x, y, and z were untouchable, invisible for the rest of the system, the situation would be considerably better. The quest for such an arrangement creates (created[‡]) the problem of *Mutual Exclusion*, which — roughly speaking — boils down to the problem of how we can see to it that arbitrary program fragments can be dealt with as if they were atomic — "indivisible" or "interference-free" during execution. Let us consider the concept of Mutual Exclusion in some more detail and investigate how it can be exploited for reducing the proof load.

*   *

*

For our investigations it suffices to consider a multiprogram with just two components, Comp.0 and Comp.1, say. They each contain two types of program fragments, viz. N-fragments and C-fragments. N-fragments and C-fragments are disjoint. We furthermore introduce two booleans, inc_0 and inc_1, which are coupled to the components by

$$inc_0 \equiv (\text{Comp.0 is engaged in one of its C-fragments})   ,$$

and similarly for inc_1. Now suppose that somehow we have succeeded in tuning the multiprogram in such a way that it maintains system invariant

$$\neg inc_0 \vee \neg inc_1   ,$$

[‡]In fact, Mutual Exclusion was the historically first means towards bridling the complexity of parallel programs.

or, equivalently,

(0) $inc_0 \wedge inc_1 \equiv false$.

(The operational interpretation of this invariant is that two components are never engaged in their respective C-fragment simultaneously; their C-fragments "mutually exclude" each other in time: hence the name Mutual Exclusion.)

Now let us focus on C-fragments, which in general will consist of a number of atomic statements each properly supplied with a pre-assertion. In Comp.0 these pre-assertions can, by definition, all be strengthened with conjunct inc_0, so that they all have shape $inc_0 \wedge P$. Likewise, the atomic statements from Comp.1's C-fragments all have a pre-assertion of shape $inc_1 \wedge Q$. Let S be such a statement of Comp.1. Then we have, thanks to (0),

$$\{inc_0 \wedge P \wedge inc_1 \wedge Q\}\ S\ \{P\}   ,$$

i.e. such an S of Comp.1 does not falsify such a P of Comp.0. As a result we have

(1)   the assertions in C-fragments of the one component are globally correct under the atomic statements of the C-fragments of the other component.

*   *
*

How much is gained by this? Quite a lot, if the components contain many C-fragments that, in addition, are large in size. Multiprograms of this kind are "coarse-grained" in the sense that, during execution, not too much parallelism is exhibited. After all, the executions of the C-fragments are supposed to exclude each other in time. In the extreme case, when each individual component is just one C-fragment, no parallelism can be exhibited at all. It is generally accepted that in multiprogramming — i.e. in the construction of parallel programs — solutions that are too coarse-grained are to be avoided, because they would be against "the nature of parallelism". They are only tolerated if there are good reasons (for instance to avoid otherwise unmanageable complexity).

Hardly anything is gained by C-fragmentation if there are only a few C-fragments that, in addition, are small in size. There are, however, application areas, most notably the area of operating systems, where the components are so "loosely coupled" that all interaction between them can be confined to the C-fragments. There we can adhere to a programming discipline such that

(i) access to shared variables is confined to C-fragments (and disallowed in N-fragments),

(ii) the C-assertions of a component are expressed in shared variables and private variables of that component only,

with as a consequence that besides (1) we also have

(2) the assertions in C-fragments of the one component are globally correct under the atomic statements of the N-fragments of the other component.

And then we can combine (1) and (2) into

(3) on the assumptions (i) and (ii), C-assertions require a proof of local correctness only.

*   *
*

Let us see how we can exploit the above in the example from the beginning of this section. If for the benefit of "maintaining" $x+y=z$, program fragment

$$x := x+1$$
$$; z := z+1$$

is embedded in a C-fragment of Comp.0 and

$$y := y+1$$
$$; z := z+1$$

say, in a C-fragment of Comp.1,   and if there are no other operations on x, y, or z, then

$$inc_0 \lor inc_1 \lor x+y=z$$

is a system invariant, and as a result

$$x+y=z$$

holds "outside C-fragments", i.e. when no component is engaged in a C-fragment. Because, if we adhere to (i) and (ii), C-fragments cannot be distinguished from genuine atomic statements, we are entitled to say: "$x+y=z$ *is* a system invariant".

*   *
*

It is by (3), that a considerable reduction in proof load can be accomplished. Program construction based on this principle of mutual exclusion has firmly settled itself in the everyday practice of computing, right from the beginning (in the early 1960s). We can find extensive accounts of this programming style in the established literature — see, for instance, [Dij68], [Hoa74], [BH73] — and that is why, in this book, we will hardly pay attention to it.

*   *
*

The *concept* of Mutual Exclusion should not be confused with what has become known as the *problem* of Mutual Exclusion. The latter refers to the question of how to *implement* Mutual Exclusion, i.e. how to tune a multiprogram so as to realize (0) with the primitive repertoire of atomic statements provided by a particular technology. The problem of finding or designing such an implementation — commonly called a *Mutual Exclusion Algorithm* — has, ever since the problem emerged, been so intriguing, appealing, and challenging, that a nearly endless stream of (often would-be) solutions has seen the light — see [Ray86]. Up to this very day, "novel" solutions are submitted for publication.

In a later chapter, we ourselves will address the problem of Mutual Exclusion as well.

6

Co-assertions and Strengthening the Annotation

This short chapter will, as a matter of fact, be at the heart of one of our main techniques for the formal derivation of multiprograms. This technique will consist in a stepwise strengthening of a too-weakly annotated multi-program, i.e. of a multiprogram that cannot be handled with just the Core rules of the Owicki/Gries theory. Each individual strengthening step will always be guided by the desire to turn one or more assertions into correct ones, i.e. correct ones according to the Core. When, after a series of such strengthenings, the entire annotation has become correct in the Core — if ever! —, the design process has come to an end, because then — by the postulate of Weakening the Annotation — the original annotation is correct as well. In this chapter we shall focus on how to strengthen the annotation so as to make a *single* assertion correct (in the Core).

* *
*

Strengthening an annotation means strengthening one or more assertions or the precondition of the multiprogram. The strengthening of any such condition amounts to adding a conjunct. Therefore, we first analyze what is involved in proving the correctness of an assertion that is a conjunction, $X \wedge Y$ say.

There are three cases to be distinguished, viz. two dealing with the local correctness of $X \wedge Y$ and one with its global correctness.

- If $X \wedge Y$ is the initial assertion of a component, then its local correctness requires a proof of

$$[\, \text{Pre} \;\Rightarrow\; X \wedge Y \,] \quad ,$$

or, equivalently, of

(i) $$[\, \text{Pre} \Rightarrow X \,] \;\text{ and }\; [\, \text{Pre} \Rightarrow Y \,] \quad .$$

- If $X \wedge Y$ is textually preceded by $\{Q\}\, S$, then the proof obligation for its local correctness has the shape

$$[\, Q \;\Rightarrow\; wlp.S.(X \wedge Y) \,] \quad .$$

Because $wlp.S$ is conjunctive, this equivales

(ii) $$[\, Q \Rightarrow wlp.S.X \,] \;\wedge\; [\, Q \Rightarrow wlp.S.Y \,] \quad .$$

- All proofs of global correctness of $X \wedge Y$ with respect to $\{Q\}\, S$ have the shape

$$[\, Q \wedge X \wedge Y \;\Rightarrow\; wlp.S.(X \wedge Y) \,] \quad ,$$

which equivales

(iii) $$[\, Q \wedge X \wedge Y \Rightarrow wlp.S.X \,] \;\wedge\; [\, Q \wedge X \wedge Y \Rightarrow wlp.S.Y \,] \quad .$$

From (i) and (ii) we see that the local correctness of a conjunction can, without loss, be handled conjunct-wise. And this is nice, because, besides being more manageable, it may also contribute to a better separation of concerns: after all, the individual conjuncts may be very unrelated.

Remark   Such conjunct-wise treatment of a conjunction has become an established and successful practice in sequential programming. Note that it is only possible thanks to the conjunctivity of the wlp.
End of Remark.

From (iii) we obtain that also the global correctness of a conjunction can be handled conjunct-wise, this time not just without loss, but even with benefit. Let us consider the first conjunct of (iii), which can be rewritten as

(0) $$[\, Y \;\Rightarrow\; (Q \wedge X \Rightarrow wlp.S.X) \,] \quad .$$

If we had to prove the global correctness of X with respect to $\{Q\}\, S$ all by itself, we would have to show the validity of

(1) $$[\, Q \wedge X \;\Rightarrow\; wlp.S.X \,] \quad .$$

Comparing (0) and (1) we see that the body of (1) occurs as the consequent in (0), which implies that in the presence of a "conmate"[†] Y of X, proving the global correctness of X via (1) can be replaced by proving the weaker (0), and this might be beneficial. Of course, the same holds for X and Y interchanged.

*   *
*

In the above, we have established that an assertion that is a conjunction can be handled conjunct-wise. We now use this property in answering a question that is fundamental to our method of stepwise strengthening of the annotation: viz. the question is how the original annotation is affected if, for some reason, the precondition Pre or an assertion X, say, receives a conmate Y. The reassuring answer is that it isn't.

- If Pre is strengthened to Pre $\wedge Y$, this does not affect the local correctness of the initial assertions of the components. All other proof obligations remain the same since Pre is not involved in them.

- If assertion X receives a conmate Y, the previous section shows that this does not affect the correctness of X: from (i) and (ii) we see that its proof obligation for local correctness remains the same, and from the analysis of (iii) we see that its proof obligations for global correctness can only become weaker in the presence of conmate Y — so that the global correctness of X cannot by violated either.

  As for the correctness of any assertion other than X we observe that if X was involved in its original proof obligations at all, again the addition of conmate Y to X can only weaken these proof obligations.

Thus we have established that adding conjuncts to assertions does not violate the correctness of the annotation.

*   *
*

Now that the above has been said we return to the original problem of how to strengthen the annotation so as to make an assertion (or an invariant), P say, correct (in the Core). Again we distinguish three cases.

[†]In $X \wedge Y$, X and Y are called "conjunctive mates" of each other, or "conmates" for short.

• Local correctness of initial assertion P

If P is the initial assertion of a component, its local correctness requires the validity of

$$[\, \text{Pre} \Rightarrow P \,] \quad .$$

If this condition is not satisfied, we have to strengthen the precondition of the multiprogram as a whole into $\text{Pre} \wedge P$, or something stronger. Thus, P becomes locally correct in the Core. Note that — as mentioned before — this strengthening does not affect the correctness of the existing annotation.

Remark In practice, condition $\text{Pre} \wedge P$ can often be simplified, but that is a different, separate concern.
End of Remark.

• Local correctness of non-initial assertion P

If P is textually preceded by $\{Q\}\, S$, its local correctness requires the validity of

$$[\, Q \Rightarrow wlp.S.P \,] \quad .$$

If this condition is not satisfied, we strengthen pre-assertion Q of S into $Q \wedge wlp.S.P$, or something stronger. Thus, P becomes locally correct in the Core.

Note that by this strengthening Q has received a conmate, which we will record in the program text as a *co-assertion* to Q , to be denoted through juxtaposition; i.e. the strengthening will become manifest by replacing

$$\{Q\}\, S \quad \text{with} \quad \{Q\}\, \{wlp.S.P\}\, S \quad .$$

We lay down this convention in the

Rule of Juxtaposition

The juxtaposition of assertions stands for their conjunction.

End of Rule of Juxtaposition.

This notational device will appear to be very important[‡] in the development of annotation and programs. For one thing, human beings can, in fact, only do one thing at a time, here: tackle one assertion after the other.

[‡]This is quite an understatement: without this notational device this book could never have been written.

For another, we have seen that in case of a conjunction, separate treatment of the conjuncts is technically feasible and even to be recommended. By juxtaposing the conjuncts, their separate treatment becomes almost imposed.

Finally note that the introduction of a new assertion like $wlp.S.P$ constitutes a new proof obligation, which in turn may require new strengthenings of the annotation, but, again, that is a separate and later concern: here we are dealing with P, and P only.

• Global correctness of assertion P

The global correctness of P under $\{Q\}\ S$ (taken from a different component) requires the validity of

(2) $[\ Q \wedge P \Rightarrow wlp.S.P\ ]$.

But what if this does not hold? Remembering (0) and (1), we can replace it by the weaker

(3) $[\ F \Rightarrow (Q \wedge P \Rightarrow wlp.S.P)\ ]$,

whenever we strengthen assertion P into $P \wedge F$, i.e. whenever we add F as a co-assertion to P. By thus strengthening the annotation and requiring (3), P becomes globally correct under $\{Q\}\ S$.

Equation (3) in F may have many solutions. In a particular application, however, finding a solution F that is a *correct* co-assertion to P may be too much to ask for. For instance, each F satisfying $[\ F \Rightarrow \neg P\ ]$ is a solution to (3), but if for particular P, Q, and S such F's are the only solutions of (3), we are in trouble, because conjoined with P they yield *false*; and *false* is an assertion that can never be established.

Fortunately, there is a different possibility for weakening (2), viz. by adding a co-assertion G to Q, i.e. by replacing

   $\{Q\}\ S$ with $\{Q\}\{G\}\ S$.

Then (2) can be replaced by the weaker

   $[\ G \wedge Q \wedge P \Rightarrow wlp.S.P\ ]$,

or, equivalently, by

(4) $[\ G \Rightarrow (Q \wedge P \Rightarrow wlp.S.P)\ ]$.

Unfortunately, it will often be impossible to find a correct conmate F of P that satisfies (3) or a correct conmate G of Q that satisfies (4). A "combination" of the two, however, will, in practice, often do. So we shall in general be willing to handle P's global correctness under $\{Q\}\ S$ by adding a co-assertion F to P and a co-assertion G to Q, such that

$$[\,G \wedge Q \wedge F \wedge P \;\Rightarrow\; wlp.S.P\,]$$

or, equivalently,

(5) $[\,F \wedge G \;\Rightarrow\; (Q \wedge P \Rightarrow wlp.S.P)\,]$

will hold. Note that, indeed, (5) is a *further* weakening of both (3) and (4).

*   *

*

And this concludes our treatment of strengthening the annotation. Many examples will follow in subsequent chapters. Here we confine ourselves to a few final remarks.

• The above technique will be our *only* mechanism for introducing new assertions into the program text. That is, in a series of approximations, the annotation becomes stronger and stronger. This may be a little reassuring as far as the convergence of the process is concerned, but it isn't a guarantee at all. Sometimes convergence can only be reached by the introduction of *new* ingredients such as auxiliary variables. (To get a feel for this, the reader is invited to try to prove the First Topology Lemma — see Chapter 5 — by the technique just described.) In our experience, it is the F and the G in (5) that usually give strong hints as to what auxiliary variables might be introduced.

• The shape of (5) is geared to the way in which we typically derive appropriate co-assertions F and G. Mostly we begin massaging the consequent

$$Q \wedge P \;\Rightarrow\; wlp.S.P$$

of (5), setting up a sequence of equivalence preserving transformations, until an expression emerges that is simple enough. This latter expression, or a strengthening thereof, will then be our choice for $F \wedge G$. The question of how to divide it over an F and a G very much depends on specifics of the example.

• Our overall strategy, however, is to choose our strengthenings as weak as possible. There are good reasons for this, to which we shall return later. One — fundamental — reason can be explained here and now: if a strengthening turns out to be too strong, there is no going back, but if it turns out to be too weak, we can always perform another strengthening later on, and it is this chapter that tells us how to do so!

7

Three Theorems and Two Examples

Now that most of the groundwork has been done, the time has come to show the formalism at work. We shall give a number of rather unrelated examples, some of which are relevant enough to acquire the status of theorems. We start with the theorems, which happen to be the simpler exercises, and we conclude with slightly more sophisticated examples, which enable us to pay attention to *the design* of a-posteriori proofs, an activity that is quite similar to our ultimate goal: the design of multiprograms.

Disjointness

The first theorem is the

Rule of Disjointness

Assertion P is (globally) correct under $\{Q\}\, S$ if

$$[\, P \wedge Q \Rightarrow false \,] \quad .$$

End of Rule of Disjointness.

The proof is extremely simple: P is (globally) correct under $\{Q\}\, S$ whenever

$$[\, P \wedge Q \Rightarrow wlp.S.P \,]$$

holds, which it does for $[\, P \wedge Q \ \Rightarrow \ false\,]$.

However simple this rule may be, it deserves a name because it will prove to be of great practical value. A proof of the global correctness of an assertion like $x = 0$ under $\{x = 1\}\ x := 7$, for instance, can now be disposed of by the catchword

"Disjointness",

which explains the situation in just a single word.

Remark   The importance of having catchwords or catchphrases for well-understood situations should not be underestimated. They capture at a stroke what is going on. We extensively employ this "technique" of using catchwords in our calculations by putting in *hints*.
End of Remark.

The Rule of Disjointness not only helps in correctness proofs, it also has its rôle in program design. A typical usage is illustrated by the following little example.

Assume we want assertion $x = 0$ in one component to be globally correct under statement $x := 7$ in another component. It is quite clear that $x := 7$ will *certainly* falsify $x = 0$. One way to preclude this is to appeal to the Rule of Disjointness by requiring $x \neq 0$, say, to be a correct pre-assertion to $x := 7$. But if, for one reason or another, pre-assertion $x \neq 0$ would be too much to ask for, there is yet another — fairly canonical — way to proceed, viz. to strengthen the annotation by adding a co-assertion C to the target assertion $x = 0$ and a pre-assertion D to culprit statement $x := 7$ and requiring $[\, C \wedge D \ \Rightarrow \ false\,]$. In such a way C and D do the job (without anything being required about the value of x prior to $x := 7$).

Remark   Operationally speaking, the Rule of Disjointness expresses that certain combinations of states (ought to) exclude each other in time, thus bringing about mutual exclusion for particular program fragments. The traditional mutual exclusion proposal with the explicitly designated critical sections pushes the idea of Disjointness to the limit.
End of Remark.

Widening

The second theorem to be dealt with is the

Rule of Widening

> Assertion $x \leq y$ — x and y integer, say — is (globally) correct under descents of x and ascents of y.

End of Rule of Widening.

Here a "descent" is a decrease of at least 0. More precisely,

$$\{F \leq x\}\ x := F$$

descends x. And likewise,

$$\{y \leq G\}\ y := G$$

ascends y. In many applications F is something like $x - 1$ and G something like $y + 1$, so that the pre-assertions are just *true*. By such assignments the (x, y)- interval gets "wider", hence the name of the rule.

The proof that $x \leq y$ is (globally) correct under, for instance, $\{y \leq G\}\ y := G$ is, again, extremely simple:

$$(y := G).(x \leq y)$$
$$\equiv \quad \{\text{substitution}\}$$
$$x \leq G$$
$$\Leftarrow \quad \{\text{transitivity of} \leq\}$$
$$x \leq y\ \wedge\ y \leq G \quad ,$$

from which we see that it is the *transitivity* of $\leq$ that plays a central rôle.

Of course the Rule of Widening comes in many variations: predicate $x \leq y$ is just one example of a relation that is (anti)monotonic in some of its arguments. Another example would be a predicate like $c \Rightarrow d$ which is globally correct under statements like $c := c \wedge f$, $d := d \vee g$, $c := false$, etc., mainly thanks to the transitivity of $\Rightarrow$. We do not formulate the Rule of Widening in its full generality here, because we don't think that would be helpful.

Again, no matter how simple the Rule of Widening is, it deserves a name: since it can be used so frequently, it will prove to be of great practical value. By the single catchword

"Widening",

the situation is again explained at a stroke.

Topology

The third theorem to be dealt with is of a completely different nature. It is the

Second Topology Lemma

The following multiprogram — with arbitrary number of components — is correctly annotated

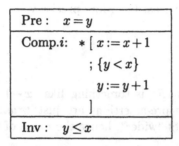

(The individual assignments are atomic.)

End of Second Topology Lemma.

We can prove the theorem in a way very similar to the proof given earlier for the First Topology Lemma. But this time we have yet another option: we can *use* the First Lemma to prove the Second, and that is what we will do. To that end, we introduce an auxiliary variable z and adjust the given multiprogram so as to make $z = x - y$ a system invariant. We thus obtain

$$
\begin{array}{|l|}
\hline
\text{Pre}: \quad x = y \ \wedge \ z = 0 \\
\hline
\text{Comp.}i: \ * [\ x, z := x + 1, z + 1 \\
\qquad \quad ; \{0 < z\} \ \{\text{hence} \ y < x \ \} \\
\qquad \quad y, z := y + 1, z - 1 \\
\qquad \quad] \\
\hline
\text{Inv}: \quad 0 \le z \ \wedge \ z = x - y, \ \text{hence} \ y \le x \\
\hline
\end{array}
$$

The invariance of $z = x - y$ is correct by construction. The invariance of $0 \le z$ and the correctness of assertion $0 < z$ follow from the First Topology Lemma by "projecting" the above program on z. The combination settles the theorem.

Topology Lemmata, too, come in many variations. For instance, in a multiprogram with N identical components — $1 \le N$ —, we have the correctness of

Pre :	$x = 0$
Comp.i:	$* [\; \{ x < N \}$
	$x := x + 1$
	$; \; x := x - 1$
	$\{ x < N \}$
	$]$
Inv :	$0 \le x \; \wedge \; x \le N$

It is almost undoable to characterize what Topology Lemmata are about in general. They usually refer to program structures in which the components increase and decrease shared variables in some strict and consistent order. When dealing with programs like that, we will often motivate the correctness of annotation by just using the catchphrase

"Program Topology".

We have learned, however, that it should not be used without care.

So much for our three theorems.

*　　　*
*

Next we consider some examples that will not be raised to theoremhood. But they serve at least three other purposes:

- They give a first performance of how the theory developed so far works in practice;

- They demonstrate how a-posteriori proofs can be designed. We will badly need this agility, because at a later stage we will have to design proofs for the absence of total deadlock — a phenomenon to be discussed in a next chapter —;

- They anticipate on what is coming, viz. program design. As will become clear, the design of programs and the design of a-posteriori proofs for existing programs are two activities of a kind. In either case auxiliary annotation will generally have to see the light; the main difference is that in program development genuine code is introduced along with it.

In the examples to follow, we will also pay some attention to the heuristics of the designs.

Example 0

We return to the artificial, random program from our initial chapter and put forward as our goal to prove the correctness of the postcondition in

Pre :	$x = 7 \; \wedge \; y = 3$	
A:	$x := y + 1$	B: $y := x + 1$
	; $x := y^2$	; $y := x^2$
	; $x := x - y$	; $y := y - x$
Post :	? $SQ.(x+y)$	

where SQ is defined by $SQ.z \equiv \langle \, \exists i :: z = i^2 \, \rangle$. (The individual assignments are atomic.)

In order not to confuse the reader with our presentation, we will largely separate the "what" and the "why". That is, we first present the fully annotated program, then explain how this annotation was chosen, and we conclude with fulfilling the major proof obligations.

Pre :	$x = 7 \; \wedge \; y = 3 \; \wedge \; \neg f \; \wedge \; \neg g$	
A: $\{\neg f\}$		B: $y := x + 1$
$x := y + 1$		; $y := x^2$
; $\{\neg f\}$		; $y, g := y - x,\ true$
$x := y^2$		$\{g\}$
; $\{SQ.x\}$		
$x, f := x - y,\ true$		
$\{f\}$		
Inv : ? P : $f \wedge g \;\Rightarrow\; SQ.(x+y)$		
Post : $SQ.(x+y)$		

Let us first explain why there is much more annotation in A than there is in B. To that end we observe that in the specification of the problem, both the multiprogram and the required postcondition are symmetric — in x versus y . Our first design decision has been to try to retain that symmetry in the proof as well. (And we succeeded, as will become clear below.) Thanks to the symmetry, however, we can now confine the whole discussion to just one component and its annotation — here: component

A. That is why most of B's annotation has been omitted. (Besides, if the need arises, B's annotation can simply be deduced from A's.)

Why this particular annotation?

- Both components certainly terminate; now the Rule of the Postcondition tells us that we have to introduce post-assertions in the individual components such that their conjunction implies $SQ.(x+y)$. We could, for instance, have tried $SQ.(x+y)$ itself as a post-assertion of A, but this assertion would have been far too vulnerable with respect to the operations in B. Therefore, we made a very neutral choice, choosing f in A and — symmetrically — g in B. But then, of course, we need that

$$f \wedge g \;\Rightarrow\; SQ.(x+y) \quad ,$$

and this we have chosen to become a system invariant — named P. (Note that P is symmetric in (f, x) versus (g, y) !)

- For P to be a system invariant, it should hold initially; that is why $\neg f$ and — symmetrically — $\neg g$ have appeared in the precondition.

- For reasons of simplicity we decided that variable f be private to A and g to B. As a result, the global correctness of assertions f and $\neg f$ in A is for free. Their local correctness is obvious.

- Assertions $\neg f$ and $SQ.x$ have been plugged in because they are useful for the invariance of P, to be dealt with shortly. Note that $SQ.x$ is obviously correct as well.

- Because f is *false* to start with and *true* at the end, statement $f := true$ has to be incorporated somewhere in A. The reason why it has been coupled to $x := x - y$ is that this is the only statement in A that "eliminates" variable y from the consequent of P, as will become apparent below.

So much for some why's.

Now we prove the invariance of P. We have to show that it holds initially — which it does by construction — and that no statement of the multiprogram violates it. Because of the symmetry, it suffices to address the statements of A only, and we now do so one after the other.

Re $\{\neg f\}\ x := y + 1$
Our proof obligation is

$$\{P \wedge \neg f\} \; x := y + 1 \; \{P\} \quad ,$$

the correctness of which follows from

$$(x := y + 1).P$$

$\equiv \qquad \{\text{substitute in } P\}$

$$f \wedge g \;\Rightarrow\; SQ.(y + 1 + y) \qquad\qquad (*)$$

$\equiv \qquad \{\neg f \text{ from the pre-assertion of } x := y + 1\}$

$\qquad true \qquad .$

Remark Here we see why $\neg f$ was introduced as a pre-assertion to $x := y + 1$. In the line marked $(*)$, the consequent is absolutely hopeless, in that it cannot follow from anything; and since g's value is unknown, the only way to "save" $(*)$ is by assuming $\neg f$.
End of Remark.

Re $\{\neg f\} \; x := y^2$

Similarly.

Re $\{SQ.x\} \; x, f := x - y, true$

$$(x, f := x - y, true).P$$

$\equiv \qquad \{\text{substitute in } P\}$

$$true \wedge g \;\Rightarrow\; SQ.(x - y + y)$$

$\equiv \qquad \{\text{simplify}\}$

$$g \;\Rightarrow\; SQ.x$$

$\equiv \qquad \{SQ.x \text{ from the pre-assertion of the statement}\}$

$\qquad true \qquad .$

End of Re's.

$$* \qquad *$$
$$*$$

From the above proof we see that neither the initial value of x or of y, nor the statements $x := y + 1$ and $y := x + 1$ play a rôle in the correctness of the postcondition. This is due to the weird example and the particular postcondition chosen. From the table of possible outcomes of this multiprogram we see that $x + y > 0$ is a correct postcondition as well. Here the initial value of x and y do play a rôle; we leave this proof as an exercise.

Example 1

The little multiprogram to be considered here is a simplified version of what has been called the "Non-Blocking Write Protocol", to which we shall return in a later chapter. Here our only goal is to prove the correctness of the assertion in:

Pre : $w \land \neg y \land \neg g$	
W: $w := false$	R: **do** $\neg g \rightarrow$
; $w := true$	$g := y$
; $y := true$	; $r := w$
	od
	$\{?\ r\}$

Version 0

(The individual assignments are atomic.)

Given the above program, it is not too difficult to show by operational reasoning that post-assertion r is, indeed, correct. The reader may have a look at it this way, and also convince himself that both in the loop body of R and in W the order of the assignments is crucial for the conclusion. When, in a later chapter, we derive a generalization of this algorithm from some specification, the order of the assignments will follow. Here our goal is to *develop*, in a number of steps, an annotation that is a strengthening of the one demanded by Version 0 — our specification — and that is correct in the Core of Owicki and Gries.

Let us first convince ourselves that component R terminates. Component W surely does, and because variable y is private to W, the final state of W satisfies y. In this state, R is guaranteed to terminate as well, since g will become stably *true*.

Now we proceed to the next, more strongly annotated version, guided by the following consideration. How can the local correctness of r — the post-assertion of a repetition — be concluded? We have little choice, viz. it has to follow from the conjunction of a loop invariant L and the negation of the guard, i.e. we need

$$L \land g \Rightarrow r$$

or, equivalently,

$$L \Rightarrow (g \Rightarrow r) \quad .$$

The weakest L thus is $g \Rightarrow r$, and that is the one we choose. With this loop invariant, the local correctness of target assertion r is guaranteed. Its global correctness is for free, since r is private to component R. We thus arrive at the next approximation for our ultimate annotation:

Pre : $w \wedge \neg y \wedge \neg g$	
W: $w := false$	R: $\{?\ \ g \Rightarrow r\}$
; $w := true$	**do** $\neg g \rightarrow$
; $y := true$	$\quad g := y$
	$\quad ; r := w$
	$\qquad \{?\ \ g \Rightarrow r\}$
	od
	$\{r\}$

Version 1

and what remains to be done is to take care of the two assertions $g \Rightarrow r$.

$$* \qquad *$$
$$*$$

The global correctness of either assertion $g \Rightarrow r$ is again for free. The local correctness of R's initial assertion $g \Rightarrow r$ follows from conjunct $\neg g$ of the multiprogram's precondition. As for the local correctness of the other assertion $g \Rightarrow r$, we demand that the preceding statement $r := w$ have precondition

$$wlp.(r := w).(g \Rightarrow r) \quad ,$$

i.e. $g \Rightarrow w$. Thus the next approximation becomes

Pre : $w \wedge \neg y \wedge \neg g$	
W: $w := false$	R: $\{g \Rightarrow r\}$
; $w := true$	**do** $\neg g \rightarrow$
; $y := true$	$\quad g := y$
	$\quad ; \{?\ \ g \Rightarrow w\}$
	$\quad\ \ r := w$
	$\qquad \{g \Rightarrow r\}$
	od
	$\{r\}$

Version 2

and what remains to be done is to take care of assertion $g \Rightarrow w$ in R.

*   *
*

The global correctness of $g \Rightarrow w$ is not for free: statements $w := false$ and $w := true$ might influence it. Statement $w := true$ is harmless to $g \Rightarrow w$: this is just Widening! As for $w := false$, we calculate[†]

$$(g \Rightarrow w) \Rightarrow (w := false).(g \Rightarrow w)$$

$\equiv$ {substitution}

$$(g \Rightarrow w) \Rightarrow (g \Rightarrow false)$$

$\equiv$ {simplification}

$$\neg g \vee \neg w$$

$\Leftarrow$ {see Remark below}

$$\neg g \qquad ,$$

and from this we see that something extra is needed for $g \Rightarrow w$ to be correct under $w := false$. We gratify this extra need by demanding that $\neg g$ be a pre-assertion of $w := false$.

Remark The last step in the above calculation looks like a strengthening, but in fact it isn't: looking a little bit ahead, we observe that w is a correct precondition of $w := false$. Thus the transition from $\neg g \vee \neg w$ to $\neg g$ is merely a simplification.
End of Remark.

We satisfy the local correctness of $g \Rightarrow w$ in R by requiring that the preceding statement $g := y$ have precondition

$$wlp.(g := y).(g \Rightarrow w) \qquad ,$$

i.e. $y \Rightarrow w$.

Thus we have arrived at

[†]See penultimate remark of Chapter 6

Pre : $w \wedge \neg y \wedge \neg g$	

W: $\{? \ \neg g\}$
 $w := false$
 ; $w := true$
 ; $y := true$
	R: $\{g \Rightarrow r\}$
	 do $\neg g \to$
	      $\{? \ \ y \Rightarrow w\}$
	      $g := y$
	      ; $\{g \Rightarrow w\}$
	      $r := w$
	      $\{g \Rightarrow r\}$
	 od
	 $\{r\}$

Version 3

and we are left with the care for assertion $\neg g$ in W and assertion $y \Rightarrow w$ in R.

$$* \qquad *$$
$$*$$

Assertion $y \Rightarrow w$ in R solely depends on private variables of W, which means that it ought to be an invariant of the "subsystem" W, and, as a result, of the entire system. We leave to the reader to check that $y \Rightarrow w$ is, indeed, a system invariant. (The topology of W is accountable for it.)

The local correctness of $\neg g$ in W follows from the precondition of the multiprogram. Its global correctness is endangered by $g := y$ in R. We calculate

$$\neg g \ \Rightarrow \ (g := y).(\neg g)$$

$\equiv$ {substitution}

$$\neg g \ \Rightarrow \ \neg y$$

$\Leftarrow$ {eliminating g — see below — }

$$\neg y \qquad ,$$

and we add this last line — $\neg y$ — as a co-assertion to target assertion $\neg g$. This new assertion only depends on private variables of W, and that is why we eliminated g in the above calculation. The local correctness of $\neg y$ is obvious.

Thus we arrive at our final version which reads

Pre : $w \wedge \neg y \wedge \neg g$	
W: $\{\neg g\} \{\neg y\}$ $w := false$; $w := true$; $\{w\}$ $y := true$	R: $\{g \Rightarrow r\}$ **do** $\neg g \rightarrow$ $\{y \Rightarrow w\}$ $g := y$; $\{g \Rightarrow w\}$ $r := w$ $\{g \Rightarrow r\}$ **od** $\{r\}$
Inv : $y \Rightarrow w$	

Version 4

*   *

*

The program above is fully documented in that anyone who wants to prove the correctness of the annotation, can now do so with just the Core rules. This will be a typical feature of almost all our designs, whether they pertain to program- or to proof construction. This should not be amazing, since — after all — the Core rules form our ultimate means for demonstrating correctness. Also typical will be that a cautiously conducted design will not produce more (annotation) than is strictly needed for the purpose. In much of the literature on a-posteriori verification we can find programs far too lavishly annotated, and needless to say this can only lead to unnecessary complication.

*   *

*

We hope that through this example we have been able to transmit some of the flavour of our intended design process. In a later chapter, the one on Concurrent Vector Writing, we will be more explicit about the details of design and presentation.

End of Example 1.

*   *

*

It is quite conceivable that at this stage some readers may be annoyed by the long-windedness and tardiness of the treatment of an example as simple as our last one. And to some extent they are right. Later on, when the reader has grown more familiar with most of the ins and outs of the design process, we will speed up the treatments, assisted by some clerical aids. The general advice, however, is not to be in a hurry, because in designing delicate artefacts — which multiprograms happen to be — hurrying may cause oversights or mistakes that are hard to recover from, and thus may seriously slow down the design process in the end. Nothing is as costly, ineffective, and frustrating as making mistakes that could have been avoided in the first place.

8

Synchronization and Total Deadlock

Most multiprograms are designed with the aim of having the components cooperate on a common task. The common task may vary from a large-scale computation divided over the various components to an orderly scheduling of the access of components to scarce common resources. Almost all applications will require information exchange — communication — between components, and almost always will the need arise for tuning the relative speeds — i.e. for synchronization — of the components. Indeed, a component that is about to perform an addition, might have to be delayed until the addends have arrived, and a component that is about to need a printer, might have to "wait" if no printer is free.

There are many technical means for implementing communication — e.g. shared memory, communication channels, message passing, etc. — and there are many ways for realizing synchronization — e.g. via busy waiting, via P- and V- operations on semaphores, via conditional critical regions, monitors, etc.. We also find the two aspects combined, as is revealed by the phrase "synchronous communication", of which C.A.R. Hoare's CSP-constructs [Hoa78, Hoa85] are a prominent representative.

In a previous chapter we already decided "how to communicate", viz. through an abstract universe of variables. Now we must decide "how to synchronize", and in the chapter on our program notation we already hinted that this would be done by means of guarded statements of the form if $B \to S$ fi   .

Here we recall that guarded statements are atomic. However, in this monograph we will not allow them to occur in our final program texts, where — by our self-imposed constraint[†] — we wish to make do with the finer-grained guarded skip

if $B \to skip$ fi   .

8.0   Guarded Statements

Before we go into some of the rationale for this choice of synchronization primitive, we first recall its semantics and its operational interpretation. The weakest liberal precondition for a guarded statement is given by

$$[\, wlp.(\text{if } B \to S \text{ fi}).R \;\equiv\; B \Rightarrow wlp.S.R \,]   ,$$

which for a guarded skip specializes to

$$[\, wlp.(\text{if } B \to skip \text{ fi}).R \;\equiv\; B \Rightarrow R \,]   .$$

In Hoare-triple notation the semantics is given by

(0) $\{B \Rightarrow R\}$ if $B \to skip$ fi $\{R\}$.

As will turn out later, relation (0) — no matter how simple it is — will play a central rôle in the way we shall be deriving multiprograms. It will be one of our prime means for establishing the local correctness of an assertion:

> in (0),   post-assertion R is locally correct whenever pre-assertion $B \Rightarrow R$ is both locally and globally correct.

This rule is most commonly applied with B (chosen to be) equal to R, i.e.

(1)   if $R \to skip$ fi $\{R\}$,

which is the way par excellence to establish the local correctness of assertion R. In our annotation-driven handling of multiprograms, it is the compelling simplicity of (0) and (1) that forms our first incentive for choosing the guarded statement (and its descendant the guarded skip) as our synchronization primitive. So much for recalling the semantics of the guarded statement.

The operational interpretation of

[†]Had we decided to admit the guarded statement as a *primitive* atomic statement, we would have written a completely different book (cf. Chapter 15).

if $B \rightarrow S$ **fi**

is that the component executing it, atomically evaluates guard B with positive frequency until it is found to be *true*; if this happens, execution of S follows within the same atomic action. Thus S takes place under "mutual exclusion" with all other statements, starting from a state satisfying B.

For the guarded skip,

if $B \rightarrow skip$ **fi** ,

one of the possible implementations is

do $\neg B \rightarrow skip$ **od** .

Now also recall that we have made no assumption about the speed with which the execution of a component proceeds, except that it is positive. So when a component is about to execute a guarded skip, we have absolutely no idea as to how frequently the guard will be evaluated, whether it is at a frequency as enabled by modern electronic circuitry or just once in a while, for instance when triggered by a scheduler. The mere fact that, thus, the guarded skip forces, and hence enables us to ignore — to a large extent — underlying scheduling mechanisms, was an important second incentive for adopting it as our synchronization primitive. In such a way, we are able to fully separate logical and strategical aspects concerning synchronization.

Remark Conditional critical regions [Hoa72, BH72] and guarded statements are quite similar, be it that the former come with a number of strategical assumptions, which causes their use to become slightly more cumbersome. They share this "fate" with the P- and V-operations on semaphores [Dij68], from which they are outgrowths. We return to the latter in a later chapter.
End of Remark.

8.1 Progress issues

In the foregoing chapters we rather emphatically abandoned operational reasoning, exchanging it for the far more static theory of Owicki and Gries. The question now arises why, with the introduction of the guarded statement, we returned to an operational model. The answer is: we have to! With the incorporation of the if-statement, a truly complifying, almost frightening, phenomenon has entered our game, as we shall explain next.

The Hoare-triple semantics for sequential programming only addresses partial correctness, i.e. it cannot deal with issues of termination of, say, a repetition. This is not regrettable at all, because termination — being a completely different concern — can be effectively dealt with by other means, viz. through variant functions [Dij76], also called bound functions [Gri81]. Along with a repetition there should always come a bound function, for instance an integer function that is bounded from below and that is decreased by each step of the repetition. Then termination is guaranteed.

Remark   We ourselves have come to consider this separation of concerns, viz. the concern for partial correctness and the concern for termination, as a highly adequate one, because the techniques for dealing with the two are so very different.
End of Remark.

The Owicki/Gries theory is to multiprogramming what Hoare-triples are to sequential programming: it can address partial correctness only. Unfortunately, in the current state of the art of multiprogramming there is no such universal technique like the bound function, for dealing with the issue of "progress", as it is called in this context.

Let us investigate the situation we are in, by considering a component containing guarded skip **if** $B \rightarrow$ *skip* **fi**. In a stand-alone sequential program, such a statement would make no sense, because there is no outside world to change the value of the guard. In a component of a *multiprogram*, however, the occurrence of **if** $B \rightarrow$ *skip* **fi** *does* make sense, since due to the activities of the other components the value of guard B may be altered. While the component is engaged in the execution of this if-statement, three things can happen due to the computations that can be evoked by the rest of the system:

(i)   There exists a computation in which the value of B oscillates an infinite number of times (between *true* and *false*).

   The component might terminate its guarded skip, viz. if B is inspected when *true*. But termination is not guaranteed: the inspection of B may all the time take place at a moment when B is *false*. There is danger of so-called

   Individual Starvation
   or   *Infinite Overtaking* .

(ii)   There exists a computation in which the value of B oscillates only a finite number of times and eventually becomes stably *false*.

   If the component has not terminated before the last alteration of B (if any), nontermination of **if** $B \rightarrow$ *skip* **fi** for

this computation is guaranteed. There is danger of so-called
(Individual) Deadlock .

(iii) In all computations the value of B oscillates only a finite number
of times and eventually becomes stably *true*.

The component is guaranteed to always terminate. It makes
Progress .

In multiprograms the danger of Individual Starvation or Deadlock is
unwanted. It is to be avoided: there is no point in having a component
that can get stuck forever in a guarded statement. We will always demand
Progress, and from (iii) above we conclude the

Rule of Progress

Statement $\{Q\}$ if $B \rightarrow S$ fi in a component is guaranteed to
terminate

if and only if

the rest of the system, when constrained to Q , will, in a finite
number of steps, converge to a state in which B is stably *true*.

End of Rule of Progress.

And this precisely tells us what we have to prove to ensure progress. Unfortunately, we don't know of a general and technically appealing technique
for proving that a system converges to some specified state. The problem
is very similar to problems of self-stabilization, which have been generally
recognized as notoriously difficult.

Remark General techniques for dealing with progress do exist. Noteworthy is temporal logic, as pioneered by Amir Pnueli [Pnu77]. Chandy and
Misra embedded this logic in their UNITY programming formalism and
provided the semantics for handling progress [CM88]. Thus, powerful formalisms for dealing with progress are available. However, the thing that
has discouraged *us* from using them in practice is, that they bring about
so much formal complexity. They are no match for the simplicity of the
bound functions of sequential programming. It could very well be that the
formalisms are to be blamed, but it is also quite possible that the problem
of progress is, in its full generality, just intrinsically complicated, and then
we should not be amazed for this to become manifest in a formal system.
At the moment, we just don't know. We have decided to investigate how
far we can get in designing multiprograms without doing *formal* justice to
progress. And as we shall see, there are quite a number of circumstances
in which we can make do without temporal logics.
End of Remark.

From the Rule of Progress we extract a very useful condition to be imposed on the shape of multiprograms, lest progress be seriously endangered. It is the following.

Ground Rule for Progress

> For each guarded statement **if** $B \to S$ **fi** in a component, it should hold that the rest of the system has the potential of ultimately truthifying B.

End of Ground Rule for Progress.

Programs that do not satisfy this requirement are wrong or make no sense: if B is a provably correct pre-assertion to **if** $B \to S$ **fi**, the guarded statement is a fake synchronization, since it can be simplified to just S, but if B can be *false*, then we are in great trouble with **if** $B \to S$ **fi** whenever the rest of the system cannot ultimately truthify B, because then individual deadlock will be the result.

Naive as the Ground Rule may at first seem, it will show to be of great heuristic value.

8.2   Some examples

We now give a series of examples that exhibit the various phenomena discussed so far in this chapter.

Example 0

Pre : $\neg x \wedge \neg y$	
A: $x := true$	B: $y := true$
; if $\neg y \to skip$ fi	; if $\neg x \to skip$ fi

Here there is danger of deadlock for each of the components individually, and even for the two of them simultaneously — which is called Total Deadlock. We trust that the reader can construct computational scenarios that confirm these claims.

Example 1

Pre : $\neg x \wedge \neg y$	
A: **if** $\neg y \rightarrow skip$ **fi** ; $x := true$	B: **if** $\neg x \rightarrow skip$ **fi** ; $y := true$

Here there is danger of individual deadlock for each of the components, but total deadlock is impossible. The reader may verify this in an operational fashion.

Example 2

In Example 0 and 1, neither component has the potential of effectively weakening the guard in the other component, and we recall that that is against the rules, viz. against the Ground Rule for Progress. Therefore, let us improve the situation and slightly extend the program of, say, Example 1.

Pre : $\neg x \wedge \neg y$	
A: **if** $\neg y \rightarrow skip$ **fi**	B: **if** $\neg x \rightarrow skip$ **fi**
; $x := true$	; $y := true$
; $x := false$	; $y := false$

By adding the assignments $x := false$ and $y := false$ we have saved the situation: both components are guaranteed to terminate. We can and shall formally prove this — see Example 4.

Example 3

We slightly extend the program of Example 2 by turning the components into cyclic ones:

Pre : $\neg x \wedge \neg y$	
A: * [**if** $\neg y \rightarrow skip$ **fi**	B: * [**if** $\neg x \rightarrow skip$ **fi**
; $x := true$	; $y := true$
; $x := false$	; $y := false$
]	]

Any satisfaction that may have been evoked by the previous example will (should) now disappear immediately, because now the danger of individual starvation is lurking around the corner, for both components. The reader can easily construct a scenario where component A only inspects its guard $\neg y$ in states where y equals *true*.

End of Examples.

And here we have seen in a nutshell what the indispensable synchronization primitives can have in store for us. We called the situation "frightening', and this is not without justification. In the next chapter, however, we shall discuss a frequently recurring situation in which we can prove individual progress of components at a bargain, but before we can do so, we first have to discuss the phenomenon of Total Deadlock.

8.3   Total Deadlock

Among all our concerns about progress, there is one that need not bother us too much and that is Total Deadlock. The reason is that we can handle it within the scope of the Owicki/Gries theory.

Total Deadlock refers to a state of the system in which *each* component has gotten stuck in a guarded statement, i.e. a state in which *each* component is at an if-statement whose guard is *false*. It is the word "each" that expresses what is so distinctive about this state of affairs: because *each* component is blocked, the state of the system can no longer change. The system is as dead as a doornail; it has entered a quiescent state.

Now consider a state of the system where each component is about to execute a guarded statement, say

$$\{Q_i\} \text{ if } B_i \rightarrow S_i \text{ fi}$$

in Component i — with Q_i a correct assertion! Then the state of the system as a whole satisfies

$$\langle \forall j :: Q_j \rangle \quad .$$

If in this state all the B's are *false*, we have a total deadlock. But if, in this state, at least one B is *true*, the show can (and will) go on: one of the components with a *true* guard will make a move and execute its guarded statement. Hence, in order to prove that this configuration of if-statements does not give rise to total deadlock, we must prove

$$(2) \qquad [\, \langle \forall j :: Q_j \rangle \;\Rightarrow\; \langle \exists j :: B_j \rangle \,] \quad .$$

And in order to prove that the multiprogram *as a whole* does not suffer from the danger of total deadlock, we have to prove (2) for each possible configuration of if-statements. In summary we have the

Rule of Absence of Total Deadlock

In a multiprogram, a configuration of guarded statements containing one such statement per component, is deadlock free whenever it is possible to supply each guarded statement in the configuration with a — correct — pre-assertion in such a way that the conjunction of the pre-assertions implies the disjunction of the guards.

The multiprogram as a whole is free of total deadlock whenever all such configurations are deadlock free.

End of Rule of Absence of Total Deadlock.

It goes without saying that the more synchronization points — guarded statements, that is — the components have, the bigger the proof load of demonstrating the absence of total deadlock is: with N components each containing 2 guarded statements, the number of configurations to be considered equals 2^N. Fortunately, we shall not encounter too many of such designs in this monograph.

8.4 More examples

We conclude this chapter with some examples in which we give or construct proofs of the absence of total deadlock. In case we *construct* such a proof, the construction process will already be quite similar to the way we will be deriving multiprograms later on.

Example 4

For the program of Example 2 we prove that both components terminate. We copy the program text while adding a number of assertions.

Pre : $\neg x \wedge \neg y$	
A: $\{\neg x\}$	B: $\{\neg y\}$
if $\neg y \rightarrow skip$ fi	if $\neg x \rightarrow skip$ fi
; $x := true$	; $y := true$
; $x := false$	; $y := false$
$\{\neg x\}$	$\{\neg y\}$

Because variable x is private to A, and y is private to B, the correctness of the assertions easily follows from the rules of sequential programming.

We added pre-assertions to the if-statements in order to show absence of total deadlock; and, indeed, we have

$$[\,\neg x \wedge \neg y \;\Rightarrow\; \neg y \vee \neg x\,]\quad.$$

Observe that, for this purpose, in fact only one of the pre-assertions is needed.

Because there is no total deadlock, at least one of the components terminates. Since the situation is so symmetric, we may say: let it be A. The final state of A satisfies $\neg x$, which means that B could not possibly get stuck in its guarded skip.

Observe that, thanks to the symmetry, here one of the post-assertions is superfluous. At later occasions we will usually be more frugal in our annotations.

Example 5

We will encounter the following two-component multiprogram a few more times later on:

Pre :	*true*		
A:	$y := false$	B:	$x := false$
	; $x := true$		; $y := true$
	; if $y \rightarrow skip$ fi		; if $x \rightarrow skip$ fi
	; $x := true$		; $y := true$

Here the situation is more complicated, because variables x and y are truly shared by A and B. We shall prove that both components terminate, but we do not ask the reader to give it a try for himself, since that would be too hard on him at this stage.

The structure of the proof is the same as in the previous example. We first show the absence of total deadlock, from which we conclude that at least one component terminates, and then we show that x is a correct post-assertion of A, implying that B terminates whenever A does. Symmetry does the rest.

• No total deadlock

In order to show the absence of total deadlock we introduce pre-assertion *RA* to A's guarded skip and pre-assertion *RB* to B's guarded skip. Now we must see to it that

(i)   *RA* and *RB* arc correct assertions,   and

(ii) $[\,RA \wedge RB \;\Rightarrow\; y \vee x\,]$.

For reasons of symmetry, we can confine our attention to the construction of RA.

By requirement (ii), RA had better be an expression in x or in y or in both. Because assertion RA is preceded by statement $x := true$,

      x

would be a good candidate for RA, because it is locally correct. This, however, is too naive, because statement $x := false$ in B falsifies it. Therefore, our next proposal is that RA have the shape

      $RA:$ $x \vee QA$ and, symmetrically,
      $RB:$ $y \vee QB$,

where QA and QB will contain fresh variables only.

Now let us investigate requirements (i) and (ii) for these choices of RA and RB. As for (i), we observe that

‒ RA is locally correct
‒ RA will be globally correct if we satisfy requirement (iii):

(iii)   Statement $x := false$ in component B ought to
              be extended so as to truthify QA.

This settles (i). As for (ii), we observe

      $RA \wedge RB$

$\equiv$ {choices for RA and RB}

      $(x \vee QA) \wedge (y \vee QB)$

$\Rightarrow$ {by requirement (iv) below}

      $y \vee x$,

where requirement (iv) reads

(iv) $[\,QA \wedge QB \;\Rightarrow\; false\,]$,

and this settles (ii). We are left with (iii) and (iv).

From requirement (iii) we see that the availability of an auxiliary variable would be very welcome, viz. for the truthification of an as yet unknown predicate QA. Requirement (iv) can be met in many ways. Because $A \neq B$, we meet (iv) by choosing

      $QA:$ $z = B$ $QB:$ $z = A$,

for a fresh variable z. With this choice, (iii) is met if we

      extend $x := false$ in B to $x, z := false, B$.

This completes our proof of the absence of total deadlock. As a summary, we give the final program with the auxiliary variable and the relevant assertions

Pre : $true$	
A: $y, z := false, A$	B: $x, z := false, B$
; $x := true$	; $y := true$
; $\{x \vee z = B\}$	; $\{y \vee z = A\}$
if $y \rightarrow skip$ fi	if $x \rightarrow skip$ fi
; $x := true$	; $y := true$

Remark At the start of this example we tried to be kind to the reader by suggesting he not try the exercise for himself. Here we would like to ask him to do something in return, viz. to be a little impressed by the above little program. First of all, the demonstration that the annotation is correct and that there is no total deadlock is a walkover. Secondly, the annotation is as crisp as it can be: there are no unnecessary assertions hanging around. The reason for this is that we *developed* the proof, starting from the demonstrandum — the proof's specification!. And this now is typical of proof- and program development: they are demand-driven activities that, when carried out cautiously, will hardly ever yield something that is not strictly needed.
End of Remark.

Exercise In the above proof we constructed RA and RB that are symmetric in the components. This is by no means necessary. The reader may try to design a proof based on the asymmetric choice

$RA :$ $x \vee y \vee b$
$RB :$ $\neg b$.

End of Exercise.

• Individual Progress

As announced earlier, we prove individual progress by proving that the postcondition of A implies x. This time we do invite the reader to design a proof for himself — still not an easy task!. There are quite a number of ways to obtain the result; this time we just give a solution at once, i.e. without discussing heuristics. It uses an auxiliary boolean.

```
Pre :   ¬d

A:    y := false            B:    {¬d}
   ; {¬y ∨ d}                   x := false
      x := true               ; y, d := true, true
   ; {¬y ∨ d}                 ; if x → skip fi
      if y → skip fi          ; y, d := true, true
   ; {d}
      x := true
      {x} {d}
```

Proving the correctness of the annotation is an easy exercise — which, in fact, can be done by heart. Because A's postcondition $x \wedge d$ implies the intended postcondition x, the result follows (from the principle of Weakening the Annotation).

Remark   Most programming or verification problems come in the form of the request to establish or to prove a number of a-priori specified assertions. When dealing with such a problem, we mostly have to add code and assertions, thereby strengthening the originally demanded annotation. This process of adding and strengthening always ends in a situation where the design is correct according to the Core of Owicki and Gries. The originally demanded annotation is then correct on account of the principle of Weakening the Annotation. We shall witness this pattern all the time, and in this example we saw an occurrence of it.
End of Remark.

The algorithm in this example is the so-called "Initialization Protocol", to which we shall return later.
End of Example 5.

*   *

*

To conclude this chapter we wish to report a little experiment that we did in a classroom, and which demonstrates how dangerously fickle the world of multiprogramming is and how poorly human intuition is equipped for it. We were considering the two-component multiprogram

```
A:   y := false            B:   x := false
   ; if y → skip fi          ; if x → skip fi
```

and we asked the class to insert statements $x := true$ in A, wherever they wanted and as many as they liked. And similarly for insertions of $y := true$ in B. The goal was, of course, to guarantee termination of both components. There was not much hesitation among the students and they quickly reached consensus: because B is waiting for x to become $true$, the best guarantee for progress would be to insert as many assignments $x := true$ in A as possible. And similarly for B. Thus they arrived at

A:	$x := true$	B:	$y := true$
	; $y := false$		; $x := false$
	; $x := true$		; $y := true$
	; if $y \rightarrow skip$ fi		; if $x \rightarrow skip$ fi
	; $x := true$		; $y := true$

But as soon as we started to *prove* termination, we quickly discovered that we could not succeed, and then we constructed a scenario in which one of the components got stuck forever. (It is the leading assignment that causes the trouble; compare Example 5.)

The whole situation was felt to be completely counterintuitive, but the moral was clear:

> In multiprogramming, *never* lean on intuition of any kind, but on rigorous proof instead.

9

Individual Progress and the Multibound

In the early decades of computing, when the speed of electronic circuitry had outgrown that of mechanical peripheral devices by some orders of magnitude, the demand for "parallelism" became louder and louder, because it was becoming more and more urgent for economic reasons. And, indeed, the excessively expensive circuitry of the time could, instead of being idle while waiting for the input of a slow card reader, much more beneficially be deployed for serving other customers of the computer installation. The idea of several programs running "simultaneously" on a single installation had been born.

It was quickly discovered then that for an orderly management of programs sharing a single installation, the concept of Mutual Exclusion was of utter importance. Thus the search for Mutual Exclusion Algorithms had begun. It was this search that brought into daylight a number of fundamental, unforeseen and seriously complicating issues coming with parallelism. And of all the issues that emerged, the problem of Individual Progress is perhaps the harshest of all.

In order to support this claim, we offer a small glance behind the scenes by giving the historically first mutual exclusion algorithm for two components, designed in the early 1960s by the numerical mathematician Th. J. Dekker.

Remark The atomic statements prevailing in this kind of algorithm — or rather the ones that one has to make do with — are the so-called *one-point-statements*, i.e. statements that contain at most one reference to at most one shared or private variable[†]. For this occasion, we indicate the grain of atomicity by surrounding the atomic statements or expressions with a pair of angular brackets.
End of Remark.

Pre : $\neg x \;\wedge\; \neg y \;\wedge\; (v = X \;\vee\; v = Y)$

X: $*\,[\; ncs.X$

   $;\, \langle\, x := true\, \rangle$

   $;\, \textbf{if}\; \langle\, \neg y\, \rangle \;\rightarrow\; skip$

    $\|\; \langle\, y\, \rangle \;\rightarrow\; \textbf{if}\; \langle\, v = X\, \rangle \;\rightarrow\; skip$

        $\|\; \langle\, v \neq X\, \rangle \;\rightarrow$

          $\langle\, x := false\, \rangle$

          $;\, \textbf{if}\; \langle\, v = X\, \rangle \;\rightarrow\; skip\;\; \textbf{fi}$

          $;\, \langle\, x := true\, \rangle$

        $\textbf{fi}$

       $;\, \textbf{if}\; \langle\, \neg y\, \rangle \;\rightarrow\; skip\;\; \textbf{fi}$

   $\textbf{fi}$

   $;\, cs.X$

   $;\, \langle\, v := Y\, \rangle$

   $;\, \langle\, x := false\, \rangle$

   $]$

Y: Component X with (x, X) and (y, Y) interchanged.

Dekker's Algorithm

We will not discuss Dekker's Algorithm in any detail; we just quote it to make several points.

First of all, we wish to point out how little of the algorithm's code is actually concerned with the (partial) correctness — or safety — of the algorithm. Mutual exclusion requires that the components not be engaged in their "critical sections" — $cs.X$ and $cs.Y$ — simultaneously. Dekker's

---

[†]More precisely, statements that can be implemented by at most one memory access to at most one shared or private variable.

algorithm meets this requirement. In fact, as we will see in a later chapter, when the Safe Sluice Algorithm will be discussed, the safety is ensured by two pieces of code only, viz. by statement $x := true$ and guard $\neg y$ — and their counterparts in Y — and by nothing else. Consequently, *all the rest* of the code is there for the sake of Individual Progress, i.e. for the sake of seeing to it that a component that has terminated its noncritical section *ncs* will eventually enter its critical one. This discrepancy may start to give some idea of the complications brought about by progress requirements.

Second, we would like to invite the reader to seriously try to set up an operational argument as to why (individual) progress is guaranteed. The argumentation should not be carried out superficially — which is what we usually observe — but carefully and meticulously; then we gather that long before the argument is completed, the reader will see the light: this is like all hell let loose.

Third, we once more point out what a *formal* approach to progress may have in store for us. Earlier we referred to temporal logics and UNITY; here we wish to draw attention to works on "fairness". In [Fra86], one can find a formal treatment of Dekker's algorithm, which convincingly reveals that something very complicated is going on.

*   *
*

Thus, when we (i.e. the authors) considered embarking on concurrent programming we knew that, if we were to go through with it at all, we had to make a decision: we had to decide whether to take formal aspects of progress into account right from the beginning, or postpone them, or forget about them altogether. We decided for a mixture of the last two options, for fear of otherwise not getting anywhere — at least not simply so. The price to be paid is that at some occasions in this monograph we will have to wave our operational hands for arguing about progress.

This attitude towards concurrent programming may very well be rated as unscientific and not contributing to the field. However, we may also find consolation in the fact that we all were able to do lots of integral calculations even though not every integral can be calculated analytically, and in the fact that we could master and use the calculus pretty well long before we were introduced to measure theory — if at all. And that is exactly the position we feel to be in with our current treatise on multiprogramming.

The Multibound

There are some circumstances where we can handle all progress issues formally without the need to introduce new formalism, and in this section we discuss those circumstances. To that purpose we consider a multiprogram with an arbitrary number of components. Let variable z_i be private to component i and let component i, projected on the operations on z_i, have the form

$$\text{Comp.}i: \quad * [\, z_i := 1 + z_i \,] \quad .$$

Furthermore assume that the components are synchronized in such a way that, for some natural U,

$$MB: \qquad \langle\, \forall i, j :: z_i \leq U + z_j \,\rangle$$

is a system invariant. If now, for one reason or another, component j comes to a definitive halt, we conclude from the structure of the components and from invariant MB that then *all* components will get stuck: because z_j becomes constant, all other variables z_i will eventually become constant as well. As a result

> either all components get stuck
> or   no component gets stuck.

Because our components can only get stuck at guarded statements (or variations thereof), we conclude that

> with components of the right shape and in the presence of a *multibound* like MB:
>
>> there is no danger of total deadlock
>>
>> $\equiv$
>>
>> individual progress for each component is guaranteed.

In other words, we can prove individual progress by proving the absence of total deadlock, and this is completely within the scope of Owicki/Gries.

Remark A relation like MB has been named a "multibound" because it mutually bounds the values of the variables involved.
End of Remark.

Of course, such "multibound scenarios" may come in many variations. The increment of z_i by 1, for instance, is just an example. Also, the invariant can take various shapes. For instance, we may have an invariant of the (more general) form

$$\langle \, \forall i,j :: z_i \le C.i.j + z_j \, \rangle \qquad ,$$

which implies MB with $U := \langle \, \uparrow i,j :: C.i.j \, \rangle^{\ddagger}$. Or, we may encounter MB in the equivalent form

$$\langle \, \uparrow i :: z_i \, \rangle \le U + \langle \, \downarrow i :: z_i \, \rangle \qquad .$$

We think that it is not very helpful (because too cumbersome) to characterize multibound scenarios in general. We just have to be a little bit alert so as not to overlook the situation when it arises.

Whenever applicable, the multibound technique is most effective. An example is given below. We will encounter quite a few more occasions for using the technique in the remainder of this text. (And recently we learnt that the idea might also be valuable in the design of asynchronous electronic circuits.)

Example We consider the classical Producer/Consumer problem, i.e. we consider a multiprogram of the form

Pre :	$in = 0 \, \wedge \, out = 0$
Prod:	$* \, [\, in := in + 1 \,]$
Cons:	$* \, [\, out := out + 1 \,]$
Inv :	$? \, P : \quad 0 \le in - out \le C$

Here, variable in records the number of portions produced and added to, say, a buffer by Prod. Likewise, variable out records the number of portions taken from the buffer by Cons. Because the buffer has finite capacity C, $1 \le C$, the components have to be synchronized so as to maintain system invariant

P: $\qquad 0 \le in - out \le C \qquad ,$

or, equivalently,

P: $\qquad out \le in \, \wedge \, in \le C + out \qquad .$

Before proceeding, we observe that in view of the structure of the components, P is a suitable multibound. As a result, individual progress is guaranteed whenever our ultimate solution is free from total deadlock — no matter what that solution will look like.

Meeting the synchronization requirements is extremely simple in this case. We leave it to the reader to verify or derive the solution given below.

$\ddagger$ $\uparrow$ denotes the maximum, $\downarrow$ the minimum

Pre :	$in = 0 \ \wedge \ out = 0$
Prod:	$* [\ \text{\textbf{if}} \ in < C + out \rightarrow skip \ \text{\textbf{fi}}$
	$; \{ in < C + out \}$
	$in := in + 1$
	$]$
Cons:	$* [\ \text{\textbf{if}} \ out < in \rightarrow skip \ \text{\textbf{fi}}$
	$; \{ out < in \}$
	$out := out + 1$
	$]$
Inv :	$P : \quad out \leq in \ \wedge \ in \leq C + out$

As for the absence of total deadlock we investigate the disjunction of the guards:

$$in < C + out \ \vee \ out < in$$

$\equiv \quad \{ \Leftarrow \text{ by transitivity}; \ \Rightarrow \text{ by } P \text{ and transitivity} \}$

$$in < C + in$$

$\equiv \quad \{ 1 \leq C \}$

$$true$$

And as a result, there is no danger of total deadlock (so that individual progress is guaranteed on-the-fly!).

End of Example.

* * *

We conclude this chapter with a variation on the theme, which pops up every so often, most notably in distributed algorithms. Our canonical form for the multibound is

(0) $\uparrow Z \leq U + \downarrow Z$,

where Z is the set of variables z_i, and $\uparrow Z$ and $\downarrow Z$ denote the maximum and the minimum of this set, respectively. Sometimes, however, the variables come in, say, two kinds, given by the sets X and Y for which we have the invariance of

(1) $\uparrow X \leq F + \downarrow Y$

(2) $\uparrow Y \leq G + \downarrow X$,

for some naturals F and G. The question is whether we can still prove
(0) for some U. Translated into (X, Y)- nomenclature, relation (0) is

(3) $(\uparrow X)\uparrow(\uparrow Y) \leq U + (\downarrow X)\downarrow(\downarrow Y)$.

Due to the symmetry in X and Y, (3) follows if we can find some U
satisfying

(4) $\uparrow X \leq U + (\downarrow X)\downarrow(\downarrow Y)$.

In order to investigate this, we start calculating with $\uparrow X$:

$$
\begin{array}{llcll}
 & \uparrow X & \qquad\qquad & & \uparrow X \\
\leq & \{(1)\} & & \leq & \{(1)\} \\
 & F + \downarrow Y & & & F + \downarrow Y \\
\leq & \{\text{``}\downarrow\text{''} \leq \text{``}\uparrow\text{''}\} & & \leq & \{0 \leq G\} \\
 & F + \uparrow Y & & & F + G + \downarrow Y \\
\leq & \{(2)\} & & & \\
 & F + G + \downarrow X & & &
\end{array}
$$

Combining the two results, we see that (4) is satisfied for $U := F + G$. This
settles the question.

The conclusion is that the weaker (1) and (2) still guarantee that we
are dealing with a proper multibound scenario. It goes without saying that
similar decomposition lemmata for the multibound exist when the various
variables come in three, or four, or five kinds. Thus with N variables x_i
and appropriate program structure, a system invariant like

$$x_0 \leq x_1 \leq \ldots \leq x_{N-1} \leq 17 + x_0$$

is readily recognized as a multibound.

$$* \qquad *$$
$$*$$

As we said before, we do not know of any simple and universal technique
for seeing to individual progress. We believe, however, that the technique
that will eventually fill the gap, will be the overall application of variant functions on well-founded sets. We can already get glimpses of this
technique in, for instance, [Dij71], and in [Dij86] — one of the first self-
stabilizing systems —, and in other non-trivial designs such as the Sliding
Window Protocol [Sne95]. The multibound itself is an application of the
use of variant functions as well.

Ideally, one would — just as in sequential programming — start by choosing a variant function and then develop the program, adhering to this choice. We have done *one* experiment of this kind, namely we designed a two-component mutual exclusion algorithm starting from a specification expressing the progress requirements. Out came G. L. Peterson's Mutual Exclusion Algorithm [Pet81], which outperforms Dekker's in simplicity by at least one order of magnitude. And this is just encouraging. We will present the experiment in one of the later chapters of this monograph, and we hope that next generations of computing scientists will create much more evidence, so that, eventually, Individual Progress will become less of a problem than it is now.

10

Concurrent Vector Writing: A First Exercise in Program Development

In the foregoing chapters we have seen a number of examples of how to use the technique of Strengthening the Annotation to show that a given, too-weakly annotated multiprogram is correct. There we strengthened the original annotation in a number of steps, until it became correct in the Core. Here, in this chapter, we will do exactly the same, be it not for a completed program, but for a program still to be completed. That is, along with a stronger annotation, new, additional code will see the light as well, and that is what we call program development. We have to admit, though, that in this first exercise not too much additional code will be developed, on the one hand because the current example is very simple and on the other hand because, in general, a development that is carried out with caution does not introduce more than needed.

Besides using the example to give a first performance of program development, we will also use it to explain more precisely our bookkeeping regime with the "Notes" and the "queries", which we have been using a number of times now without much ado. We will also be more explicit about the status of the intermediate versions that emerge during the approximation process, which starts at the specification and ends in the ultimate solution.

* * *

The problem of Concurrent Vector Writing is the following. We consider an array $x[0..N)$, $0 \leq N$, and two components A and B. Component A writes zeroes into x, and component B ones. We wish to synchronize the components such that the multiprogram terminates and delivers a final state satisfying $\vec{x} = \vec{0}$.

A more precise specification of this problem is given by the figure below.

Pre : $i = 0 \wedge j = 0$	
A: **do** $i \neq N \rightarrow$ $\quad x.i := 0$ $\quad ; i := i + 1$ **od**	B: **do** $j \neq N \rightarrow$ $\quad x.j := 1$ $\quad ; j := j + 1$ **od**
Post : $\quad ? \langle \forall k : 0 \leq k < N : x.k = 0 \rangle$	

Version 0

(The individual assignments are atomic.)

This specification is more precise in that it reveals *how* the components write into x. We shall refer to the combination of the precondition Pre and the program texts for A and B as the *Computation Proper*.

Remark   The legal status of the computation proper is that it is owned by someone else, who needs it for some purpose that is not of our concern. This implies that no matter how we proceed, we are not entitled to interfere with this computation in any other way than needed for the purpose of synchronization.
End of Remark.

Version 0 also contains a notational device that we shall use all the time, namely the query. A query indicates that something remains to be done — here, taking care of the correctness of the postcondition. As we go along, we will also encounter queried assertions and queried system invariants (as we did in earlier examples).

Taking care of a queried item means accomplishing its correctness (in the Core). This will always be achieved by extending the program text — be it with code, assertions, or invariants. However, these extensions are constrained by the rule that

> the computation proper is not to be changed.

This rule prohibits, for instance, that we replace the parallel composition of A and B with the sequential program B; A , which would trivially establish the required postcondition. This would not do: the legal proprietor has handed in a *parallel* program.

The rule also prohibits that we plug in further changes to x , i , or j . Inspections, however, of the variables of the computation proper will, in general, be allowed — sometimes they are even unavoidable (for instance in termination detection algorithms). In many circumstances, though, the additional code will be phrased in terms of fresh (synchronization) variables.

Given the above conventions regarding the status of the computation proper and given our appreciation of queried items, Version 0 acts as the formal specification of the programming task ahead of us.

Remark Admittedly, the repertoire of atomic statements that we may draw from to solve the problem has been left unspecified; in particular, nothing has been said about the grain of atomicity in the guards and in the assignments. Our general pursuit is for quite fine-grained solutions, but we do not want to commit ourselves in too early a stage. We want to tackle the logic of the design first and see what kind of expressions emerge in the additional code. Only then will we be concerned with "implementation issues" like making solutions more fine-grained — if necessary and technically feasible.
End of Remark.

*   *
*

The simplest solution to our current problem is one that *mimics* the behaviour of the sequential program B; A . This can be achieved at the expense of one fresh boolean, f say. A solution is

$$\text{Pre}: \quad i=0 \ \land \ j=0 \ \land \ \neg f$$

A:	**if** $f \to$ *skip* **fi**	B:	**do** $j \neq N \to$
	; **do** $i \neq N \to$		$x.j := 1$
	$x.i := 0$		; $j := j+1$
	; $i := i+1$		**od**
	od		; $f :=$ *true* .

It is a nice exercise to prove that this program, indeed, establishes the required postcondition.

Although there is no logical objection to this solution, there is a strategical one: all the potential parallelism has been killed. Component A starts idling for f to become *true*, i.e. it is denied progress until B has terminated, whereas there seems to be no good reason for this delay. This is not quite decent (towards the legal owner of the computation proper), and therefore we will always try to obey the rule that

> the computation proper is not to be hampered (i.e. delayed) without good reasons.

Sometimes there are good reasons for hampering the progress of the computation proper, and near the end of this chapter we will encounter one such reason, which is of a rather quantitative nature. It stands to reason, however, that the best reason for hampering progress is when otherwise the required synchronization, i.e. the (partial) correctness of the design, would be endangered. Safety first!

*   *

*

After these preliminaries, we now proceed with our problem by making a first design decision, namely the decision to restrict our solution to a multiprogram of the form

Pre : $i = 0 \land j = 0$	
A: **do** $i \neq N \rightarrow$	B: **do** $j \neq N \rightarrow$
S_0	T_0
; $x.i := 0$	; $x.j := 1$
; S_1	; T_1
; $i := i+1$	; $j := j+1$
; S_2	; T_2
od	**od**
Post : $? \, \langle\, \forall k : 0 \leq k < N : x.k = 0 \,\rangle$	

Version 1

The S's and the T's serve as *placeholders* for the additional code: they indicate the *only* places where we (have decided to) allow synchronization code to be inserted. With the above choice of placeholders we have been quite generous, but not completely so: we have ruled out the "sequential" solution suggested earlier, by offering no placeholders before or after the repetitions.

Remark It is, in general, a good habit to be explicit in the matter of placeholders, and in our current example we are — and will be until the very end. Drawing from experience, however, we know that they are mostly well-understood, so that we can afford to leave them implicit. But when in doubt, we had better not leave them out.

In the rest of this monograph, we will only occasionally feel the need to introduce placeholders, and fortunately so because, in fact, they are a notational mistake. It would be far more efficient and elegant to have a notational device for indicating where *no* additional code may be inserted, but we have not been able to design a notation that would be plain enough to be adopted and put into practical use.
End of Remark.

*　　*
*

Version 1 contains one queried item, viz. the postcondition. From the Rule for the Postcondition we know that its correctness is guaranteed whenever it follows from the conjunction of the postconditions of the individual components. Now observe that

$$\langle\, \forall k : 0 \leq k < N : x.k = 0 \,\rangle$$
$$\Leftarrow$$
$$\langle\, \forall k : 0 \leq k < i : x.k = 0 \,\rangle \,\wedge\, i = N \quad.$$

From the structure of component A we see that $i = N$ is a correct post-condition of A, variable i being private to A. So what remains is the correctness of

$$P: \qquad \langle\, \forall k : 0 \leq k < i : x.k = 0 \,\rangle$$

as a postcondition of A or B. We enforce it — and again this is a design decision — by demanding that P be a system invariant. With these choices it suffices to take *true* as a postcondition of B, and because *true* is a correct assertion anywhere in a multiprogram, we never write it down.

Thus we arrive at our next version:

Pre : $i = 0 \; \wedge \; j = 0$	
A: **do** $i \neq N \rightarrow$ S_0 ; $x.i := 0$; S_1 ; $i := i+1$; S_2 **od** $\{i = N\}$	B: **do** $j \neq N \rightarrow$ T_0 ; $x.j := 1$; T_1 ; $j := j+1$; T_2 **od**
Inv : ? P : $\langle \, \forall k : 0 \leq k < i : x.k = 0 \, \rangle$	
Post : $\langle \, \forall k : 0 \leq k < N : x.k = 0 \, \rangle$	

Version 2

Observe that the postcondition has lost its query, because in passing from Version 1 to Version 2 we turned it into one that is correct in the Core, be it at the expense of a — here obviously correct — assertion $i = N$ in A and a new queried item, viz. system invariant P.

This is the place to draw attention to what we think is an important methodological issue. Version 2 tells us in a very precise and compact way what has been achieved — viz. the correctness of assertion $i = N$ and of the postcondition — and what remains to be achieved — viz. the correctness of the queried items, here system invariant P . Thus the figure named Version 2 acts as the *precise* interface between the past and the future of the development process. As a result, Version 2 is the specification of the programming problem ahead of us, and it is absolutely irrelevant how we arrived at it. This is important because, as the development evolves from one version to the next, we at any time only need to be concerned with the question of how to transform the current version into a next one. Thus the procedure is very similar to the method of stepwise refinement (and, in a way, very similar to calculation, where, at any time, we are — to a large extent — only concerned with how to transform the current expression into a next one).

This, too, is the place to argue once more why such a transformation is correct in the light of the Owicki/Gries theory. In transforming Version 1 into Version 2, we have clearly strengthened the annotation: the latter contains assertion $i = N$ and — queried — system invariant P, which were both absent from the former. Now suppose that in the end we succeed in removing the queries from Version 2 by appropriate choices for the S's and the T 's ; then Version 2 will have turned into a correctly annotated multiprogram. But thanks to the postulate of Weakening the Annotation, Version 1 will have turned into a correctly annotated multiprogram as well, and that is what we were after!

*   *
*

After these intermediate remarks, the time has come to resume our development. Version 2 requires that we take care of the invariance of P . To that end we have to investigate whether P holds initially and under what additional conditions it is maintained by the atomic statements of the multiprogram. We record these investigations as follows:

Re   Inv P " $\langle\ \forall k : 0 \leq k < i : x.k = 0\ \rangle$ "

Init: correct, from $i = 0$ in Pre

- $\{true\}\ x.i := 0$
- $\{?\ x.i = 0\}\ i := i + 1$
- $\{?\ i \leq j\}\ x.j := 1$

End of Re.

Because the situation is so simple, we have given the additional preconditions at once, i.e. without giving the calculations leading to those preconditions. Observe that we tacitly used the Rule of Orthogonality by ignoring all statements that could not possibly affect P ; these are $j := j + 1$ and the S 's and the T 's , which were supposed to not change the computation proper, i.e. to not change x , i , or j .

Remark   During class-room sessions on this example, students were asked what precondition ought to be supplied to $x.j := 1$ in order that P not be violated. Quite a few came up with the answer $i < j$, and that is correct. It is just a tiny little bit stronger than our $i \leq j$. However minor this difference may seem, it has major consequences: with condition $i < j$, (individual) deadlock will become unavoidable. We urge the reader to check this after he has studied the rest of this chapter. The moral is that multiprograms are unusually delicate artefacts and that their design is a highly critical activity. When in our chapter on Strengthening the Annotation we said that we always wanted the *weakest* additional condition, we meant just that. The consequence is that well-versedness in the predicate calculus is indispensable for playing this game at all, and there is no escaping it.
End of Remark.

The incorporation of these new pre-assertions leads us to the next version. It reads

Pre :	$i = 0 \ \wedge \ j = 0$	
A: **do** $i \neq N \rightarrow$		B: **do** $j \neq N \rightarrow$
S_0		T_0
$; x.i := 0$		$; \{?\ i \leq j,\ \text{Note } 0\}$
$; S_1$		$x.j := 1$
$; \{?\ x.i = 0\}$		$; T_1$
$i := i + 1$		$; j := j + 1$
$; S_2$		$; T_2$
od		**od**
$\{i = N\}$		
Inv :	$P : \quad \langle\, \forall k : 0 \leq k < i : x.k = 0 \,\rangle$	
Post :	$\langle\, \forall k : 0 \leq k < N : x.k = 0 \,\rangle$	

Version 3

In moving to the next version we have to remove one or more queries. In general, the choice of how many and which ones to remove is completely free. We indicate the ones that are chosen by supplying them with a reference to a Note. Thus, Version 3 expresses our intention to tackle $i \leq j$ first, leaving $x.i = 0$ for later.

Note 0   " $i \leq j$ "

We ensure the correctness of $i \leq j$ by requiring it to be a system invariant.

End of Note 0.

Why this design decision, which looks much stronger than necessary? The alternative would have been to ensure the local correctness of $i \leq j$ in B through guarded skip **if** $i \leq j \rightarrow$ *skip* **fi** , but this would not accord with the Ground Rule for Progress: component A has no potential for truthifying $i \leq j$. Hence the "choice" of letting $i \leq j$ be a system invariant is more or less imposed on us.

Remark   Here, the adoption of guarded skip **if** $i \leq j \rightarrow$ *skip* **fi**   would nevertheless have led to a happy end, but that is just a stroke of very good luck. We would like to encourage the reader to trace that alternative derivation after he has studied this one.

End of Remark.

Now we should write down the next version, with " $? \ i \leq j$ " appearing under the heading "Inv", but in order to shorten our treatment a little bit, we skip this intermediate version and deal with the invariance of $i \leq j$ right away. We will apply this form of *cascading* more often.

Re   Inv " $i \leq j$ "

Init: correct, from Pre

* $\{?\ i < j\}\ i := i+1$

End of Re.

Thus we arrive at

Pre : $i = 0 \wedge j = 0$

A: **do** $i \neq N \rightarrow$
   S_0
   ; $x.i := 0$
   ; S_1
   ; $\{?\ x.i = 0,\ \text{Note 0}\}\ \{?\ i < j,\ \text{Note 1}\}$
   $i := i+1$
   ; S_2
  od
  $\{i = N\}$

B: **do** $j \neq N \rightarrow$
   T_0
   ; $\{i \leq j\}$
   $x.j := 1$
   ; T_1
   ; $j := j+1$
   ; T_2
  od

Inv : P : $\quad \langle \forall k : 0 \leq k < i : x.k = 0 \rangle$, $\qquad\qquad i \leq j$
Post : $\quad \langle \forall k : 0 \leq k < N : x.k = 0 \rangle$

Version 4

We continue with the remaining obligations.

Note 0   "$x.i = 0$", with co-assertion $i < j$

L: Choose *skip* for S_1. Then $x.i = 0$ follows from the textually preceding $x.i := 0$.

G: Only $x.j := 1$ in B can violate $x.i = 0$. We calculate

$$(x.j := 1).(x.i = 0)$$

$\equiv$ {substitution}

$$x.i = 0 \ \wedge \ i \neq j$$

$\equiv$ {$i < j$ is a co-assertion of $x.i = 0$}

$$x.i = 0 \quad .$$

Hence, $x.i = 0$ is not violated, thanks to its co-assertion $i < j$ —
see Remark below.

End of Note 0.

Remark   From our earlier chapter on Strengthening the Annotation we
recall that in showing the global correctness of an assertion we are allowed
to use its co-assertions, and that is what happens in the above. Nevertheless,
the reader might feel somewhat uneasy about using a co-assertion — $i < j$
— that still carries a query. But here we should not forget that in the end
such a query (like all queries) will be gone.
End of Remark.

Note 1   " $i < j$ ", with co-assertion $x.i = 0$

L: Because we have chosen S_1 equal to skip (see Note 0), we ensure the
local correctness of $i < j$ by demanding

$$\{? \ i < j, \text{ Note 2}\} \ x.i := 0 \quad .$$

G: Widening.

End of Note 1.

Note 2   " $i < j$ "

L: Choose guarded skip **if** $i < j \rightarrow$ *skip* **fi** for S_0.

G: Widening.

End of Note 2.

Observe that, again, we used cascading, by handling the new assertion
$i < j$ emerging in Note 1.L right away.

Now we are done: all queries have been removed! Before writing down
our solution, however, we have to admit that we played a tricky game
with the order in which the assertions $x.i = 0$ and $i < j$ in Version 4
were tackled. Had we first dealt with $i < j$ and decided to establish its
local correctness by choosing **if** $i < j \rightarrow$ *skip* **fi** for S_1, the design would
have become much more complicated. (The reason is that $i < j$ is really

needed for the global correctness of $x.i = 0$.) We invite the reader to try this alternative.

The final solution, in which the remaining placeholders are now omitted — or rather: replaced by skips — is as follows:

Pre : $\quad i = 0 \ \wedge \ j = 0$	
A: **do** $i \neq N \rightarrow$ $\qquad$ **if** $i < j \rightarrow skip$ **fi** $\qquad ; \{i < j\}$ $\qquad x.i := 0$ $\qquad ; \{x.i = 0\} \ \{i < j\}$ $\qquad i := i+1$ $\quad$ **od** $\quad \{i = N\}$	B: **do** $j \neq N \rightarrow$ $\qquad \{i \leq j\}$ $\qquad x.j := 1$ $\qquad ; j := j+1$ $\quad$ **od**
Inv : $\quad \langle \forall k : 0 \leq k < i : x.k = 0 \rangle$ $\qquad\quad i \leq j$	
Post : $\quad \langle \forall k : 0 \leq k < N : x.k = 0 \rangle$	

Version 5

Our only remaining task is to show that the multiprogram terminates. Component B surely does, thus establishing $j = N$. Then, guard $i < j$ of A's guarded skip is stably *true*, because $i < N$ is a correct precondition of the guarded skip. Hence, A terminates as well.

$$* \qquad *$$
$$*$$

Herewith we conclude the formal development of an — admittedly — very simple multiprogram. Our main purpose was

- to show in very small steps how such a development evolves,
- to show how the validity of such a development is carried by the theory of Owicki and Gries,
- to exhibit the similarity with "stepwise refinement" and its induced benefits: the stimulation of a better separation of concerns, and
- to present some of the notational and clerical aids used in organizing such a development.

A few final remarks are in order.

• Again, our final version is fully documented in that its annotation is correct in the Core. But this need no longer amaze us, because it is intrinsic to the game. Do observe, however, how crisp the annotation is; here we are reaping the fruits of a cautious *development* of the program: nothing is encountered that is not strictly needed.

• In our presentation we proceeded from one version to the next in *very* small steps. We did so in order to explain the rules of the game. Sometimes, when the situation had become simple and transparent, we accelerated the design process a little by what we called "cascading", thus combining several successive versions into one. Such a combination of steps certainly shortens the presentation, but it may also evoke oversights or mistakes. It is always a matter of good taste how coarse- or how fine-grained one chooses one's steps. In this respect we have one rule of thumb that we ourselves learned from sad experience: when one is on the verge of making mistakes or loosing one's grip, the advice is: Slow Down.

• Presenting a development like this on the blackboard is much simpler and faster, because with a little orchestration and preparation there will be no need to copy the successive versions, as is necessitated here since paper is such a linear medium. On the blackboard we can begin by writing down the computation proper, leaving conspicuous space for the placeholders and for the assertions, and then fill up the space with code and assertions as the development evolves. As for the queries: instead of erasing a query from its item, we can extend it with its mirror image, thus forming symbol $\heartsuit$, to indicate that the item has become sound. Because in this way program texts can only grow, one never needs an eraser. This may be nice to know for the teacher reader.

*   *

*

And this concludes our first program derivation.

Postscript (for the circuit designer)

In our solution — Version 5 —, the synchronization runs under control of the originally given program variables i and j. In fact, only the difference $j - i$ matters — see the guarded skip in component A. In the algorithm, this difference is an $(N+1)$- valued entity, because $0 \le j - i \le N$ is a system invariant. For circuit design, it could be advantageous if $j - i$ were just 2-valued, because that would enable a transformation into the boolean domain. For this (good) reason, we shall now "hamper" the computation proper by strengthening system invariant $i \leq j$ to

$$Q: \qquad i \leq j \,\wedge\, j \leq i+1 \qquad .$$

This has an impact on the code of component B, which increments j. We give the adjusted B at once, leaving to the reader to check that relation Q has, indeed, become a system invariant. We also insert two obviously correct assertions for later usage.

Pre : $i=0 \,\wedge\, j=0$	
A: **do** $i \neq N \to$ **if** $i < j \to$ *skip* **fi** ; $x.i := 0$; $\{i < j\}$ $i := i+1$ **od**	B: **do** $j \neq N \to$ **if** $j \leq i \to$ *skip* **fi** ; $x.j := 1$; $\{j \leq i\}$ $j := j+1$ **od**
Inv : $Q: \quad i \leq j \,\wedge\, j \leq i+1$	

For reasons to become clear shortly, B has been given the same syntactic structure as A has.

By inserting a guarded skip in B, we may have hampered progress, so the question is: does this program still terminate? It does, because

- at least one of the guards of the two guarded skips is *true*, so that
- $i+j$ increases, and
- since $i \leq j \leq N$ is a system invariant, B will terminate in a state satisfying $j = N$, so that
- as before, A will terminate as well.

Now we transform the program according to the coordinate transformation given by the *coupling invariant*

$$c \equiv (i=j) \qquad , \text{ or } - \text{ equivalently, see } Q -$$
$$\neg c \equiv (i+1=j) \qquad .$$

Then we can eliminate the guards thanks to

$$i < j \equiv \neg c \qquad \text{and} \qquad j \leq i \equiv c \qquad .$$

Statement $\{i < j\}\ i := i+1$ can now be replaced with

$$\{\neg c\}\ c, i := \neg c, i+1$$

or — using pre-assertion $\neg c$ — by

   $c, i := true, i+1$.

The raw program code thus becomes

Pre : $i = 0 \wedge j = 0 \wedge c$	
A: **do** $i \neq N \rightarrow$	B: **do** $j \neq N \rightarrow$
if $\neg c \rightarrow skip$ **fi**	**if** $c \rightarrow skip$ **fi**
; $x.i := 0$	; $x.j := 1$
; $c, i := true, i+1$	; $c, j := false, j+1$
od	**od**

*　　*

*

And now the situation has become so symmetric that if we want the above machinery to deliver $\vec{x} = \vec{1}$ instead of $\vec{x} = \vec{0}$, we only need to flip c's initial value. And if we want $\vec{x} = \vec{0}$ or $\vec{x} = \vec{1}$, i.e. if we don't care, we simply leave c's initial value unspecified. It is with this regime that two individual processors can write a bit stream, bit by bit, into one and the same memory location, such that the result is as if they had done so in some unspecified order.

*　　*

*

We conclude this postscript with two remarks.

- We will discuss coordinate transformations like the one applied above with more precision in a later chapter.

- We achieved the two-valuedness of $j - i$ by strengthening the annotation via introduction of invariant Q, thus reducing the degree of parallelism that can be displayed by the program. We will encounter this trade-off more often and then discuss it at greater length.

11

More Theorems and More Examples

This is the last chapter of the first half of this text. In the second half we will almost exclusively be occupied with program derivation, using the vocabulary and the techniques introduced so far. There is, however, one final issue that we have hardly touched upon, viz. the problem of how to make programs more *fine-grained*. We already alluded to this issue when specifying the problem of Concurrent Vector Writing, but now the time has come to become a little more articulate about it.

An important aspect of the theory of Owicki and Gries is that the coarser-grained the atomic statements, the smaller the proof load. This phenomenon has its match in program development: the coarser-grained the repertoire of atomic statements, the easier the task becomes. As said earlier, granularity issues are not our first concern when we develop a program: instead, we usually start by focusing on the logic of the design. However, in many situations we will sooner or later *have* to be concerned with granularity, because the architecture of the executing machinery requires us to. Therefore it would be nice to have means or techniques for making programs more fine-grained without impairing their correctness. The main purpose of this chapter is to provide a number of theorems dealing with correctness-preserving program transformations, by which coarse-grained statements can sometimes be turned into finer-grained ones. We shall illustrate this in a number of examples.

Remark   Here we have to admit that, to our regret, we only have a very limited number of techniques for reducing the granularity of our programs. Additional — simple! — techniques are most welcome.
End of Remark.

*   *
*

Our first two theorems are about substitution of equals for equals. Because they are two sides of the same coin, they are both named Rule of Leibniz. Substitution of equals for equals being what it is, we present them without proof.

Rule of Leibniz

> Program fragment $\{F = G\}\ x := F$ may be replaced by
> $\{F = G\}\ x := G$ with impunity, i.e. without affecting progress properties or correctness of the annotation.

End of Rule of Leibniz.

We already tacitly used this rule at the very end of our treatment of Concurrent Vector Writing, when we replaced $\{\neg c\}\ c, i := \neg c, i+1$ by $c, i := true, i+1$.

In the same vein we have

Rule of Leibniz

> Program fragment $\{C \equiv D\}$ **if** $C \rightarrow S$ **fi** may be replaced by
> $\{C \equiv D\}$ **if** $D \rightarrow S$ **fi** with impunity.

End of Rule of Leibniz.

This rule, too, was used in our treatment of Concurrent Vector Writing, viz. when we replaced **if** $i < j \rightarrow skip$ **fi** by **if** $\neg c \rightarrow skip$ **fi** , such on account of the coupling invariant $i < j \equiv \neg c$.

Of course, the Rule of Leibniz comes in many forms. The transformations are so reasonable, that we shall usually apply them without much ado.

*   *
*

The next two theorems, though simple, happen to be very useful for unraveling too coarse-grained atomic statements. They are the two Guard Strengthening lemmata:

First Guard Strengthening Lemma

> Program fragment

  if $B \to S$ **fi**

may be replaced by

  $\{C \Rightarrow B\}$ **if** $C \to S$ **fi**

without impairing the correctness of the annotation, provided
the added assertion $C \Rightarrow B$ is correct.

End of First Guard Strengthening Lemma.

and

Second Guard Strengthening Lemma

  Program fragment

    $\{C \Rightarrow B\}$ **if** $B \to S$ **fi**

  may be replaced by

    $\{C \Rightarrow B\}$ **if** $C \to S$ **fi**

without impairing the correctness of the annotation.

End of Second Guard Strengthening Lemma.

Before we discuss these lemmata and use them in some examples, let us
first prove them.

Proof of First Each proof obligation involving the new fragment
$\{C \Rightarrow B\}$ **if** $C \to S$ **fi** has the form

  $[\, P \wedge (C \Rightarrow B) \;\Rightarrow\; wlp.(\text{if } C \to S \text{ fi}).Q \,]$,

which equivales — definition of *IF* —

  $[\, P \wedge C \wedge B \;\Rightarrow\; wlp.S.Q \,]$,

and this follows from the stronger

  $[\, P \wedge B \;\Rightarrow\; wlp.S.Q \,]$,

which is the corresponding proof obligation for the original fragment
if $B \to S$ **fi**.

End of Proof of First.

Proof of Second The proviso of the First Lemma, viz. the correctness of
assertion $C \Rightarrow B$, is fulfilled through the assertion $C \Rightarrow B$ in the original
fragment.

End of Proof of Second.

Remark So, in fact, the Second Lemma is just a corollary of the First,
be it a useful one. In the beginning we ourselves only knew of the Second
Lemma, and it was our former student Perry D. Moerland who discovered

that in particular applications it was insufficiently strong. He then designed the First Lemma: the difference is a very subtle one.
End of Remark.

Both lemmata tell us that the guard of a guarded statement can be strengthened without endangering the partial correctness of a design. We should be aware, however, that their application may have consequences for progress: the stronger a guard, the less probable it is that a component can find it *true*. And indeed, one may even introduce total deadlock, as we shall see in our next example.

In most of our applications we shall use the Second Guard Strengthening Lemma rather than the First, and when doing so we will simply announce this by the phrase "Strengthening the Guard". Only when we appeal to the First Lemma we will say so explicitly.

Example 0   (from "The Safe Sluice", Chapter 13)

Consider the following two-component multiprogram

Pre : $\neg x.p \land \neg x.q$
Comp.p: $* \, [\, \textbf{if } \neg x.q \rightarrow x.p := true \textbf{ fi}$ $; \, x.p := false$ $]$
Comp.q: $* \, [\, \textbf{if } \neg x.p \rightarrow x.q := true \textbf{ fi}$ $; \, x.q := false$ $]$

(The guarded statements and the individual assignments $x.p := false$ and $x.q := false$ are atomic.)

Exercise   The reader may prove that there is no danger of total deadlock. He may also verify that individual progress is, however, not guaranteed.
End of Exercise.

There are quite a number of machine architectures in which an atomic statement like

$$\textbf{if } \neg x.q \rightarrow x.p := true \textbf{ fi}$$

is not readily implemented, for instance those machines that only offer one-point statements as atomic statements. (Recall that a one-point statement is a statement that can be implemented by at most one access — for instance one read or one write — to a shared or private variable.) On such installations, the inspection of $\neg x.q$ and the assignment $x.p := true$ cannot take place indivisibly, i.e. combined within one and the same atomic statement, and we, therefore, have to separate them: we have to eliminate the guarded statements from the above multiprogram and turn them into finer-grained ones, of course without affecting the correctness of the — invisible — annotation. Here we can use the technique of Strengthening the Guard, which we shall now show in a number of small steps.

We first introduce fresh, auxiliary variables $y.p$ and $y.q$ to "take over the rôles of $x.p$ and $x.q$ ", respectively, the intention being that in Comp.p guard $\neg x.q$ is to be replaced with $\neg y.q$. Our Guard Strengthening Lemmata tell us that this can be done safely if we can see to the correctness of $\neg y.q \Rightarrow \neg x.q$, or — equivalently — of

$$x.q \Rightarrow y.q$$

as a precondition to the guarded statement. In our next intermediate version of the multiprogram we shall accomplish this by making it a system invariant. Likewise,

$$x.p \Rightarrow y.p$$

will be a system invariant.

Because we are aiming at a replacement of if $\neg x.q \rightarrow x.p := true$ fi by if $\neg y.q \rightarrow x.p := true$ fi , we should not try to maintain the invariance of $x.p \Rightarrow y.p$ by changing $x.p := true$ into $x.p, y.p := true, true$, because that would be begging the question: it would give rise to

if $\neg y.q \rightarrow x.p, y.p := true, true$ fi   ,

a statement in which the y's are just as entangled as the x's were before. So assignment $y.p := true$ had better occur in isolation. The topology of the program then hardly leaves us any choice:

Pre :	$\neg x.p \wedge \neg x.q \wedge \neg y.p \wedge \neg y.q$
Comp.p:	$* [\, y.p := true$
	; if $\neg x.q \rightarrow x.p := true$ fi
	; $x.p := false$
	; $y.p := false$
	$]$
Comp.q:	Comp.p with p and q interchanged
Inv :	$(x.p \Rightarrow y.p) \wedge (x.q \Rightarrow y.q)$

Now, thanks to Inv we can strengthen the guards and replace, in Comp.p, $\neg x.q$ with $\neg y.q$. Then Comp.p becomes

```
Comp.p:  * [ y.p := true
         ; if ¬y.q → x.p := true fi
         ; x.p := false
         ; y.p := false
         ]
```

and Comp.q likewise. And from this program text we see that execution
no longer runs under control of the variables x but under control of the
variables y instead: the originally auxiliary variables y have become
genuine ones, and the originally genuine x's have become auxiliaries and
can, therefore, be removed from the program text altogether:

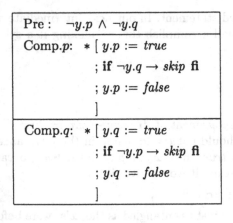

```
Pre :    ¬y.p ∧ ¬y.q

Comp.p:  * [ y.p := true
         ; if ¬y.q → skip fi
         ; y.p := false
         ]

Comp.q:  * [ y.q := true
         ; if ¬y.p → skip fi
         ; y.q := false
         ]
```

*   *

*

We conclude this example with a few remarks.

- The transformation of the original program into the above final one introduces the danger of total deadlock indeed, but that is a separate
  concern and is not what the example was about. Moreover, the original
  program was not too fine a specimen either, because it lacks the property
  of individual progress.

- Once the above program transformation has been grasped, it can be
  carried out in one or two steps at later occasions, and we will do so,
  because the transformation is a fairly standard one.

- The original coarse-grained program serves some partial-correctness requirement unknown to us. The transformed finer-grained one satisfies

that same requirement. However, an a-posteriori proof that it does will, in general, be harder to find, because it will, at best, require a reversal of the transformation process given above. For us, this particular example has, in fact, been the first indication that in multiprogramming verification might feasibly be exchanged for derivation. We will return to this observation in more detail in our chapter on the Safe Sluice.

End of Example 0.

Example 1   (from "Phase Synchronization", Chapter 17)

We consider the following two-component multiprogram

Pre : $x \wedge y$	
A: $*$ [**if** $x \rightarrow$ *skip* **fi**	B: $*$ [**if** $y \rightarrow$ *skip* **fi**
$; x, y := \neg y, true$	$; y, x := \neg x, true$
]	]

(The guarded skips and the multiple assignments are atomic.)

Our purpose is to eliminate the multiple assignments, exchanging them for simple assignments, without impairing the correctness of the invisible annotation. Again we can use the technique of Strengthening the Guard. The transformation is guided by the desire to replace guard x in A by a stronger f, and guard y in B by a stronger g. We now give the intermediate, hybrid version at once

Pre : $x \wedge y \wedge f \wedge g$
A: $*$ [**if** $x \rightarrow$ *skip* **fi**
$; f := false$
$; x, y, g := \neg y, true, true$
]
B: $*$ [**if** $y \rightarrow$ *skip* **fi**
$; g := false$
$; y, x, f := \neg x, true, true$
]
Inv : $(f \Rightarrow x) \wedge (g \Rightarrow y)$

Exercise 0   It is a — nice — exercise to prove that $(f \Rightarrow x) \land (g \Rightarrow y)$ is, indeed, a system invariant. To that end one has to introduce an auxiliary annotation, which can be found constructively by the technique of Strengthening the Annotation.
End of Exercise 0.

Because of system invariant Inv, we can now replace guard x with f and guard y with g, after which variables x and y have become auxiliaries and can be eliminated from the program text. We thus obtain

Pre : $f \land g$	
A: $* [$ **if** $f \to$ *skip* **fi**	B: $* [$ **if** $g \to$ *skip* **fi**
; $f :=$ *false*	; $g :=$ *false*
; $g :=$ *true*	; $f :=$ *true*
]	]

Exercise 1   It is a — nice — exercise to prove that the above program does not suffer from the danger of total deadlock.
End of Exercise 1.

Finally, as an aside, we wish to inform the reader that the original program has an invisible multibound, expressed in invisible variables, associated with it. Because the technique of Strengthening the Guard does not affect the partial correctness, that same invisible multibound has remained intact. As a result we can immediately conclude individual progress in the fine-grained algorithm above from the absence of total deadlock. No operational reasoning and no temporal logic are required.

End of Example 1.

*   *
*

Our next theorem tells us uncircumlocutorily about refinement. It is the

Guard Conjunction Lemma

   For globally correct B, (atomic) program fragment

   if $B \land C \to S$ **fi**

   may be replaced by the composition

>   if $B \rightarrow$ *skip* fi
>   ; if $C \rightarrow S$ fi

of the two finer-grained (atomic) statements, without impairing the *total* correctness of the design, i.e.

(i)   without impairing the correctness of the annotation, and
(ii) without introducing total deadlock, and
(iii) without endangering individual progress.

End of Guard Conjunction Lemma.

Proof

(ii) & (iii) Unfortunately, our formalism is not suited for proving this. Fortunately, Dr. Jozef Hooman proved it for us (when the Lemma was still a conjecture). He did so by considering the sets of all possible computations that can be evoked by the original and by the new system, respectively, and then showing that the two systems have the same properties as far as deadlock and individual progress are concerned. The proof is not for free and we are grateful to him for having designed it for us [Hoo93].

(i)   The proof of (i) is within the scope of our formalism. We will show that the original fragment can be transformed (indicated by " $\sqsubseteq$ ") into the new one by exhibiting a series of already established transformations:

>   if $B \wedge C \rightarrow$ *skip* fi

$\sqsubseteq$ {adding a skip is harmless}

>   if *true* $\rightarrow$ *skip* fi
>   ; if $B \wedge C \rightarrow S$ fi

$\sqsubseteq$ {strengthening the guard}

>   if $B \rightarrow$ *skip* fi
>   ; if $B \wedge C \rightarrow S$ fi

$\sqsubseteq$ {introducing the globally (and locally) correct
>   intermediate assertion B}

>   if $B \rightarrow$ *skip* fi
>   ; {B}
>   if $B \wedge C \rightarrow S$ fi

$\sqsubseteq$ {Leibniz}

$$\textbf{if } B \rightarrow skip \textbf{ fi}$$
$$; \{B\}$$
$$\textbf{if } C \rightarrow S \textbf{ fi}$$

$\sqsubseteq$ {weakening the annotation}

$$\textbf{if } B \rightarrow skip \textbf{ fi}$$
$$; \textbf{if } C \rightarrow S \textbf{ fi}$$

End of Proof.

Examples in which the Guard Conjunction Lemma can be applied tend to be the more complicated ones, and therefore we refrain from illustrating its use here.

*   *
*

The last theorem of this chapter has nothing to do with program transformation. It is the

Rule of Modus Ponens

For globally correct C , the post-assertion in

$$\{B \Rightarrow C\} \textbf{ if } B \rightarrow skip \textbf{ fi } \{C\}$$

is correct whenever the pre-assertion is.

End of Rule of Modus Ponens.

One may justly wonder why this rule is worthy of a name: it is nothing more than the definition of the correctness of an assertion. However, the reason to introduce it nevertheless is that a bell should start ringing whenever some stable (i.e. globally correct) state of a system has to be detected, the bell being the Rule of Modus Ponens.

Consider, for instance, the following programming problem

Pre : $true$	
X: S_0 ; {? T_0 has terminated} S_1	Y: T_0 ; T_1

in which component X has to "detect" the stable state "T_0 has terminated".
Now the intention is that in this situation we grab, without much hesitation,

the Modus Ponens, introduce a variable y and — for instance — system invariant

$$y \Rightarrow \text{``}T_0 \text{ has terminated''} \quad ,$$

and write down as our solution

Pre : $\neg y$	
X: S_0 ; if $y \rightarrow skip$ fi ; $\{T_0$ has terminated$\}$ S_1	Y: T_0 ; $y := true$; T_1
Inv : $y \Rightarrow \text{``}T_0 \text{ has terminated''}$	

The Modus Ponens captures what in more operationally inclined circles is commonly phrased as "If the component has observed the validity of B, we can be sure that event so-and-so (viz. the truthification of C) must have taken place".

In short: the Modus Ponens serves to signal stable states; and more importantly: when stable states are to be signalled remember the Modus Ponens.

*   *
*

And this concludes the last chapter of the first half of this book.

12

The Yellow Pages

This chapter forms a true divide in this monograph, in that the preceding part was mainly concerned with the *description* of multiprograms whereas the following part will deal with their *construction*. What we did so far was introduce and discuss a body of concepts, techniques, and rules of thumb that together form the basic ingredients for our method of multiprogramming. Since these ingredients are rather scattered over the various chapters, it seems appropriate that, on this divide of the book, we give a brief and rough summary of them. And this, indeed, is the primary purpose of these "Yellow Pages".

When we (the authors) conceived the flavour of this book, we decided it to become a (research) monograph rather than a textbook. As a result no exercises were planned, apart from a few in the running text. When, in a late stage of writing, prof. David Gries heard about this, he strongly recommended to include exercise sections nevertheless. We then decided to (partly) follow his advice and to "misuse" the Yellow Pages for this other purpose as well.

12.0   A Summary

This summary is arranged thematically. For most items quoted, we refer to a chapter where it is discussed more elaborately and precisely.

12.0.0   Predicate Calculus

The reader is assumed to be familiar with the rules of the predicate calculus. ([DS90], for instance, gives a fairly exhaustive treatment.) However, we adopted a few conventions diverging from what is common.

- Function application:

  Function application is denoted by an infix dot. Its distinctive property is Leibniz' Rule: for function f

  $$x = y \;\Rightarrow\; f.x = f.y \qquad , \text{ for all } x, y.$$

- The "Everywhere"-operator:

  The Everywhere-operator is a unary operator on predicates, and it is denoted by a pair of square brackets. Its "semantics" is given by

  $$[\,P\,] \equiv (P \text{ yields value } \textit{true} \text{ for all states of the state space}).$$

  The operator plays an important rôle in treating the semantics of program notations.

- Binding powers:
  - The logical operators in order of decreasing binding power are $\neg$, then $\land$ and $\lor$ (with equal binding power), then $\Rightarrow$ and $\Leftarrow$ (with equal binding power), and finally $\equiv$ and $\not\equiv$ (also with equal binding power).
  - The arithmetic operators and relators bind more strongly than the logical ones.
  - Of all operators, function application binds strongest.

- The equivalence-operator:

  The equivalence-operator, denoted $\equiv$, is an infix operator on predicates. Its most important properties are:
  - it is symmetric (commutative) and associative;
  - it has *true* as its left and right identity;

– disjunction distributes over it, i.e.
$$[\, P \vee (X \equiv Y) \equiv P \vee X \equiv P \vee Y \,] \quad ;$$

– it is related to negation by
$$[\, \neg(P \equiv Q) \equiv \neg P \equiv Q \,] \quad ;$$

– for predicate transformer f, it satisfies
$$[\, P \equiv Q \,] \;\Rightarrow\; [\, f.P \equiv f.Q \,] \quad ,$$

which is an instance of Leibniz' Rule.

12.0.1 Our computational model (cf. Chapters 1 and 18)

A multiprogram is a set of sequential programs — called components. Execution of a single component results in a sequence of atomic actions, prescribed by the state and the program text. Execution of a multiprogram results in a sequence of atomic actions that is a fair interleaving of the sequences generated by the individual components. What "fair" boils down to is that each component that has not terminated will, within a finite number of steps of the rest of the system, contribute a next action to the interleaving, irrespective of whether this action is a guard evaluation or an assignment.

Our use of the model is confined to produce scenarios for supporting or refuting progress claims.

12.0.2 Annotation

Its shape (cf. Chapters 2, 3, 5.1)

A *fully-annotated* multiprogram is annotated with assertions such that

– there is a precondition of the multiprogram as a whole;

– there is a postcondition of the multiprogram as a whole, in case all components terminate;

– each individual atomic statement of each individual component carries a pre-assertion;

– it mentions the (relevant) system invariants.

Its correctness (cf. Chapters 3, 4, 5.1)

In principle, correctness of annotation can only be established via the Core rules of the Owicki/Gries theory, which require a fully annotated multiprogram.

Of course, there are also some correctness-preserving program transformations, like Guard Strengthening (cf. Chapter 11), or special theorems stating correctness, like Topology Lemmata.

Manipulating correct annotation (cf. Chapters 4, 5.1, 6)

- Correctness of annotation is not affected by weakening an assertion, weakening an invariant, weakening the postcondition, or strengthening the precondition. By the weakening operations, the correctness according to the Core rules may, however, be lost.
- Adding a correct conjunct to an assertion, an invariant or the postcondition preserves the correctness of the existing annotation. For proving the correctness of the added conjunct, the correctness of the existing annotation can be used (cf. Chapter 6).
- An invariant may be added as a correct conjunct to each individual assertion.

12.0.3   The Core of the Owicki/Gries theory (cf. Chapters 3, 6)

Consider a fully annotated multiprogram. The annotation is correct (in the Core) whenever

(i)   each individual assertion is correct, and
(ii) the postcondition is correct, if present, and
(iii) the invariants are correct.

Re (i)
An assertion is correct whenever it is both locally and globally correct — for definitions, see Chapter 3.

What the correctness proof of an assertion P amounts to is proving the validity of a number of Hoare-triples $\{X\} S \{P\}$. We emphasize that, for this purpose, pre-assertions X may always be strengthened with the system invariants.

Re (ii)
The postcondition is correct whenever

- it is implied by the conjunction of the post-assertions of the individual components, and

- all components are guaranteed to terminate.

Re (iii)

An invariant P is correct whenever

- it is implied by the precondition, and

- it is maintained by each atomic statement $\{Q\}$ S of the multiprogram, i.e. $\{P \wedge Q\}$ S $\{P\}$ is a correct Hoare-triple. We emphasize that in proving the correctness of these Hoare-triples, the pre-assertions may always be strengthened with other invariants.

12.0.4 Variables

There are two independent classifications for the variables we encounter, one that is related to their accessibility, and one that is related to their rôle in the "flow of control".

- *Auxiliary* variables are those that have no influence on the flow of control. They usually enter the game in a-posteriori proofs and in program transformations. In the latter case they tend to switch rôle with the "genuine" (i.e. non-auxiliary) variables (cf. Chapters 10, 11).

- *Shared* variables are those that can be changed by more than one component.

- *Private* variables are those that can be changed by one component only, but can be inspected by all.

- *Local* variables are those that can be changed by one component only and cannot be inspected by the others.

12.0.5 Atomicity

Unless stated otherwise, our only atomic program fragments are

- the (multiple) assignment statement
- the guarded skip
- the guard of a repetition.

In the process of program development, we may, of course, temporarily use coarser-grained fragments, but in the end they will have to be replaced with the above ones.

Our finest-grained atomic fragments are

- the one-point-statements, and
- the one-point-guards;

they contain at most one reference to a shared or private variable. Many algorithms in this book are "one-point".

12.0.6 Progress (cf. Chapters 8, 9)

- Individual Progress:

    Statement $\{Q\}$ if $B \rightarrow S$ fi in a component terminates

    > if and only if

    the rest of the system, when constrained to (states satisfying) Q will, in a finite number of steps, converge to a state in which B is stably *true*.

- (Absence of) Total Deadlock:

    - When all components arc "at" a guarded statement, progress of the multiprogram is guaranteed

        > if and only if

        in that state of the system at least one of the guards is *true*.

    - If in such a state all guards are *false* the multiprogram has (the Danger of) Total Deadlock (which is to be avoided).

- The Multibound:

    If all components have the shape

    $$* [\, x.i := 1 + x.i \,]$$

    and if

    MB: "the x- values are mutually bounded"

    is a system invariant, then

    > individual progress for each component is guaranteed
    >
    > $\equiv$
    >
    > there is no total deadlock.

12.0.7   Rules and Lemmata

- **(Hoare-triple) Semantics** (cf. Chapter 2):

  - $\{Q\}$ *skip* $\{Q\}$

  - $\{(x := E).Q\}\ x := E\ \{Q\}$

  - $\{P\}\ S_0; S_1\ \{Q\}$
    $\Leftarrow$
    for some H: $\{P\}\ S_0\ \{H\} \wedge \{H\}\ S_1\ \{Q\}$

  - $\{B \Rightarrow Q\}$ if $B \rightarrow$ *skip* fi $\{Q\}$

  - $\{P\}\ S\ \{Q\} \equiv [\ P \Rightarrow wlp.S.Q\ ]$

  - the correctness of a Hoare-triple is preserved by strengthening the pre-assertion and by weakening the post-assertion.

- **Orthogonality** (cf. Chapter 5):

  An assertion that doesn't depend on variable x is maintained by all assignments to x.

- **Disjointness** (cf. Chapter 7):

  Assertion P is maintained by $\{Q\}\ S$ if
  $$[\ P \wedge Q \Rightarrow false\ ]$$

- **Widening** (cf. Chapter 7):

  Assertion $x \leq y$ is maintained by "descents" of x and by "ascents" of y.

- **(Second) Guard Strengthening Lemma** (cf. Chapter 11):

  Program fragment
  $$\{C \Rightarrow B\}\ \text{if}\ B \rightarrow S\ \text{fi}$$
  may be replaced with
  $$\{C \Rightarrow B\}\ \text{if}\ C \rightarrow S\ \text{fi}$$
  without impairing the correctness of (all of) the annotation.

- **Guard Conjunction Lemma** (cf. Chapter 11):

  For globally correct B, (atomic) program fragment
  $$\text{if}\ B \wedge C \rightarrow S\ \text{fi}$$

may be replaced by

> if $B \rightarrow$ *skip* fi
> ; if $C \rightarrow S$ fi

without impairing the (total) correctness of the program.

- **Gouda's Guard Disjunction Lemma** (cf. Chapter 24):

  For globally correct B, the guard in (atomic) program fragment

  > if $B \vee C \rightarrow$ *skip* fi

  may be evaluated disjunct-wise without impairing the (total) correctness of the program.

- **Modus Ponens** (cf. Chapter 11):

  For globally correct C, the post-assertion in

  > $\{B \Rightarrow C\}$ if $B \rightarrow$ *skip* fi $\{C\}$

  is correct, whenever the pre-assertion is.

- **Topology Lemmata** (cf. Chapters 5, 7)

12.1 Exercises

The exercises in this section pertain to the entire book. However, many of them can be done with the material discussed so far; they are the ones in which no program construction is demanded. For the other ones, we recommend that the reader has studied at least the first half of the second part of this book.

Where do the exercises come from? The majority is taken from our own own archives, but some were borrowed from [Luk98] and from [Sch97]. However, in Schneider's text, one can find a wealth of exercises that would not be out of place here. Instead of copying those, we rather refer the interested reader to that text, because, besides these exercises, it also contains an in-depth logical treatment of annotated multiprograms.

Most instructive and rewarding of all however is, to consider self-made synchronization problems (for instance, variations on the ones we dealt with) or to revisit existing protocols or algorithms. However instructive or rewarding this can be, it is not without danger either. From experience we know that multiprogramming problems tend to be extremely simple or forbiddingly difficult. The layer in between is just very thin.

*   *
*

Before the reader embarks on this series of exercises, he should be informed that they are not arranged in the order of increasing difficulty or laboriousness, and that they are not classified by theme either. This may at first seem cruel, but we think it is more challenging, and more truthfully reflecting real life as well. Our advice to the reader is that he not allow himself to get discouraged too quickly, since, after all, *multiprogramming just isn't a simple activity.*

Exercise 0   Derive for which integers c and d

$$x \leq y+c \ \wedge \ y \leq x+d$$

is a system invariant of

Pre: $x=0 \ \wedge \ y=0$	
A: $*[\ x:=y$	B: $*[\ y:=x$
$;\ x:=x+1$	$;\ y:=y+1$
$]$	$]$

Exercise 1   Show the correctness of the postcondition in

Pre: $i=0 \ \wedge \ j=0$	
A: **do** $i \neq 47 \rightarrow$	B: **do** $j \neq 47 \rightarrow$
$i := i+1$	$x.j := i$
od	$;\ j := j+1$
	od
Post: $\langle \forall k : 1 \leq k < 47 : x.(k-1) \leq x.k \rangle$	

(Hint: define auxiliary element $x.(-1)$, such that $x.(-1) \leq 0$.)

Exercise 2   Show the correctness of the postcondition in

Pre :	*true*	
A: $x := x+2$	B: $x := 0$	
Post : $x=0 \lor x=2$		

Exercise 3   Show the correctness of the postcondition in

Pre :	*true*

A: **if** $\langle x \le y \rangle \rightarrow \langle m := x \rangle$
  ▌ $\langle y \le x \rangle \rightarrow \langle m := y \rangle$
  fi
	B: $\langle m := x \rangle$
	  ; **if** $\langle m \le y \rangle \rightarrow skip$
	  ▌ $\langle y \le m \rangle \rightarrow \langle m := y \rangle$
	  fi

Post : $m = x \downarrow y$	

in which $\downarrow$ denotes the minimum operator. (The angular brackets indicate the intended atomicity.)

Exercise 4   Show the correctness of the postcondition in

Pre : $i=0 \land j=0$	

A: **do** $i \ne 100 \rightarrow$
      $i := i+1$
    ; $x := i$
  od
	B: **do** $j \ne 100 \rightarrow$
	      $j := j+1$
	    ; $x := j$
	  od

Post : $x = 100$	

Exercise 5   Show the correctness of the postcondition in

Pre : $\neg x$	
A: $x := true$	B: **if** $x \rightarrow x := false$ **fi**
Post : $\neg x$	

If component A is changed into

A: $x := true$

   ; $x := true$,

postcondition $\neg x$ is no longer guaranteed. Check how this becomes manifest in the proof.

Exercise 6   Consider two-component multiprogram

Pre : $x=0 \ \wedge \ y=0 \ \wedge \ \neg p \ \wedge \ \neg q$

A: $p := true$
    ; $x := x+1$
    ; **if** $1 \leq y \rightarrow y := y-1$ **fi**
    $\{q\}$

B: $q := true$
    ; $y := y+1$
    ; **if** $1 \leq x \rightarrow x := x-1$ **fi**
    $\{p\}$

Show

a. the correctness of the given annotation;

b. the absence of total deadlock;

c. that both components terminate;

d. the invariance of $0 \leq x \leq 1 \ \wedge \ 0 \leq y \leq 1$;

e. that $x=0 \ \wedge \ y=0$ is a correct postcondition;

f. that, without loss of correctness, the guarded skip in A can be replaced with the finer-grained

        if $1 \leq y \rightarrow$ *skip* **fi**

        ; $y := y-1$

Exercise 7   Consider

Pre : $x=0 \ \wedge \ y=0$

A: $* [\ x := x+1$
     ; **if** $0 < y \rightarrow$ *skip* **fi**
     ; $y := y-1$
     ]

$$B: \quad *[\ y := y+1$$
$$; \textbf{if } 0 < x \rightarrow skip \textbf{ fi}$$
$$; x := x-1$$
$$]$$

Show

a. the invariance of $x \le 2$.

b. individual progress.

Exercise 8   Show the correctness of the postcondition in

Pre :	$true$	
A: **do** $1 \le x \rightarrow$		B: $x := 1$
$x := x-1$		
od		
Post :	$x = 0 \ \lor \ x = 1$	

In particular, show termination by constructing a suitable variant function.

Exercise 9

a. Show termination of

Pre :	$true$
A: **do** $x \lor y \rightarrow x := false$ **od**	
B: **do** $x \lor y \rightarrow y := false$ **od**	

b. Show that termination is no longer guaranteed if A and B are changed into

A: **do** $y \rightarrow x := false$ **od**
B: **do** $x \rightarrow y := false$ **od**

(This illustrates that strengthening the guard of a repetition or weakening the guard of a guarded statement can be detrimental to progress.)

c. How is the situation if A and B are changed into

$$
\begin{array}{ll}
\text{A:} & \textbf{do } y \rightarrow x := \textit{false } \textbf{od} \\
& ; x := \textit{false} \\
\hline
\text{B:} & \textbf{do } x \rightarrow y := \textit{false } \textbf{od} \\
& ; y := \textit{false}
\end{array}
$$

Exercise 10 Show mutual exclusion of $cs.A$ and $cs.B$ in

Pre : $\neg x \wedge \neg y$	
A: $* [\textbf{do } \neg x \rightarrow x := \neg y \textbf{ od}$	B: $* [\textbf{do } \neg y \rightarrow y := \neg x \textbf{ od}$
$; cs.A$	$; cs.B$
$; x := \textit{false}$	$; y := \textit{false}$
$]$	$]$

Exercise 11 Show the invariance of $x + y \leq z$ in

Pre : $x = 0 \wedge y = 0 \wedge z = 0$	
A: $* [y := y - 1$	B: $* [z := z + 1$
$; x := x + 1$	$; y := y + 1$
$]$	$]$

What if the multiprogram contains several components of the form A and of the form B?

Exercise 12 Show the invariance of $x + y \leq z^2$ in

Pre : $x = 0 \wedge y = 0 \wedge z = 0$	
A: $* [y := y - 1$	B: $* [d := 2 * z + 1$
$; x := x + 1$	$; z := z + 1$
$]$	$; y := y + d$
	$]$

Next, we change component B into

B:　*[$d := 2*z+1$
　　　; $z := z+1$
　　　; do $d \neq 0 \rightarrow$
　　　　　$d := d-1$
　　　　　; $y := y+1$
　　　od
　　　]

Show that $x+y \leq z^2$ still is an invariant.

Exercise 13　Show the invariance of $0 \leq s$ in

Pre :　$s=0$
A:　*[$s := s+1$]
B:　*[if $2 \leq s \rightarrow skip$ fi 　　; $s := s-1$ 　　]
C:　*[if $2 \leq s \rightarrow skip$ fi 　　; $s := s-1$ 　　]

Exercise 14　Consider a multiprogram with one component of type A and 47 components of type B.

Pre :　$s=0$	
A:　*[$s := s+1$]	B:　*[if $K \leq s \rightarrow skip$ fi 　　; $s := s-1$ 　　]

Derive for what values of K it will hold that $0 \leq s$ is a system invariant.

Exercise 15　Show the correctness of the postcondition for each of the following multiprograms

a.

Pre : $x = 0$	
A: $x := x+a$	B: $x := x+b$
Post : $x = a+b$	

b.

Pre : $x = 0$	
A: $y := x$	B: $x := x+b$
; $x := x+a$	
Post : $x = a \lor x = a+b$	

c.

Pre : $x = 0$	
A: $r := x$	B: $s := x$
; $r := r+a$	; $s := s+b$
; $x := r$	; $x := s$
Post : $x = a \lor x = b \lor x = a+b$	

Exercise 16   Let X be a component of some multiprogram. If the system without component X has system invariant P, then P is a correct pre-assertion of X. Prove this.

(This is a very simple "composition" theorem, which can sometimes be used at great advantage. The reader may now wish to revisit the previous exercise.)

Exercise 17   Consider the following two-component multiprogram:

Pre : $x = X \land y = Y$	
A: $f := y$	B: $g := x$
; $x := f$	; $y := g$

Synchronize, using one-point-statements only, the components such that the postcondition will imply

a. $x = Y$

b. $x = Y \land y = X$

c. $x = X \land y = X$

d. $x = y$

Exercise 18   Show that atomic statement

    if $B \to S$ fi

of some component can be replaced with the finer grained

     if $B \to skip$ fi

   ; S

without affecting correctness, provided B is globally correct.

(Hint: use the Guard Conjunction Lemma.)

(In operational terms, this theorem tells us that execution of S can be postponed, whenever B cannot be falsified by the rest of the system.)

Exercise 19   Consider the following multiprogram:

Pre : $n = 0 \ \wedge\ s = 0$

A: $*\,[\ n := n + 1$
      $;\ s := s + 1$
      $]$

B: $*\,[\ \mathbf{if}\ 1 \leq s \to s := s - 1\ \mathbf{fi}$
      $;\ n := n - 1$
      $]$

C: $*\,[\ \mathbf{if}\ 1 \leq s \to s := s - 1\ \mathbf{fi}$
      $;\ n := n - 1$
      $]$

(Note that the operations on s mimic P- and V-operations.)

Show the invariance of $0 \leq n$. What if the guarded skips in B and C are replaced by the finer grained

    if $1 \leq s \to skip$ fi

   ; $s := s - 1$?

   Next, we split "semaphore" s in the above algorithm into "semaphores" sb and sc via the coordinate transformation

    $0 \leq sb\ \wedge\ 0 \leq sc\ \wedge\ s = sb + sc$

We may thus obtain

$$
\begin{array}{|l|}
\hline
\text{Pre}: \quad n=0 \;\wedge\; sb=0 \;\wedge\; sc=0 \\
\hline
\begin{array}{l}
\text{A:} \;\; *[\, n := n+1 \\
\qquad ; \textbf{if } \langle\, true\, \rangle \rightarrow \langle\, sb := sb+1\, \rangle \\
\qquad \;\; [\![\; \langle\, true\, \rangle \rightarrow \langle\, sc := sc+1\, \rangle \\
\qquad \textbf{fi} \\
\qquad]
\end{array} \\
\hline
\begin{array}{l}
\text{B:} \;\; *[\, \textbf{if } 1 \le sb \rightarrow sb := sb-1 \;\textbf{fi} \\
\qquad ; n := n-1 \\
\qquad]
\end{array} \\
\hline
\begin{array}{l}
\text{C:} \;\; *[\, \textbf{if } 1 \le sc \rightarrow sc := sc-1 \;\textbf{fi} \\
\qquad ; n := n-1 \\
\qquad]
\end{array} \\
\hline
\end{array}
$$

(The angular brackets in A indicate the intended granularity of that if-statement.)

Argue why $0 \le n$ still is a system invariant. Show that the guarded statement in B can be replaced with the finer grained

   $\textbf{if } 1 \le sb \rightarrow skip \;\textbf{fi}$
   $; sb := sb-1$

Likewise for C.

Exercise 20   Consider two-component multiprogram

$$
\begin{array}{|l|l|}
\hline
\multicolumn{2}{|l|}{\text{Pre}: \quad x=0 \;\wedge\; y=0} \\
\hline
\text{A:} \;\; *[\, x := x+1\,] & \text{B:} \;\; *[\, y := y+1\,] \\
\hline
\end{array}
$$

Synchronize the components — using guarded skips only — such that $x \le y$ will be a system invariant. How to do this if x or y are not allowed to occur in the synchronization protocol? What if there are several components of type A and several of type B?

Exercise 21   Consider the following multiprogram, with 23 components of type A and 47 components of type B:

Pre : $s = 0$	
A: $*[\, s := s+1 \,]$	B: $*[\, s := s-1 \,]$

Synchronize the components — using guarded skips only — such that $0 \leq s \leq 100$ will be a system invariant.

Exercise 22   Show the invariance of Inv in

Pre : $x = 0 \wedge y = 0 \wedge z = 0$
A: $*[\, x := x+1;\ y := y-1 \,]$
B: $*[\, y := y+1;\ z := z-1 \,]$
C: $*[\, z := z+1;\ x := x-1 \,]$
Inv : $0 \leq x + y + z \leq 3$

Next, synchronize the components such that they will maintain

$$0 \leq x \ \wedge \ x \leq y \ \wedge \ y \leq z \quad .$$

Discuss individual progress.

Exercise 23   Consider the following many-component multiprogram:

Pre : $\langle \, \forall q :: \neg x.q \, \rangle$
Comp.p: $*[\, x.p := \textit{true}$
$;\ \textbf{if}\ \langle \, \forall q : q \neq p : \neg x.q \, \rangle \rightarrow \textit{skip}\ \textbf{fi}$
$;\ S.p$
$;\ x.p := \textit{false}$
$\,]$

Show mutual exclusion of the S- fragments.

(Hint: the easiest way of showing this is by deriving this program, which is just a generalization of the Safe Sluice for two components (cf. Chapter 13).)

Exercise 24   Consider the following N-component multiprogram $(2 \leq N)$:

Pre :   *true*

Comp.p: $*\,[\, v := p$
       ; **if** $v \neq p \rightarrow skip$ **fi**
       ; $S.p$
       $]$

Show that the number of components engaged in their S-fragment is at most $N-1$.

Show that the same holds for the following multiprogram

Pre : $\langle\, \forall q :: \neg x.q\, \rangle$

Comp.p: $*\,[\, x.p := true$
       ; **if** $\langle\, \exists q : q \neq p : \neg x.q\, \rangle \rightarrow skip$ **fi**
       ; $S.p$
       ; $x.p := false$
       $]$

How is the situation if the components are changed into

Comp.p: $*\,[\, x.p := true$
       ; $v := p$
       ; **if** $v \neq p \vee \langle\, \exists q : q \neq p : \neg x.q\, \rangle \rightarrow skip$ **fi**
       ; $S.p$
       ; $x.p := false$
       $]$

Exercise 25   Consider the following multiprogram, in which variables c, d, x and y are fresh with respect to the fragments cs and ncs:

Pre : $\quad \neg c \wedge \neg d \wedge x = 0 \wedge y = 0$	
A:	B:
$*\,[\ ncs.\mathrm{A}$	$*\,[\ ncs.\mathrm{B}$
$;\ c := true$	$;\ d := true$
$;\ x := 1 + y$	$;\ y := 1 + x$
$;\ \mathbf{if}\ \neg d \vee x < y \rightarrow skip\ \mathbf{fi}$	$;\ \mathbf{if}\ \neg c \vee y < x \rightarrow skip\ \mathbf{fi}$
$;\ cs.\mathrm{A}$	$;\ cs.\mathrm{B}$
$;\ c := false$	$;\ d := false$
$]$	$]$

Show

a. Mutual exclusion of the fragments $cs.\mathrm{A}$ and $cs.\mathrm{B}$.

b. Absence of total deadlock.

c. Individual progress, even if the disjuncts in the guards are evaluated disjunctwise.

(Hint: in fact, the above algorithm admits a derivation that is very similar to the derivation of Peterson's mutual exclusion algorithm (cf. Chapter 14). Carrying out such a derivation is the easiest way to tackle this exercise.)

Exercise 26   Consider the following three-component multiprogram:

Pre : $\quad \neg x \wedge \neg y \wedge \neg z$
X: $*\,[\ ncs.\mathrm{X}$
$\quad ;\ x := true$
$\quad ;\ u, w := \mathrm{X}, \mathrm{X}$
$\quad ;\ \mathbf{if}\ (\neg y \vee u \neq \mathrm{X}) \wedge (\neg z \vee w \neq \mathrm{X}) \rightarrow skip\ \mathbf{fi}$
$\quad ;\ cs.\mathrm{X}$
$\quad ;\ x := false$
$\quad]$

Y: * [ncs.Y

    ; $y := true$

    ; $v, u := Y, Y$

    ; if $(\neg z \lor v \neq Y) \land (\neg x \lor u \neq Y) \rightarrow skip$ fi

    ; cs.Y

    ; $y := false$

    ]

Z: * [ncs.Z

    ; $z := true$

    ; $w, v := Z, Z$

    ; if $(\neg x \lor w \neq Z) \land (\neg y \lor v \neq Z) \rightarrow skip$ fi

    ; cs.Z

    ; $z := false$

    ]

Show

a. Mutual exclusion between the cs- fragments.

b. Absence of total deadlock.

c. Individual progress.

d. That the guards can be evaluated conjunctwise, and each conjunct disjunctwise.

From (d) it follows that the algorithm is very fine-grained, almost one-point, except for the multiple assignments. Show that splitting of the multiple assignments into two simple assignments inevitably introduces the danger of total deadlock.

(Hint: in fact, the above algorithm was derived in exactly the same way as Peterson's (cf. Chapter 14).)

Exercise 27   Consider the following multiprogram for implementing mutual inclusion:

Pre : $\quad a = b \wedge x \wedge y$
A: $\;*\,[\,$ **if** $a \leq b \rightarrow$ *skip* **fi** $\quad;\;\{a = b\}$ $\quad x := false$ $\quad;\;$ **if** $\neg y \vee a < b \rightarrow$ *skip* **fi** $\quad;\; x, a := true,\, a+1$ $\quad]$
B: $\;*\,[\,$ **if** $b \leq a \rightarrow$ *skip* **fi** $\quad;\;\{b = a\}$ $\quad y := false$ $\quad;\;$ **if** $\neg x \vee b < a \rightarrow$ *skip* **fi** $\quad;\; y, b := true,\, b+1$ $\quad]$

a. Show the correctness of the two assertions.

b. Make the program finer-grained by splitting the multiple assignment into two simple ones.

c. For this refined program, show individual progress.

d. From the proof in (a) it may become clear how the program was derived. Try to give such a derivation.

Exercise 28   Show the invariance of $0 \leq x$ in the following many-component multiprogram:

Pre : $\quad 1 \leq x \wedge \langle \forall j :: \neg d.j \rangle \wedge c$
Comp.i: $\;*\,[\,$ **do** $\neg d.i \rightarrow d.i,\, c := c,\, d.i$ **od** $\quad;\; x := x - 1$ $\quad;\; x := x + 1$ $\quad;\; c,\, d.i := d.i,\, c$ $\quad]$

Exercise 29   Consider a multiprogram with two components of type A:

```
Pre :   x

A:  * [ if x → x := false fi

      ; cs

      ; x := true

      ]
```

in which the fragments cs don't mention x .

a. Show mutual exclusion between the cs- fragments.

b. Show absence of total deadlock.

c. What about individual progress?

d. Extend the components, using fresh variables and guarded skips only, so as to achieve that the number of completed cs- fragments in the one component differs by at most 7 from that in the other component.

Exercise 30   Transform, through Guard Strengthening, the following multiprogram into one in which only variable x occurs:

Pre : $x \wedge y$	
A: * [if ¬x → skip fi	B: * [x := false
; x, y := true, false	; if ¬y → skip fi
]	; y := true
	]

Exercise 31   Remove, through Guard Strengthening, the multiple assignment from component C of the following multiprogram:

Pre : $\neg x \wedge y$
A: * [if x → skip fi
; x := false
]
B: * [y := ¬x]
C: * [if y → skip fi
; x, y := true, false
]

Exercise 32   Remove, through Guard Strengthening, the multiple assignments from:

Pre : $x \wedge \neg y \wedge \neg z$
A: $*\,[\,$ **if** $x \rightarrow$ *skip* **fi** $\quad ; x,y := false, true$ $\quad]$
B: $*\,[\,$ **if** $y \rightarrow$ *skip* **fi** $\quad ; y,z := false, true$ $\quad]$
C: $*\,[\,$ **if** $z \rightarrow$ *skip* **fi** $\quad ; z,x := false, true$ $\quad]$

Exercise 33   We consider the following multiprogram with arbitrary number of components:

Pre : $m=0 \wedge n=0$
Comp.p: $*\,[\,$ *ncs.p* $\quad ; x.p, m := m, m+1$ $\quad ;$ **if** $x.p = n \rightarrow$ *skip* **fi** $\quad ; cs.p$ $\quad ; n := n+1$ $\quad]$

Show mutual exclusion between the *cs*- fragments. Show absence of total deadlock. What about individual progress?

(This is a very coarse-grained variation on Lamport's Bakery Algorithm [Lam74].)
(Try to derive the algorithm, starting from $x.p = n$ as a precondition of *cs.p* .)

Exercise 34   Consider the following three-component multiprogram, in which the communication is realized through two pebbles (p and q) and one token (t):

Pre : $p = A \land q = B \land t = C$
A: $*\,[\,ncs.A$ $;\,p := C$ $;\,\text{if } t = A \to skip \text{ fi}$ $;\,cs.A$ $;\,t := C$ $\,]$
B: $*\,[\,ncs.B$ $;\,q := C$ $;\,\text{if } t = B \to skip \text{ fi}$ $;\,cs.B$ $;\,t := C$ $\,]$
C: $*\,[\,\text{if } \langle\, p = C\,\rangle \land \langle\, t = C\,\rangle \to \langle\, p, t := A, A\,\rangle$ $\quad\quad \| \; \langle\, q = C\,\rangle \land \langle\, t = C\,\rangle \to \langle\, q, t := B, B\,\rangle$ $\quad \text{fi}$ $\,]$

(The if-statement in C is a guarded statement with two alternatives. The angular brackets indicate the intended atomicity.)

a. Statement $p := C$ in component A symbolizes the sending of pebble p from A to C. However this is only "permissible" if A "owns" p, i.e. if $p = A$ is a correct precondition of $p := C$. Now show that all pebble and token traffic in the above algorithm is "permissible".

b. Show mutual exclusion between $cs.A$ and $cs.B$.

c. Show individual progress of A and B, if the selection in C is fair.

d. Show that "permissibility", mutual exclusion, and individual progress are not affected if multiple assignment $p, t := A, A$ is split into the finer-grained $p := A; \; t := A$ (and $q, t := B, B$ into $q := B; \; t := B$).

e. What if, in this splitting, the assignments to p and t (or q and t) are reversed?

Exercise 35   Given multiprogram

Pre : $c \wedge d \wedge p \wedge q$	
A:	B:
$* \, [\, \textbf{if} \; p \rightarrow skip \; \textbf{fi}$	$* \, [\, \textbf{if} \; q \rightarrow skip \; \textbf{fi}$
$\quad ; c, d, p := \neg d, true, false$	$\quad ; d, c, q := \neg c, true, false$
$\quad ; q := E$	$\quad ; p := E$
$\quad]$	$\quad]$

design E such that

$$(p \Rightarrow c) \wedge (q \Rightarrow d)$$

will be a system invariant (of course without introducing the danger of deadlock).

Exercise 36   Consider two-component multiprogram

Pre : $x = 0 \; \wedge \; y = 0 \; \wedge \; c$	
A: $* \, [\, \textbf{if} \; c \rightarrow skip \; \textbf{fi}$	B: $* \, [\, \textbf{if} \; \neg c \rightarrow skip \; \textbf{fi}$
$\quad ; x, c := x + 1, false$	$\quad ; y, c := y + 1, true$
$\quad]$	$\quad]$

a. Show that $x \leq y \; \wedge \; y \leq x + 1$ is a system invariant.

b. Eliminate the multiple assignments through Guard Strengthening. (Hint: use the First Guard Strengthening Lemma, cf. Chapter 11.)

c. Transform the algorithm such that it will be expressed in one-point-statements and private variables only (of course, without introducing deadlock).

Exercise 37

a. Given the following two-component multiprogram

Pre : *true*	
A: $x := 0$	B: $x := 1$
$\quad ; y := 0$	$\quad ; y := 1$

synchronize the components such that the postcondition will imply

$$x = 0 \ \wedge \ y = 1 \quad .$$

b. Next we consider multiprogram

Pre :	*true*		
A:	$v := 0$	B:	$v := 1$
	$; w := 0$		$; w := 1$
	$; x := 0$		$; x := 1$
	$; y := 0$		$; y := 1$

Synchronize the components such that the postcondition will imply
$$v = 0 \ \wedge \ w = 1 \ \wedge \ x = 0 \ \wedge \ y = 1 \quad .$$

Exercise 38   Given three-component multiprogram

Pre :	*true*				
A:	$x := 0$	B:	$x := 1$	C:	$x := 2$
	$; y := 0$		$; y := 1$		$; y := 2$
	$; z := 0$		$; z := 1$		$; z := 2$

synchronize the components such that the postcondition will imply
$$x = 0 \ \wedge \ y = 1 \ \wedge \ z = 2 \quad .$$

Exercise 39   Given an array $x[0 \ldots N), 0 \leq N,$ and multiprogram

Pre :	$i = 0 \ \wedge \ j = 0$	
A: **do** $i \neq N \rightarrow$		B: **do** $j \neq N \rightarrow$
$x.i := 0$		$x.j := 1$
$; i := i + 1$		$; j := j + 1$
od		**od**

synchronize the components such that the postcondition will imply
$$\langle \ \forall k : 0 \leq k < N : x.k = k \ \text{mod} \ 2 \ \rangle \quad .$$

Exercise 40 Consider the following multiprogram with arbitrary number of components:

$$
\begin{array}{|l|}
\hline
\text{Pre}: \quad f \\
\hline
\begin{array}{ll}
\text{Comp}.p: & *\,[\ ncs.p \\
& ;\ x := p \\
& ;\ \textbf{if}\ f \rightarrow skip\ \textbf{fi} \\
& ;\ f := false \\
& ;\ \textbf{if}\ x = p \rightarrow skip\ \textbf{fi} \\
& ;\ cs.p \\
& ;\ f := true \\
& \ ]
\end{array} \\
\hline
\end{array}
$$

a. Show mutual exclusion between the cs- fragments.

b. Show that there is danger of total deadlock.

c. Show that Comp.p will make progress if all other components remain in their ncs- fragments.

Exercise 41 Consider a sequential program of the form

$$X: \quad S_0\,;\,(S_1, S_2, S_3)\,;\,S_4 \quad ,$$

in which (S_1, S_2, S_3) is an ad-hoc notation for expressing that the order in which to execute the thtee included program fragments is totally irrelevant. In order to speed up the computation we farm out some of these fragments to co-components (cf. Chapter 20).

a. Farm out S_2 to Co-X_2 and S_3 to Co-X_3.

b. Farm out (S_2, S_3) to Co-X_{23}, which in turn farms out S_3 to Co-Co-X_3.

c. How to do this for a program of the form

$$*\,[\ S_0\,;\,(S_1, S_2, S_3)\,;\,S_4\ ] \quad ?$$

Exercise 42 Consider Solution II for the distributed computation of a spanning tree:

Pre :	$\langle \forall q :: white.q \rangle$
Comp.p:	**if** $q :: q \in \mathcal{N}.p \wedge red.q \rightarrow skip$ **fi**
$(p \neq R)$	; $f.p := q$
	; $red.p := true$
	; $S.p$
Comp.R:	$red.R := true$
	; $S.R$

Now synchronize the components in such a way that they only initiate their S when the entire spanning tree has been computed, this subject to the constraint that components can only communicate with their neighbours.

Exercise 43   Consider two-component multiprogram

Pre :	$\neg x \wedge \neg y$	
A:	* [$x := true$	B: * [$y := true$
	; $x := false$	; $y := false$
	]	]

a. Synchronize, using one-point operations on booleans only, the components such that

$$\neg x \vee \neg y$$

will be a system invariant.

b. How to do this if we add a third component

$$C: \quad * [\, z := true; \ z := false \,] \qquad ,$$

strengthen the precondition with $\neg z$, and strive for the invariance of

$$\neg x \vee \neg y \vee \neg z \qquad ?$$

13

The Safe Sluice: A Synthesis Emerging

As a matter of fact, this chapter is not really about the Safe Sluice. It has more of a methodological flavour, mainly because it tells the story of how a method can emerge from a careful study of a judiciously chosen, simple algorithm like the Safe Sluice. For us, authors, the exploration of this algorithm created the first evidence that the Owicki/Gries theory could, somehow, effectively be put at work for the formal derivation of multi-programs [Fei87]. The original theme of that exploration was to compare the various correctness proofs that, at the time, we could give for the Safe Sluice. Here, we are happy to have the opportunity to let the reader share in this experience, and to show how seemingly tiny little details can give rise to unforeseen developments.

We first give the algorithm and explain what it is supposed to do. We then present three a-posteriori correctness proofs, commenting on them as we go along, and we conclude with two derivations of the algorithm.

$$* \qquad *$$
$$*$$

The Safe Sluice is a stepping stone towards a two-component mutual exclusion algorithm. It is merely a stepping stone, because it lacks all sorts of progress properties. In particular, it suffers from the danger of total deadlock, but for the time being this should not bother us. Its positive feature is that it correctly implements the property of mutual exclusion. The program reads

Pre : $\neg x.p \land \neg x.q$	
Comp.p:	Comp.q:
$* \lceil ncs.p$	$* \lceil ncs.q$
$; x.p := true$	$; x.q := true$
$; \textbf{if } \neg x.q \rightarrow skip \textbf{ fi}$	$; \textbf{if } \neg x.p \rightarrow skip \textbf{ fi}$
$; cs.p$	$; cs.q$
$; x.p := false$	$; x.q := false$
$\rfloor$	$\rfloor$

The Safe Sluice

Fragments *ncs* are commonly called the "noncritical sections", and fragments *cs* the "critical sections". Variables $x.p$ and $x.q$ do not occur in these fragments. We shall now give three proofs of the property that

> Component p and Component q are not engaged in their critical sections simultaneously.

Proof 0

This is a very old, yet nicely designed proof, which emerged shortly after the Owicki/Gries theory had become known. It is a slightly adapted version of the proof in EWD554 — "A Personal Summary of the Gries-Owicki Theory" — [Dij82]. Its main characteristic is that it is constructed via an operational understanding of the algorithm. In this respect it is typical of how the Owicki/Gries theory has mostly been used.

The proof starts with the introduction of two (fresh) auxiliary boolean variables $y.p$ and $y.q$, for the purpose of marking the beginning and the end of the critical sections.

Pre : $\neg x.p \land \neg x.q \land \neg y.p \land \neg y.q$
Comp.p: $*[\ \{P_0\}\ ncs.p$
$;\ \{P_0\}\ x.p := true$
$;\ \{P_1\}\ \textbf{if}\ \neg x.q \to y.p := true\ \textbf{fi}$
$;\ \{P_2\}\ cs.p$
$;\ \{P_2\}\ x.p, y.p := false, false$
$\{P_0\}$
$]$
Comp.q: Comp.p with p and q interchanged

Because variables $x.p$ and $y.p$ are private to Comp.p, we can safely choose the P_i's to be

$P_0 :$ $\neg x.p \land \neg y.p$
$P_1 :$ $x.p \land \neg y.p$
$P_2 :$ $x.p \land y.p$.

Indeed, their (local) correctness is obvious.

Next, we observe that each P_i implies condition P given by

$P :$ $x.p \lor \neg y.p$.

Thus relation P is a system invariant. By symmetry, we also have that

$Q :$ $x.q \lor \neg y.q$

is a system invariant. We are heading for the invariance of

$R :$ $\neg y.p \lor \neg y.q$,

since, on account of the Program Topology, we have

    $\neg y.p \Rightarrow$ Comp.p is outside $cs.p$.

The only statement that can falsify R is assignment $y.p := true$ (and, by symmetry, $y.q := true$). However, we see that

    $wlp.(\textbf{if}\ \neg x.q \to y.p := true\ \textbf{fi}).R$

$\equiv$ {definition of $wlp.IF$}

    $x.q \lor (y.p := true).R$

$\equiv$ {substitute in R}

    $x.q \lor \neg y.q$

$\equiv$ {definition of Q}

$$Q$$

$\equiv$ $\{Q$ is system invariant$\}$

    true   ,

so that R is a system invariant as well.

End of Proof 0.

There is no point in commenting on the details of the above proof, but we do wish to observe that it is totally "bottom-up": starting at the raw code, it first collects information as strong as possible about the individual components, in the form of the Pi's , then it summarizes this information, by weakening it into P , and only at the very end does target relation R enter the picture.

Proof 1

This is a "top-down" proof, which means that the very first thing we do is formalize what the algorithm has to achieve. For reasons of comparison, we choose the same auxiliary variables and the same program modification as in Proof 0. For the time being, the annotation should be ignored.

Pre : $\neg x.p \wedge \neg x.q \wedge \neg y.p \wedge \neg y.q$

Comp.p: $*\,[\;\{\neg y.p\}\;ncs.p$
     ; $\{\neg y.p\}\; x.p := true$
     ; $\{x.p\}$ **if** $\neg x.q \to y.p := true$ **fi**
     ; $\{x.p\}\; cs.p$
     ; $\{x.p\}\; x.p, y.p := false,\ false$
     $\{\neg y.p\}$
     $]$

Comp.q: Comp.p   with p and q interchanged

Again, our proof obligation is the invariance of

$R:$ $\neg y.p \vee \neg y.q$.

To that end we observe that R can only be falsified by the assignments $y.p := true$ and $y.q := true$. We investigate one of them, $y.q := true$ in component q , say

    $wlp.(\textbf{if}\ \neg x.p \to y.q := true\ \textbf{fi}).R$

$\equiv$ $\{$definition of $wlp.IF$ and substitution in $R\}$

$$x.p \lor \neg y.p \quad .$$

The variables mentioned in the resulting condition, $x.p \lor \neg y.p$, are private to component p, and therefore it suffices to demand this condition to be an invariant of that component in isolation. And, indeed, it is, on account of the obviously correct annotation, which we may consider now.

End of Proof 1.

Proof 1 is shorter than Proof 0, but this need not amaze us. By starting at target relation R we did not encounter the overspecific P_i's that appear in Proof 0. This is typical of a "top-down" approach, in which one usually encounters just what is needed. Proof 1 is an old proof, and by the standards of its day its annotation is quite sparse. By our current standards, however, one could even argue that the annotation can be left out altogether, because the emerging relation $x.p \lor \neg y.p$ is a system invariant on account of the topology of the program. Given in this way, Proof 1 is, in fact, already quite close to the structure of one of the formal derivations of the Safe Sluice to be considered shortly.

Proof 2

This is a very short proof. Here it is, pulled out of the magic hat. We introduce (fresh) auxiliary variable z and modify the program as follows:

Pre : $\neg x.p \land \neg x.q$
Comp.p: $* \lceil ncs.p$ $; x.p := true$ $; \text{if } \neg x.q \to z := p \text{ fi}$ $; \{x.p\} \ \{z = p\}$ $\quad cs.p$ $; x.p := false$ $\rfloor$
Comp.q: Comp.p, with p and q interchanged

The reader may care to prove the correctness of the assertions for himself. The annotation is effective for the purpose of proving mutual exclusion, since we have

$\quad$ (Comp.p in $cs.p$) $\land$ (Comp.q in $cs.q$)

$\Rightarrow \quad$ {by the annotation}

$$z = p \ \land \ z = q$$

$$\equiv \quad \{p \neq q\}$$

$$false \quad .$$

End of Proof 2.

Observe the crisp annotation in Proof 2: $z = p$ is needed for the conclusion and $x.p$ for the (global) correctness of $z = p$. Proof 2 outperforms Proof 0 by at least one order of magnitude as far as simplicity and, in its wake, efficiency is concerned. How come? We said that we pulled Proof 2 out of the magic hat, but that is not true: Proof 2 was the outcome of our very first effort to derive the Safe Sluice, a derivation that we shall briefly give now.

Derivation 0

In a derivation, the first thing that should always be done is to cast the specification into a formal setting (in order that formalism can do the work). Here, we have to ensure that the two components are not engaged in their critical sections simultaneously. We can formulate this, for instance, by introducing a fresh variable z and requiring that $z = p$ be a correct precondition to $cs.p$ (and $z = q$ to $cs.q$). Thus, our components get the shape

$$\vdots \qquad\qquad \vdots$$
$$; \{? \ z = p\} \quad \text{and} \quad ; \{? \ z = q\}$$
$$cs.p \qquad\qquad cs.q$$
$$\vdots \qquad\qquad \vdots$$

Next, in order to ensure the local correctness of the assertions, we transform the components into

$$\vdots \qquad\qquad\qquad \vdots$$
$$\text{if } C \rightarrow z := p \text{ fi} \quad \text{and} \quad \text{if } B \rightarrow z := q \text{ fi}$$
$$; \{? \ z = p\} \qquad\qquad\qquad ; \{? \ z = q\}$$
$$cs.p \qquad\qquad\qquad\qquad cs.q$$
$$\vdots \qquad\qquad\qquad\qquad \vdots$$

Remark Embedding the assignments to z in a guarded statement is not far-fetched at all: a component will presumably not be able to enter its critical section unconditionally.
End of Remark.

For the global correctness of $z = p$ in component p, we calculate

$$wlp.(\textbf{if } B \to z := q \textbf{ fi}).(z = p)$$

$\equiv$ {definition of $wlp.IF$}

$\neg B \ \lor \ (z := q).(z = p)$

$\equiv$ $\{p \neq q\}$

$\neg B$.

Recalling our regime of Strengthening the Annotation, we can

- either add $\neg B$ as a pre-assertion to **if** $B \to z := q$ **fi** , which makes no sense, since this would guarantee deadlock for component q
- or add $\neg B$ as a co-assertion to $z = p$, which does make sense and which results in the design of Proof 2, be it with a change in nomenclature, viz. $x.p$ taken for $\neg B$.

End of Derivation 0.

Derivation 1

We will present this derivation in slightly more detail. We are given the following computation proper, which is a two-component multiprogram

Pre : *true*	
Comp.p:	Comp.q:
$*\lceil ncs.p$	$*\lceil ncs.q$
; $cs.p$	; $cs.q$
]	]

Our task is to synchronize the components in such a way that

Comp.p and Comp.q are not engaged in their cs- fragments simultaneously.

Our first step is to introduce (fresh) auxiliary variables $y.p$ and $y.q$ such that these can be interpreted as

$y.p \ \equiv \ $ (Comp.p is engaged in $cs.p$)
$y.q \ \equiv \ $ (Comp.q is engaged in $cs.q$)   .

This interpretation for $y.p$ is valid whenever we surround $cs.p$ with assignments $y.p := true$ and $y.p := false$ (and disallow any other assignments to $y.p$).

In terms of these auxiliary variables, the synchronization requirement can now be rephrased as the required system invariance of

R : $\neg y.p \vee \neg y.q$.

We thus obtain as a first approximation

Pre : $\neg y.p \wedge \neg y.q$
Comp.p: $* \lceil ncs.p$ $\quad\quad ; y.p := true$ $\quad\quad ; cs.p$ $\quad\quad ; y.p := false$ $\quad\quad \rfloor$
Comp.q: Comp.p with p and q interchanged
Inv :   ? R : $\neg y.p \vee \neg y.q$

Next we deal with R. Because of the ubiquitous symmetries in the program and in R, we can confine our attention to Comp.p.

- $y.p := false$ doesn't falsify R: Widening
- $y.p := true$ requires precondition $\neg y.q$, which we realize by embedding $y.p := true$ in guarded statement

  if $\neg y.q \rightarrow y.p := true$ **fi**   .

We thus obtain

Pre : $\neg y.p \wedge \neg y.q$
Comp.p: $* \lceil ncs.p$ $\quad\quad ; $ **if** $\neg y.q \rightarrow y.p := true$ **fi** $\quad\quad ; cs.p$ $\quad\quad ; y.p := false$ $\quad\quad \rfloor$
Comp.q: Comp.p with p and q interchanged
Inv : R : $\neg y.p \vee \neg y.q$

Coarse-grained Safe Sluice

(Observe how little annotation has been introduced so far!)

As a last step, let us now eliminate the too coarse-grained guarded statements from the program. We do so by means of the technique of Guard Strengthening. We introduce variables $x.p$ and $x.q$ to take over the "rôles" of the y's , first seeing to it that $\neg x.p \Rightarrow \neg y.p$ and $\neg x.q \Rightarrow \neg y.q$ become system invariants and then eliminating the y's . The moral of Example 0 in Chapter 11 was that we can now perform such a program transformation in one go. And thus we arrive at

Pre : $\neg x.p \wedge \neg x.q$
Comp.p: $*\lceil ncs.p$; $x.p := true$; if $\neg x.q \rightarrow skip$ fi   ; $cs.p$; $x.p := false$ $\rceil$
Comp.q: Comp.p with p and q interchanged

The Safe Sluice

(Observe that there is *no* annotation attached.)

Remark The phrase that variables x take over the rôles of variables y should not be taken too literally: whereas the original y's satisfied $\neg y.p \vee \neg y.q$, variables x really don't satisfy $\neg x.p \vee \neg x.q$. By the elimination of the y's from the program we have lost sight of the still valid invariant R .
End of Remark.

And this concludes our second derivation of the Safe Sluice. We would like to emphasize that its explanation, in a pub say, would not require more space than the fringe of a beermat.

End of Derivation 1.

$$* \qquad *$$
$$*$$

The moral of the above was clear at the time the above experiments were carried out, and it is clear now: derivation of multiprograms with just the Owicki/Gries theory can, in principle, be done, it might become rewarding, and it might become great fun.

14

Peterson's Two-Component Mutual Exclusion Algorithm

Ever since the emergence of Dekker's mutual exclusion algorithm for two components and Dijkstra's for an arbitrary number of components [Dij65], the search for new, better or different such algorithms has continued. It took the computing community about twenty years to come up with a beautiful — because genuinely simple — mutual exclusion algorithm for two components. It is the one invented by G. L. Peterson [Pet81], and we shall be glad to discuss it here, not only because of its compelling elegance but also because we think that each educated computing scientist should be familiar with all the ins and outs of this algorithm.

In this chapter we present a derivation of the algorithm, hopefully in such a way that we will enable the reader to rapidly reconstruct the algorithm whenever the need arises. We first give the derivation and then discuss it.

*   *

*

As a starting point we take the Safe Sluice, developed in the preceding chapter:

Pre : $\neg x.p \land \neg x.q$
Comp.p: $*\,[\,ncs.p$
$;\ x.p := true$
$;$ **if** $\neg x.q \rightarrow skip$ **fi**
$;\ cs.p$
$;\ x.p := false$
$]$
Comp.q: Comp.p with p and q interchanged

Although the algorithm correctly implements mutual exclusion for the cs
fragments, it is not acceptable, because it suffers from the danger of total
deadlock. What we are after is an algorithm in which a component that
has terminated its non-critical section is guaranteed to enter its critical
section within a finite number of steps of the multiprogram. In the Safe
Sluice algorithm, the guards are just too strong to meet this requirement.
We therefore propose — and this is a design decision — to weaken the
guards, with disjuncts still to be determined. This leads to the following
version:

Pre : $\neg x.p \land \neg x.q$
Comp.p: $*\,[\,ncs.p$
$;\ x.p := true$
$;$ **if** $\neg x.q \lor H.p.q \rightarrow skip$ **fi**
$;\ \{?\ R.p.q\}\ cs.p$
$;\ x.p := false$
$]$
Comp.q: Comp.p with p and q interchanged

Restoring Mutual Exclusion

By weakening the guards, we have endangered safety, that is, mutual exclusion of the critical sections. We therefore have to re-address this issue,
and that is why we plugged in the assertions R . Mutual exclusion is guaranteed, if we can see to it that R satisfies the requirements

(i)   Assertion $R.p.q$ in Comp.p is correct

(and so is $R.q.p$ in Comp.q), and

(ii) $R.p.q \land R.q.p \Rightarrow p = q$ (i.e.: $\Rightarrow$ *false*).

Then, (i) expresses that the state of the system satisfies $R.p.q$ when component p is in its critical section, and, given (i), (ii) expresses mutual exclusion of the critical sections.

In view of (ii), it is advantageous to choose the R's as strong as possible. The strongest possible choice for $R.p.q$ that we can justify on account of local considerations in Comp.p is

$R.p.q$: $x.p \land (\neg x.q \lor H.p.q)$:

the first conjunct follows from the topology of Comp.p, and the second conjunct is just its guard. But is this assertion globally correct as well?

Only $x.q := true$ in component q may falsify it. In order to preclude this we require that

(iii) $x.q := true$ in Comp.q is to be extended
             such that it truthifies $H.p.q$.

This then settles (i), at the investment of (iii).

As for (ii), we observe

    $R.p.q \land R.q.p$
$\equiv$ {choice of R}
    $x.p \land (\neg x.q \lor H.p.q) \land x.q \land (\neg x.p \lor H.q.p)$
$\equiv$ {predicate calculus}
    $x.p \land H.p.q \land x.q \land H.q.p$
$\Rightarrow$ {we don't know anything about the x's}
    $H.p.q \land H.q.p$
$\Rightarrow$ {adopting (iv) below}
    $p = q$,

where the H's are required to satisfy

(iv) $H.p.q \land H.q.p \Rightarrow p = q$.

This then settles (ii), at the investment of (iv).

Remark One may very well wonder whether anything has been gained by exchanging (ii) for the very similar (iv). The difference, however, is that R , being an assertion, is very much constrained by the program structure,

while H is not. Thus, we have more freedom in choosing H than in choosing R.
End of Remark.

There are a number of ways to satisfy (iv). One of them is the following, which is strongly suggested by the transitivity of "$=$": introduce a fresh variable v and choose, for instance,

$H.p.q$: $v = q$.

Thus, (iv) is satisfied. And (iii) is met if we replace $x.q := true$ with the multiple assignment $x.q, v := true, q$. Summarizing, we have arrived at

Pre : $\neg x.p \land \neg x.q$
Comp.p: $* [\, ncs.p$; $x.p, v := true, p$; **if** $\neg x.q \lor v = q \to$ **skip** **fi**   ; $cs.p$; $x.p := false$ $]$
Comp.q: Comp.p with p and q interchanged

*   *
*

Now we are done with the derivation, except for the removal of the multiple assignments, which are commonly considered too coarse-grained in this kind of game. (There is a common preference for one-point statements.)

We eliminate the multiple assignments by applying our technique of Strengthening the Guards. (Recall that this does not affect the partial correctness of the design, here: the mutual exclusion.) We introduce boolean variables y to take over the rôle of the x's , in such a way that the guards can be strengthened, i.e. such that $\neg y.p \Rightarrow \neg x.p$ and $\neg y.q \Rightarrow \neg x.q$. This gives rise to the following intermediate, hybrid version:

Pre :	$\neg x.p \land \neg x.q \land \neg y.p \land \neg y.q$

Comp.p: $*\,[\ ncs.p$

   ; $y.p := true$

   ; $x.p, v := true, p$

   ; if $\neg x.q \lor v = q \to skip$ fi

   ; $cs.p$

   ; $x.p, y.p := false, false$

   ]

Comp.q: Comp.p with p and q interchanged

Inv : $(\neg y.p \Rightarrow \neg x.p) \land (\neg y.q \Rightarrow \neg x.q)$

Finally, we replace guard $\neg x.q \lor v = q$ by the stronger $\neg y.q \lor v = q$, so that the variables x turn into dummies and can be removed from the program text. Thus we arrive at

Pre :	$\neg y.p \land \neg y.q$

Comp.p: $*\,[\ ncs.p$

   ; $y.p := true$

   ; $v := p$

   ; if $\neg y.q \lor v = q \to skip$ fi

   ; $cs.p$

   ; $y.p := false$

   ]

Comp.q: Comp.p with p and q interchanged

Peterson's Mutual Exclusion Algorithm

Remark   In the above, we used the technique of Strengthening the Guard to split up the multiple assignment. The outcome was that first assigning to the boolean and then to variable v is safe. This outcome is, however, much more enforced than one might think, because reversing the order of the two assignments would yield an algorithm in which mutual exclusion is no longer guaranteed. We invite the reader to construct a scenario demonstrating this. The moral is twofold: first, the outcome of Guard Strengthening is not to be ignored lightly, and second, this example once more shows what a tricky sort of artefacts multiprograms are (in which seemingly harmless transformations like swapping two independent assignments can kill an entire design).
End of Remark.

Progress

Our development of the algorithm was *prompted*, but not *guided* by the requirement of individual progress. That is, the requirement of individual progress was not included in the specification; only mutual exclusion was. Therefore, we now have to investigate — as an afterthought — whether or not individual progress has been achieved. Because, at this point, we do not have a formalism to address this issue, we will have to resort to operational reasoning. Fortunately, this is quite feasible in the current example, thanks to the algorithm's simplicity.

In showing individual progress we proceed as follows.

- First, we observe that there is no total deadlock: both guarded skips have $v = p \lor v = q$ as an obviously correct pre-assertion, and the conjunction of these pre-assertions implies the disjunction of the guards.

- Second, we show that a component that has terminated its noncritical section will, within a finite number of steps of the rest of the system, be enabled to enter its critical section. We do so by showing that its guard, if not *true*, will be made *stably true* by the other component.

To that end, let us assume that Comp.q is blocked in its guarded skip, which has guard

$$\neg y.p \lor v = p \quad .$$

We show that, then, Comp.p converges to a state in which this guard is stably *true*. We observe that

- Comp.p's guarded skip terminates, because of the absence of total deadlock
- $cs.p$ terminates (by assumption),

so that the computation of Comp.p boils down to

$$* [\ \{\neg y.p\} \ ncs.p$$
$$; \ y.p := true$$
$$; \ v := p$$
$$; \ y.p := false$$
$$] \quad .$$

From this we see that, within a finite number of steps, Comp.p will make $v = p$ — and hence Comp.q's guard — stably *true*, or it will become engaged in a non-terminating execution of $ncs.p$, in which case $\neg y.p$ — and hence Comp.q's guard — will become stably *true*.

This settles individual progress, and herewith we conclude this treatment of Peterson's Mutual Exclusion Algorithm. However ...

Final Remarks

A final discussion is appropriate; it really is, because one may very well wonder what kind of a derivation we have been presenting here.

First of all, the derivation started from the defective Safe Sluice, which suffers from the danger of total deadlock, but it is by no means clear why the decision to weaken the guards — thereby potentially violating the safety of the algorithm — should lead to a successful conclusion. It was just a guess, a try. That it worked out well surely was a stroke of good luck.

Second, by another stroke of good luck we ended up with an algorithm that not only displays mutual exclusion (which is not amazing because the derivation was driven by this requirement), but also exhibits the desired progress properties. Progress requirements were not formally specified, so the development could not possibly be driven by them. Nevertheless things worked out well, and it is this phenomenon that we will encounter more often in the remaining chapters and to which we will return in more detail later.

Even though the above treatment may be debatable from a formalistic and puristic point of view, it *is* a development of Peterson's — beautiful — mutual exclusion algorithm and it is short enough to be remembered and reconstructed, should the need arise. Towards the end of this book we will learn more about Peterson's algorithm, when a totally different development is given, viz. one that is primarily driven by progress requirements.

15

Re-inventing a Great Idea

As mentioned before, the concept of mutual exclusion has, ever since the early days of computing, been recognized as a central issue in taming the complexity brought about by multiprograms run on a shared installation. The reason why it became a central issue is that the primitive statements provided by actual machinery often were — and are — far too fine-grained to make multiprogramming practically feasible. Thus, the mutual exclusion problem, i.e. the problem of how to build (arbitrary) coarse-grained atomic statements out of finer-grained ones, did become an urgent one. In its canonical form, the problem is:

> Given a number of components, each of the form
>
> $* [\; ncs; cs \;]$,
>
> synchronize them in such a way that at any moment in time,
> at most one component is engaged in its cs- fragment.

Thus the cs- fragment, generally known as the "critical section", is the epitome of a coarse-grained atomic statement.

*   *
*

In a foregoing chapter we had a glimpse at Dekker's mutual exclusion algorithm, and we dealt with Peterson's in detail. However, these algorithms implement mutual exclusion for just two components. But what if an arbitrary number of components are involved? Without going into any detail, we can say that solutions solving this general case with one-point statements only, invariably embody a great intellectual achievement and usually are forbiddingly complex from an operational point of view. Ever since the emergence of the first general mutual exclusion algorithm [Dij65], computing scientists have been attracted, fascinated, and challenged by the problem, and have submitted a nearly endless stream of better or different solutions.

*   *
*

Now, let us investigate what is really involved in solving this problem and let us try to take a first step towards its solution, ignoring the one-point requirement. In order to come to formal grips with the problem, we introduce a variable r to keep track of the number of components engaged in their critical section. In terms of this variable, the mutual exclusion problem can then be phrased as the required invariance of $r \leq 1$. We thus obtain as a first approximation

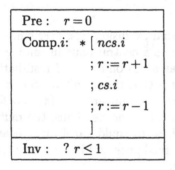

$$
\begin{array}{|ll|}
\hline
\text{Pre}: & r=0 \\
\hline
\text{Comp}.i: & *\ [\ ncs.i \\
& \quad ; r:=r+1 \\
& \quad ; cs.i \\
& \quad ; r:=r-1 \\
& \quad] \\
\hline
\text{Inv}: & ?\ r \leq 1 \\
\hline
\end{array}
$$

How can we enforce the invariance of $r \leq 1$? Statement $r := r-1$ is harmless — Widening —, but statement $r := r+1$ requires precondition $r \leq 0$. Therefore, we propose to embed $r := r+1$ in an atomic guarded statement with $r \leq 0$ as its guard. We thus obtain

$$
\begin{array}{|l|}
\hline
\text{Pre}: \quad r=0 \\
\hline
\text{Comp}.i: \quad *[\ ncs.i \\
\qquad\qquad ;\ \textbf{if}\ r\leq 0 \rightarrow r:=r+1\ \textbf{fi} \\
\qquad\qquad ;\ cs.i \\
\qquad\qquad ;\ r:=r-1 \\
\qquad\qquad] \\
\hline
\text{Inv}: \quad\quad r\leq 1 \\
\hline
\end{array}
$$

And we would be done, if only the guarded statement and statement $r:=r-1$ were one-point! We return to this in a moment, but first ask the reader to verify that this solution

(i) is free from the danger of total deadlock,
(ii) but does not guarantee individual progress.

For historical reasons, we now subject the above solution to a coordinate transformation. We introduce variable s, to be coupled to r by system invariant $s=1-r$. This enables us to eliminate r, and the solution phrased in terms of s becomes

$$
\begin{array}{|l|}
\hline
\text{Pre}: \quad s=1 \\
\hline
\text{Comp}.i: \quad *[\ ncs.i \\
\qquad\qquad ;\ \textbf{if}\ 1\leq s \rightarrow s:=s-1\ \textbf{fi} \\
\qquad\qquad ;\ cs.i \\
\qquad\qquad ;\ s:=s+1 \\
\qquad\qquad] \\
\hline
\text{Inv}: \quad 0\leq s \\
\hline
\end{array}
$$

And again: if only the guarded statement and assignment $s:=s+1$ were one-point! This forms a genuine problem here, indeed.

Now let us, as a means towards an end, take a brave step and require our primitive repertoire to be extended with *just these two* atomic statements, while giving them a name:

$$
\begin{array}{|l|}
\hline
P(s): \quad \textbf{if}\ 1\leq s \rightarrow s:=s-1\ \textbf{fi} \\
\hline
V(s): \quad s:=s+1 \\
\hline
\end{array}
$$

Thus, the P- and V-operations on "semaphores" (s) have re-arisen, and in terms of them the mutual exclusion problem, which first was so difficult, has vanished into thin air:

Pre : $s = 1$
Comp.i: $*[\ ncs.i$
$;\ P(s)$
$;\ cs.i$
$;\ V(s)$
$]$
Inv : $0 \leq s$

And apart from the issue of individual progress — to be addressed shortly — we see that the P- and V-operations are the synchronization primitives par excellence to implement general mutual exclusion. In fact, they were invented for this purpose in the early 1960s, by Edsger W. Dijkstra — [Dij68].

A little anecdote During the late 1960s and 1970s, Dijkstra taught fascinating courses on "Communication and Synchronization" at Eindhoven University of Technology. In such a course he would usually explain one of the general mutual exclusion algorithms. One year he explained Eisenberg and McGuire's [EM72] — the historically first more or less explainable solution. When thereafter he presented the solution with P- and V-operations, a clearly flabbergasted and confused student addressed him after the lecture, wondering what miraculous things these P- and V-operations were and why it was that by their use all complexity had vanished. One of us (WF) overheard the very short conversation, including Dijkstra's answer: "Because they were specially invented for this purpose.". The student left, filled with admiration, definitely impressed, but — quite likely — as flabbergasted as before. WF stood rooted to the spot as well. We hope that this chapter gives some of the (calculational) rationale behind Dijkstra's answer.
End of A little anecdote.

*   *
*

The above captures the mathematical essence of the P- and V-operations in their capacity of solving mutual exclusion, and the primary objective of this chapter has been to show how they can be re-invented (by calculation) precisely for this purpose.

But there was a little more to them when they were first introduced, and for reasons of completeness we wish to briefly make mention of it here.

- First of all, there is the concern about progress. To that end the P- and V-operations came with a postulate stating that in the presence of a sufficiently large number of V-operations on a semaphore s, a component that has got stuck in a P-operation on s will eventually complete this P-operation. Through this postulate, which later became known as a "strong fairness requirement", the danger of individual starvation in the above mutual exclusion algorithm vanishes. Many years later, it was Alain J. Martin who weakened this postulate — to mathematical advantage. We refer the reader to the seminal paper [Mar81], and also to Martin and Burch [MB85].

- Second, by using P- and V-operations as the only synchronization primitives, it became possible to eliminate the so-called — and certainly at the time so undesirable — "busy form of waiting". A component that has got stuck in a P-operation is guaranteed to remain stuck as long as the rest of the system does not perform a V-operation on the corresponding semaphore — a very detectable event!. So there is an entire span of time in which it makes no sense at all for a blocked component to inspect the value of the semaphore, and thus consume precious processor time. A blocked component can thus, until further notice, be put "asleep", i.e. ignored as a candidate for processor time. Such an arrangement may offer great economic advantages when a lot of components are to be run on an installation with only a few processors.

- Third, the P- and V-operations proved to be far more useful than just for implementing mutual exclusion. In fact, they acquired the status of universal synchronization primitives, general enough to solve any synchronization problem. (In this respect they compare with the Universal Turing Machine, capable of computing any computable function.) Due to their generality, they also acquired the status of canonical primitives. At many occasions later on, when new synchronization mechanisms were proposed, their designers

  - would check that the P- and V-operations could be implemented with these mechanisms, thus demonstrating the generality of the new proposal, and

  - they would check that their new mechanisms could be implemented by P- and V-operations, thus demonstrating the realizability of the proposal.

- Finally, a word must be spent on the implementability of the P- and V- operations. On installations where they do not belong to the primitive repertoire, embedding them in special-purpose critical sections is a viable implementation. This is, in principle, not begging the original mutual exclusion question, because the operations have a very specific, recognizable and uniform syntactic shape. Considering how useful the P- and V- operations are for program design, the programmer is greatly served if the hardware designer provides facilities for their implementation (if possible, of course). Fortunately, most computing installations nowadays possess these facilities. And this is in accordance with an old verdict of Dijkstra's: "It is not a program's purpose to instruct our computers, but the computer's purpose to execute our programs.".

*   *
*

In this monograph we will not pursue programming with P- and V- operations, because that has been done extensively elsewhere, most notably in the design of operating systems. Indeed, P- and V- operations and their variations and outgrowths have conquered the computing science world. And this is what happens to a great idea.

16

On Handshake Protocols

A frequently recurring theme in the area of communication is the transmission of information from one place to another while there is no buffering facility in between. Such situations, for instance, occur in electronic circuits where wires must carry signals from one end to the other. The problem also pops up when synchronous communication has to be implemented by asynchronous means. The algorithms that take care of such a "bufferless" information transmission are known as *handshake* protocols, and they are at the heart of the (physical) realization of communication and synchronization between otherwise autonomous computer installations. Also, they are nowadays beneficially used as a starting point for the construction of asynchronous circuitry [Mar96].

In this chapter we shall first derive a skeleton solution for a handshake protocol, and subsequently discuss various refinements.

A skeleton solution

As a starting point for our treatment we take the following, fairly general situation, viz. we consider the two-component multiprogram given by

Pre : $p = p_0$	
A: $* [\, p := f.p \,]$	B: $* [\, print(p) \,]$

The Computation Proper

(Statements $p := f.p$ and $print(p)$ are atomic.)

Component A produces information. Starting from p_0 it generates the stream

$$p_0, \quad f.p_0, \quad f^2.p_0, \quad f^3.p_0, \quad \ldots \quad .$$

Function f is just an abstraction: $f.p$ can be the next portion produced by a producer or the next character or record extracted from a file owned by the environment, etc.. Neither the type of p nor the specific nature of f are relevant for our purpose.

This purpose is to synchronize the two components in such a way that B prints exactly the same sequence as is generated by A, i.e.

$$p_0, \quad f.p_0, \quad f^2.p_0, \quad f^3.p_0, \quad \ldots \quad .$$

In order to achieve this goal we must formalize the problem statement, and this time we do so by a little trick, viz. by changing B in such a way that it mimics the behaviour of A, i.e. — for the time being — we act as if B were equipped with clairvoyance:

Pre : $p = p_0 \ \wedge \ q = p_0$	
A: $* [\, p := f.p \,]$	B: $* [\, \{?\ p = q\}$
	$print(p)$
	$;\ q := f.q$
	$]$

Now it should be beyond any doubt that B prints the required sequence whenever we can see to the correctness of pre-assertion $p = q$ to statement $print(p)$. Of course, we will ultimately have to eliminate f from B, because clairvoyance is not available in our toolbox.

If f has to disappear from B's program, so has q . Considering this, it doesn't seem to be a bad idea to replace target assertion $p = q$ with something that implies it, for otherwise q might sooner or later pop up in a guard. Because by construction q can — like p — be expressed as something of the form $f^i.p_0$, we introduce integers in order to be able to become more explicit about this.

Pre :	$p = p_0 \;\wedge\; q = p_0 \;\wedge\; u = 0 \;\wedge\; v = 0$
A:	$* [\, p, u := f.p,\; u + 1\,]$
B:	$* [\, \{?\; p = q\}$
	$print(p)$
	$;\; q, v := f.q,\; v + 1$
	$]$
Inv :	$p = f^u .p_0 \;\wedge\; q = f^v .p_0$

(The multiple assignments are atomic.)

Relation Inv is a system invariant by construction. In view of this invariant and in view of the fact that nothing is known about function f, the only safe way to cater for the correctness of assertion $p = q$ is by replacing it with the stronger $u = v$ (on account of Leibniz's Rule we have $u = v \;\Rightarrow\; f^u .p_0 = f^v .p_0$). Because by this replacement, q is eliminated from the target assertion, q and f can now be removed from B's text:

Pre :	$p = p_0 \;\wedge\; u = 0 \;\wedge\; v = 0$
A:	$* [\, p, u := f.p,\; u + 1\,]$
B:	$* [\, \{?\; u = v\}$
	$print(p)$
	$;\; v := v + 1$
	$]$

Our next move is to disentangle new target assertion $u = v$ by rewriting it into conjunction $u \le v \;\wedge\; v \le u$, and to handle the two conjuncts separately.

Remark It is a common — because usually beneficial — strategy to decompose an equality into two inequalities. It can be beneficial since the individual inequalities are each weaker than the original equality and, therefore, mostly easier to handle — think of Widening —; but more importantly, they sometimes cover entirely different aspects of the problem. As a consequence, treating the conjuncts of a conjunction separately may yield a better separation of concerns. (This holds for mathematics and programming alike.)
End of Remark.

So in component B we now ensure target assertion $u = v$ by replacing it with

$$u \leq v \,\land\, v \leq u \quad .$$

Of these two, only $v \leq u$ is a suitable candidate for a guard — see the Ground Rule for Progress —, and because its global correctness is for free (Widening), we can indeed see to its correctness by guarded skip **if** $v \leq u \rightarrow$ *skip* **fi** in B.

For the other assertion, $u \leq v$, — it being stable in B — we have no choice but to make it a system invariant (cf. Concurrent Vector Writing), and we prevent statement $u := u+1$ in component A from violating it by adding guarded skip **if** $u+1 \leq v \rightarrow$ *skip* **fi** to A's code. Thus we arrive at

Pre : $p = p_0 \,\land\, u = 0 \,\land\, v = 0$

A: $*\,[$ **if** $u+1 \leq v \rightarrow$ *skip* **fi**
      $; \{u+1 \leq v\}$
      $p, u := f.p,\, u+1$
      $]$

B: $*\,[$ **if** $v \leq u \rightarrow$ *skip* **fi**
      $; \{u = v\}\ \{v \leq u\}\ \{u \leq v,$ from Inv $\}$
      $print(p)$
      $; v := v+1$
      $]$

Inv : $u \leq v$

Note that with the adoption of $u \leq v$ as an invariant, we have on-the-fly created a multibound for the above system, because by the structure of the program, $v \leq u+1$ is a system invariant as well:

- it holds initially;
- A doesn't falsify it (Widening);
- $v := v+1$ in B doesn't falsify it, since this statement has (correct) precondition $v \leq u$.

So no matter what our ultimate solution will be, our task of proving progress has been reduced to proving absence of total deadlock.

$$* \qquad *$$
$$*$$

This completes our skeleton solution, except for the fact that we wish to eliminate the multiple assignment in A, since it might be undesirable to burden the computation proper — $p := f.p$ — with the task of indivisibly performing synchronization code. For the purpose of elimination, we introduce a fresh variable x to take over the rôle of u, and apply the technique of Strengthening the Guard.

We can replace guard $v \le u$ in B by $v \le x$ if $x \le u$ is a system invariant. We see to this invariance by choosing $x = 0$ as a precondition and by postfixing statement $u := u + 1$ in component A with $x := x + 1$ (cf. Topology). Now both x and u are private to component A, and we see that $x = u$ is a correct pre-assertion of guarded skip $\textbf{if } u + 1 \le v \to skip \textbf{ fi}$. As a result, we can replace guard $u + 1 \le v$ by the equivalent $x + 1 \le v$, thus turning u into a dummy that can now be eliminated. For cosmetic reasons we rename v into y, and thus we arrive at — temporarily ignore the annotation —

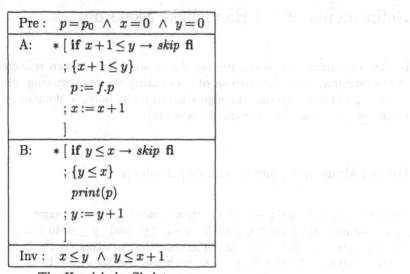

Pre : $\quad p = p_0 \;\wedge\; x = 0 \;\wedge\; y = 0$
A: $\quad *[\textbf{ if } x + 1 \le y \to skip \textbf{ fi}$ $\quad ; \{x + 1 \le y\}$ $\qquad p := f.p$ $\quad ; x := x + 1$ $\quad]$
B: $\quad *[\textbf{ if } y \le x \to skip \textbf{ fi}$ $\quad ; \{y \le x\}$ $\qquad print(p)$ $\quad ; y := y + 1$ $\quad]$
Inv : $\quad x \le y \;\wedge\; y \le x + 1$

The Handshake Skeleton

A few remarks are in order.

- In our previous program, the one phrased in (u, v)-nomenclature, we had the invariance of $u \le v \;\wedge\; v \le u + 1$, i.e. the difference $v - u$ was just 2-valued. It was not clear at the outset that the transition to the (x, y)-nomenclature would retain this property for the difference $y - x$, but the — obviously correct — annotation in the above skeleton shows that it did. We will use this property shortly to further transform the program, carrying it into the boolean domain.

- The skeleton does not suffer from the danger of deadlock — for integers x and y, $x + 1 \le y \;\vee\; y \le x$ is just $true$ —, so that individual progress

is guaranteed, thanks to our (original!) multibound $u \leq v \ \wedge \ v \leq u+1$
(which hasn't been damaged by guard strengthening).

- Earlier we said that statement $p := f.p$ — the production of the information — was atomic, and the same holds for $print(p)$ — the consumption of the information. Now we can see from the above skeleton solution that it is irrelevant whether these activities are atomic or not, because thanks to their preconditions $x+1 \leq y$ and $y \leq x$, respectively, they exclude each other in time. So their "atomicity" is "automatically" guaranteed by the Handshake Protocol.

Refinements of the Handshake Skeleton

In the remainder of this chapter we derive some well-known refinements of the skeleton, with the purpose of eliminating the ever-growing integers x and y , and of carrying the algorithm into the boolean domain (which might be appreciated by electrical engineers).

Handshaking with one (common) boolean

Because $x \leq y \ \wedge \ y \leq x+1$ is a system invariant, the difference $y-x$ is just 2-valued, and from the guards $x+1 \leq y$ and $y \leq x$ in the components we see that it is only this difference that matters for the "control" of the program. We therefore try to rephrase the algorithm in terms of a single boolean b , coupled to x and y by (system invariant)

$$b \ \equiv \ (x=y) \quad \text{(and hence also by)}$$
$$\neg b \ \equiv \ (x+1=y) \quad ,$$

relations that show the two "flavours" for $x-y$.

For guard $y \leq x$ in component B we now obtain

$\quad y \leq x$

$\equiv \quad \{x \leq y, \text{ from invariant Inv}\}$

$\quad y = x$

$\equiv \quad \{\text{coupling } b/(x,y)\}$

$\quad b \quad .$

So guard $y \leq x$ can be rewritten into the *equivalent* guard b. Likewise, guard $x+1 \leq y$ in A can be rewritten into the *equivalent* guard $\neg b$.

Remark   Unlike in the case of guard strengthening, there is no need to re-address the danger of deadlock when guards are rewritten equivalently. And since our skeleton does not suffer from deadlock, neither will our subsequent refinement.
End of Remark.

So much for the elimination of x and y from the guards. Next we deal with the assignments to x and y. Along with statement $y := y+1$ in B, an adjustment of boolean b may be necessary. We therefore extend the statement to $y, b := y+1, E$, and investigate for which expressions E the coupling between b, x, and y is maintained:

$$(y, b := y+1, E).(b \equiv x = y)$$
$$\equiv \quad \{\text{substitution}\}$$
$$E \equiv (x = y+1)$$
$$\equiv \quad \{\text{by Inv,} \quad x = y+1 \equiv \textit{false}\}$$
$$E \equiv \textit{false} \quad .$$

Likewise, we find that $\{x+1 \leq y\}$ $x := x+1$ in A has to be replaced by $x, b := x+1, \textit{true}$. Thus, x and y are reduced to auxiliaries and can be removed altogether:

Pre : $p = p_0 \wedge b$
A: $* [$ **if** $\neg b \rightarrow$ *skip* **fi** $; \{\neg b\}$ $p := f.p$ $; b := \textit{true}$ (or: $b := \neg b$) $]$
B: $* [$ **if** $b \rightarrow$ *skip* **fi** $; \{b\}$ $print(p)$ $; b := \textit{false}$ (or: $b := \neg b$) $]$

Single-Boolean Handshake Protocol

(The obviously correct assertions have been added to demonstrate that the assignments to b can both be replaced by "flippings" of b, thus making the components more alike.)

Distributed Handshaking

In the above protocol, the synchronization and communication between the two components runs under control of one single boolean. This is readily implemented on a shared-memory installation and also in electronic circuitry where the manipulation and inspection of the boolean can be realized through appropriate wiring. But in cases where the components are physically too far apart, say, one might prefer a more distributed solution, in which components can only manipulate private variables — and "private wires" for that matter. Such a distribution can be achieved by "distributing the value of boolean b " in our protocol over two booleans c and d, c private to A and d private to B. In view of the operations on b — viz. flippings of its value —, the coupling[†]

$$b \equiv c \equiv d$$

is highly attractive, because b's flipping in A can then be effected by a flipping of c. Thus we obtain

Pre : $\quad p = p_0 \ \wedge \ (c \equiv d)$
A: $\quad * [\ \textbf{if}\ \neg(c \equiv d) \rightarrow skip\ \textbf{fi}$ $\quad\quad ; p := f.p$ $\quad\quad ; c := \neg c$ $\quad\quad]$
B: $\quad * [\ \textbf{if}\ c \equiv d \rightarrow skip\ \textbf{fi}$ $\quad\quad ; print(p)$ $\quad\quad ; d := \neg d$ $\quad\quad]$

Distributed Handshake Protocol

Remark Here we have presented the Distributed Handshake Protocol as a refinement of the Single-boolean Handshake. We could also have derived it

---

[†]Equivalence is symmetric and associative, and it is related to negation by $[\ \neg(c \equiv d) \equiv \neg c \equiv d\ ]$.

directly from the Handshake Skeleton, for instance by choosing the coupling
$c \equiv d \equiv (x = y)$.
End of Remark.

Four-phase Handshaking

Each of the above two protocols is commonly called a "two-phase handshake
protocol". The addendum "two-phase" stems from the original operational
appreciation of the algorithms. For our protocols, this is as follows: B starts
printing, and then it "signals" A that it has finished doing so — tic! —;
then A receives the signal, starts producing via $p := f.p$, and then signals
B that it has finished producing — tac! —, after which B can start printing
again. So for B the rhythm is:

print,   tic,   tac,   print,   tic,   tac,   print,   ...   ,

and for A it is:

tic,   produce,   tac,   tic,   produce,   tac,   tic, ...

Thus, in each component there are *two* synchronization acts (tic and tac)
in between any two successive activities of the computation proper; hence
the name *two*-phase.

For reasons to become clear in a moment, electrical engineers prefer the
so-called "four-phase handshake protocol", which has four synchronization
acts in between successive printings or productions. As a first step towards
such an algorithm, we expand our distributed protocol using the rule

$$* [\, S \,] = * [\, S; S \,]\ .$$

For the initial state we arbitrarily choose to satisfy $c \equiv d$ by $c \wedge d$. We
also plug in a number of trivially correct assertions about c and d for
later use, and, on the fly, we use these assertions to simplify the guards and
the statements.

Pre:	$p = p_0 \wedge c \wedge d$		
A:	$* [\ \{c\}$ **if** $\neg d \to skip$ **fi**	B:	$* [\ \{d\}$ **if** $c \to skip$ **fi**
⓪ →	$;\ \{c\}\ p := f.p$	② →	$;\ \{d\}\ print(p)$
	$;\qquad c := false$		$;\qquad d := false$
	$;\ \{\neg c\}$ **if** $d \to skip$ **fi**		$;\ \{\neg d\}$ **if** $\neg c \to skip$ **fi**
① →	$;\ \{\neg c\}\ p := f.p$	③ →	$;\ \{\neg d\}\ print(p)$
	$;\qquad c := true$		$;\qquad d := true$
	$\qquad \{c\}$		$\qquad \{d\}$
	$]$		$]$

We transform the above program into a four-phase protocol by omitting one of the two printings at ② and ③ and one of the productions at ⓪ and ①. To see why, let us focus on, for instance, component B. It is quite likely that in B's wired version, the printing at ② is initiated upon detection of state $c \wedge d$, whereas the printing at ③ is triggered by $\neg c \wedge \neg d$. As a result, the printing mechanism should be fired when on both "wires" c and d a *transition* of the voltage level, say, has taken place. In general, however, electrical engineers prefer their circuitry to run under control of unambiguous states rather than transitions. Because at either of the places ② and ③ the *state* is unambiguous, viz. $c \wedge d$ and $\neg c \wedge \neg d$, respectively, we can satisfy the electrical engineer's preference by removing either the print statement at position ② or the one at ③. And, similarly, in component A we can remove the production at ⓪ or the one at ①. The question is, which of the four possible combinations preserves the correctness of the algorithm.

Our multiprogram has a very sequential behaviour, viz. we have

$* [\text{ print } ②; \quad \text{prod } ⓪; \quad \text{print } ③; \quad \text{prod } ①]$.

What we need is $* [\text{ print}; \text{prod}]$, and because in our multiprogram the first printing activity precedes the first production, retaining the print operation at ② is always harmless. So, retaining the pairs ②-⓪ and ②-① preserves the correctness. So does the pair ③-①. The only faulty combination is ⓪-③, which fails to print p_0!

All three correct combinations have received a name and have been the subject of study. Further elaboration on the matter, however, falls outside the scope of this monograph. Just for fun, we conclude this chapter with the raw code of one of the three four-phase handshake protocols.

Pre : $p = p_0 \wedge c \wedge d$	
A: $* [\text{ if } \neg d \rightarrow skip \text{ fi}$	B: $* [\text{ if } c \rightarrow skip \text{ fi}$
$; c := false$	$; print(p)$
$; \text{ if } d \rightarrow skip \text{ fi}$	$; d := false$
$; p := f.p$	$; \text{ if } \neg c \rightarrow skip \text{ fi}$
$; c := true$	$; d := true$
$]$	$]$

A Four-Phase Handshake Protocol

17

Phase Synchronization for Two Machines

This monograph emphasizes the construction of *correct* (multi)programs. However, along with every program comes the question of "performance", addressing such aspects as efficiency, demand on storage space, degree of parallelism, communication density, robustness, etc.. Although these issues definitely fall outside the scope of this text, we nevertheless wish to include a very modest touch on them.

One of the purposes of this chapter is to illustrate in a simple setting a number of such rather quantitative phenomena that can be displayed by a multiprogram under execution. More in particular, we will illustrate how the degree of parallelism can be enhanced by non-unique representation of data, and how storage space can be traded for parallelism and vice versa.

Our setting is a highly simplified version of the problem of phase synchronization, which we learned about from Jayadev Misra [Mis91]. In a few later chapters we will re-address the problem, then taking into account several extensions and generalizations. Here we deal with the simplified version in isolation, because with this example alone, we can already illustrate some of the quantitative phenomena alluded to above. In addition, it provides a next simple example showing the design of multiprograms at work. So, all in all, the message of this chapter is largely of a methodological flavour.

First approximation of the problem

We consider the following two-component multiprogram

Pre : *true*	
A: $*[\,S\,]$	B: $*[\,T\,]$

The computation proper

Our task is to synchronize the components in such a way that, for all natural x, component A does not start the $(x+1)^{\text{st}}$ execution of its — phase — S before B has completed at least x executions of its T, and the other way around. In order to render this specification more formally, we introduce fresh variables x and y to record the number of completed phases in A and in B, respectively, and we also number the phases. Then a more formal specification of our problem is

Pre : $x=0 \wedge y=0$	
A: $*[\,\{?\ RA\}$	B: $*[\,\{?\ RB\}$
$S.x$	$T.y$
$;\ x:=x+1$	$;\ y:=y+1$
$]$	$]$

where RA and RB are given by

RA: $\langle\,\forall i:0\leq i<x:\ T.i\text{ has terminated}\,\rangle$

RB: $\langle\,\forall i:0\leq i<y:\ S.i\text{ has terminated}\,\rangle$.

However, we wish to formalize the specification a little further, because the phrase "has terminated" is still rather verbal. To that end we observe that (by construction) we have the system invariants

PA: $\langle\,\forall i:0\leq i<x:\ S.i\text{ has terminated}\,\rangle$ and

PB: $\langle\,\forall i:0\leq i<y:\ T.i\text{ has terminated}\,\rangle$,

so that

$$RA \ \Leftarrow\ PB \wedge x\leq y \quad\text{and}$$
$$RB \ \Leftarrow\ PA \wedge y\leq x \quad.$$

As a consequence, target assertions RA and RB are satisfied whenever we replace them with $x \leq y$ and $y \leq x$, respectively. Now our formal specification becomes — we remove the phase numbers again —

Pre : $x = 0 \ \wedge \ y = 0$	
A: $* \, [\, \{? \ x \leq y\}$	B: $* \, [\, \{? \ y \leq x\}$
S	T
$; \, x := x + 1$	$; \, y := y + 1$
$]$	$]$

A Formal Specification

Remark The specification would have been even more formal — and more correct for that matter — had we included place holders for the synchronization code to be added (cf. Concurrent Vector Writing). For reasons of simplicity they were omitted, on the understanding that the only constraint to be obeyed is that $x \leq y$ is to become a correct pre-assertion to S (and $y \leq x$ to T).
End of Remark.

From our formal specification we can already infer that by realizing the correctness of the target assertions $x \leq y$ and $y \leq x$, we will automatically also realize system invariant

$x \leq y + 1 \ \wedge \ y \leq x + 1$,

which, in combination with the structure of the components, yields a perfect multibound for our system. Hence, as far as individual progress is concerned the only thing we need to prove of our ultimate solution is that it is free from the danger of total deadlock.

*   *

*

Before starting our development, we first perform a coordinate transformation, in order to simplify the formulae and to show more explicitly that for our problem only the difference $x - y$ matters. To that end we introduce (fresh) variable d, coupled to x and y by[†]

$d = x - y + 1$.

In terms of d, the specification and the multibound are rephrased as

---

[†]The "+1" in $d = x - y + 1$ is just cosmetic: it makes d into a natural number.

Pre : $d=1$	
A: $*[\{? \ d \leq 1\}$ S $; d:=d+1$ $]$	B: $*[\{? \ 1 \leq d\}$ T $; d:=d-1$ $]$
Inv : $0 \leq d \ \wedge \ d \leq 2$	

$$*\qquad *$$
$$*$$

Now we proceed to our first approximation, focussing on target assertion $d \leq 1$ in A, which is globally correct — Widening. The structure of A shows that for its *local* correctness, we hardly have any choice but to make $d \leq 1$ a loop invariant of A, i.e. an invariant of A's repetition. Because it holds as a precondition to component A, the only thing needed for its correctness is that it is a postcondition of A's loop body. And similarly for assertion $1 \leq d$ in B. Thus, the specification is satisfied by the following approximation:

Pre : $d=1$	
A: $*[\{d \leq 1\}$ S $; d:=d+1$ $\{? \ d \leq 1\}$ $]$	B: $*[\{1 \leq d\}$ T $; d:=d-1$ $\{? \ 1 \leq d\}$ $]$
Inv : $0 \leq d \ \wedge \ d \leq 2$	

Approximation 0

It is this approximation that we shall take as our point of departure for developing three different solutions.

Solution 0

Our first solution starts with a straightforward move. Because the target assertions are globally correct (Widening), we only need to see to their local correctness, which we do by inserting appropriate guarded skips. We thus obtain

Pre : $d=1$	

A: ∗[$\{d \le 1\}$
    S
  ; $d := d+1$
  ; if $d \le 1 \rightarrow$ *skip* fi
    $\{d \le 1\}$
  ]
	B: ∗[$\{1 \le d\}$
	    T
	  ; $d := d-1$
	  ; if $1 \le d \rightarrow$ *skip* fi
	    $\{1 \le d\}$
	  ]

Inv : $0 \le d \;\wedge\; d \le 2$	

Version 0.0

There is no total deadlock, and, in principle, we are therefore done.

∗   ∗

∗

However, we wish to proceed a little further and transform the algorithm into the boolean domain, which is possible thanks to d's limited range. Since d is 3-valued, we need at least two booleans. Therefore, let us introduce fresh x and y coupled to d by

Px: $x \;\equiv\; d \le 1$ and

Py: $y \;\equiv\; 1 \le d$.

This choice is inspired by the shape of the guards: A's guarded skip, for instance, now simply translates into if $x \rightarrow$ *skip* fi. However, along with changes in d, both x and y may need adjustment in order for Px and Py to be maintained. Thus we have to investigate an altered statement

$\qquad d, x, y := d+1, F, G$

in A, and find out for which F and G relations Px and Py are maintained.

Re Px We calculate

$\qquad (d, x, y := d+1, F, G).Px$

$\equiv \qquad \{\text{substitution in } Px\}$

$\qquad F \;\equiv\; d+1 \le 1$

$\equiv \qquad \{\text{arithmetic}\}$

$\qquad F \;\equiv\; d \le 0$

$\equiv \qquad \{\text{invariant } Py\}$

$$F \equiv \neg y \quad .$$

Re P_y We calculate

$\quad (d, x, y := d+1, F, G).P_y$

$\equiv \quad$ {substitution in P_y}

$\quad G \equiv 1 \leq d+1$

$\equiv \quad$ {arithmetic}

$\quad G \equiv 0 \leq d$

$\equiv \quad$ {invariant $0 \leq d$}

$\quad G \equiv true \quad .$

End of Re's.

As a result,   A's assignment statement becomes

$\quad d, x, y := d+1, \neg y, true \quad .$

The corresponding adjustment in B follows by symmetry. Our program, from which d can now be eliminated, becomes

Pre : $x \wedge y$	
A: $*\,[\,\{x\}$	B: $*\,[\,\{y\}$
$\quad S$	$\quad T$
$\quad ;\, x, y := \neg y,\, true$	$\quad ;\, y, x := \neg x,\, true$
$\quad ;\, \text{if } x \rightarrow skip \text{ fi}$	$\quad ;\, \text{if } y \rightarrow skip \text{ fi}$
$\quad \{x\}$	$\quad \{y\}$
$\quad]$	$\quad]$

Version 0.1

Because in transforming the d- program into the (x, y) -program we have rewritten the guards *equivalently*, the latter program is as free from total deadlock as the former.

*   *

*

Next we wish to eliminate the multiple assignments from Version 0.1, with the purpose of making the program more fine-grained. We do so via the technique of Strengthening the Guard which in this example is carried out by introducing fresh booleans f and g , and maintaining the system invariants $f \Rightarrow x$ and $g \Rightarrow y$. Apart from minor details, this is exactly the program transformation that we dealt with in Example 1 of Chapter 11. The result is

Pre : $f \wedge g$	
A: $*[\,S$	B: $*[\,T$
$;\ f := false$	$;\ g := false$
$;\ g := true$	$;\ f := true$
$;\ \textbf{if } f \rightarrow skip \textbf{ fi}$	$;\ \textbf{if } g \rightarrow skip \textbf{ fi}$
$\,]$	$\,]$

Version 0.2

Of course, we can no longer rely on the deadlock freedom of Version 0.2, because the guards have been strengthened. Therefore, we have to re-investigate the danger of total deadlock. Its absence was dealt with in Example 1 of Chapter 11 also — by way of Exercise 1. So we are done.

*   *
*

Let us now have a look at the performance of the above algorithm. Our original specification is satisfied by each computation in which one of the components is one (complete) phase ahead of the other. Version 0.0 (and hence Version 0.1) can indeed display *all* computations that agree with the specification, i.e. all parallelism that is permitted in the computation proper can be exhibited. Through our guard strengthening, this situation has become different for the ultimate solution, Version 0.2.

Consider the following interleaving:
- first, A performs $S\,;\ f := false\,;\ g := true$; then A is one phase ahead of B;
- next, B performs $T\,;\ g := false\,;\ f := true$, thus falsifying its own guard.

Now the only way in which B can proceed to its next phase is by finding its guard *true*, which can only happen after A has performed its next $S\,;\ f := false\,;\ g := true$. And from then onwards the story repeats. As a result, component B can *never* again get one phase ahead of A, although this would perfectly agree with the specification.

Thus, under control of our algorithm the computation can degenerate — here to some sort of handshake protocol —, thus unnecessarily reducing the degree of parallelism permitted. Here the degeneration is a consequence of the guard strengthening in our last transformation, and we are lucky that the reduction in parallelism has not turned out to be disastrous — which would have been the case had we ended up with a solution exhibiting the danger of total deadlock. The message is that the technique of guard strengthening, no matter how valuable, should be used with some reluctance and with caution. Our overall strategy is to appeal to it when we can't think of anything else to be done anymore, which means that usually it is the last transformation step in a design process.

Remark Our algorithm *can* exhibit degeneration in behaviour, but it *need* not do so. The latter is the case whenever $f := false$ and $g := false$ are executed in "lock-step". Or, to put it more precisely, whenever $g := true$ in A is not started before the corresponding $g := false$ in B has been completed, and vice versa for the assignments to f. This would require extra synchronization, and it is good to realize that sometimes it may be unavoidable to superimpose a protocol on a protocol in order to rule out misbehaviours of the latter. The reader is encouraged to carry out this superposition in the current example.
End of Remark.

Solution 1

When Frans W. van der Sommen learned about the above solution and its degeneration phenomenon, he immediately spotted the place where we had gone astray. The first step — Version 0.0 — was still okay; so we copy it:

Pre : $d = 1$	
A: $*\,[\,\{d \le 1\}\ S$	B: $*\,[\,\{1 \le d\}\ T$
$;\ d := d+1$	$;\ d := d-1$
$;$ **if** $d \le 1 \rightarrow skip$ **fi**	$;$ **if** $1 \le d \rightarrow skip$ **fi**
$\{d \le 1\}$	$\{1 \le d\}$
$]$	$]$

Version 1.0

But then we made a "mistake", by the unfortunate decision to represent d's value by two booleans through

$$x \equiv d \le 1 \quad \text{and} \quad y \equiv 1 \le d \quad .$$

The problem with this choice is that each value of d *uniquely* defines the values of x and y, and since d is 3-valued one of the four possible values for the pair (x, y) — viz. $(false, false)$ — cannot be utilized. Due to this lack of slack, each alteration of d potentially necessitates alterations in both x and y, and that is where the, in retrospect troublesome, multiple assignments in our previous solutions entered the picture.

Van der Sommen then proposed a different coordinate transformation, viz. by coupling two booleans x and y to d via

$$d = \#[x, y] \quad ,$$

where $\#[x, y]$ counts how many of the two booleans x and y have value *true*. Then we have, for the guards,

$$d \leq 1 \equiv \neg x \vee \neg y \quad \text{and}$$
$$1 \leq d \equiv x \vee y \quad ,$$

and statement $\{d \leq 1\}\ d := d+1$ in A can then be translated into the as yet atomic

$$\{\neg x \vee \neg y\}$$
if $\neg x \rightarrow x := true$
$\llbracket\ \neg y \rightarrow y := true$
fi .

We thus obtain for our program — in (x, y)- terminology —

Pre : $x \not\equiv y$	
A: * [$\{\neg x \vee \neg y\}$ S	B: [$\{x \vee y\}$ T
; **if** $\neg x \rightarrow x := true$	; **if** $x \rightarrow x := false$
$\llbracket\ \neg y \rightarrow y := true$	$\llbracket\ y \rightarrow y := false$
fi	**fi**
; **if** $\neg x \vee \neg y \rightarrow skip$ **fi**	; **if** $x \vee y \rightarrow skip$ **fi**
$\{\neg x \vee \neg y\}$	$\{x \vee y\}$
]	]

Version 1.1

Remark   We need not be bothered by the coarse-grained atomic alternative constructs, because they need not be as coarse-grained as they look: the alternative construct in, for instance, component A can be correctly annotated as

if $\neg x \rightarrow \{\neg x\}\ x := true$
$\llbracket\ \neg y \rightarrow \{\neg y\}\ y := true$
fi ,

which implies that in guarded command

$$\neg x \rightarrow x := true$$

the inspection of the guard and the assignment need not take place indivisibly.
End of Remark.

*   *
*

Because in transforming Version 1.0 into Version 1.1, we have rewritten the guards equivalently, no reduction in the potential degree of parallelism of the computation proper has crept in. This is in sharp contrast with the protocol of Solution 0. It is the non-unique — the redundant — representation of d's value that opened the door to a larger manoeuvring space. This is not coincidental. It is a general phenomenon that non-unique representation of data creates an opportunity for more computational freedom, which may manifest itself in the form of more parallelism in the case of multiprograms. Frans van der Sommen surely was aware of this when he proposed the above solution.

Solution 2

This little problem of Phase Synchronization is paradigmatic, indeed: our third development serves to illustrate yet another quantitative phenomenon, viz. it shows how parallelism can be "traded" for storage space. This kind of trading may sometimes come in handy for economical or technical reasons. This time, the development starts from Approximation 0 again, which we, therefore, copy here:

Pre : $d = 1$	
A: $*\,[\ \{d \leq 1\}\ S$	B: $*\,[\ \{1 \leq d\}\ T$
$;\ d := d+1$	$;\ d := d-1$
$\{?\ d \leq 1\}$	$\{?\ 1 \leq d\}$
$]$	$]$
Inv : $0 \leq d\ \wedge\ d \leq 2$	

Version 2.0

While we ourselves were focussing on solutions symmetric in the components — What a bias! —, it was our former student Toon Wijnands who was brave enough to investigate an asymmetric solution. He observed that the alternative way to ensure the local correctness of assertion $d \leq 1$ in A would be to require $d \leq 0$ as a precondition to $d := d+1$. Following this suggestion we get:

Pre :	$d = 1$	
A: $*[\{d \leq 1\}\ S$		B: $*[\{1 \leq d\}\ T$
$;\ \{?\ d \leq 0\}$		$;\ d := d - 1$
$\quad d := d+1$		$\{?\ 1 \leq d\}$
$\quad \{d \leq 1\}$		$]$
$]$		
Inv :	$0 \leq d\ \wedge\ d \leq 2$	

Version 2.1

Thanks to the global correctness of the remaining queried assertions in A and B — Widening —, this specification is readily implemented by

Pre :	$d = 1$	
A: $*[\{d \leq 1\}\ S$		B: $*[\{1 \leq d\}\ T$
$;$ if $d \leq 0 \rightarrow$ skip fi		$;\ d := d - 1$
$;\ \{d \leq 0\}$		$;$ if $1 \leq d \rightarrow$ skip fi
$\quad d := d + 1$		$\{1 \leq d\}$
$\quad \{d \leq 1\}$		$]$
$]$		
Inv :	$0 \leq d\ \wedge\ d \leq 2$	

Version 2.2

And there is no total deadlock.

*   *
*

We have included intermediate Version 2.1, because something noteworthy happened in the transition from Version 2.0 to Version 2.1; any solution satisfying the latter will inevitably also satisfy the *stronger* system invariant

$$0 \leq d\ \wedge\ d \leq 1\quad :$$

$0 \leq d$ is invariant like before and $d \leq 1$ is invariant thanks to (queried) pre-assertion $d \leq 0$ of $d := d+1$ in A. As a result, d has become two-valued instead of three-valued, and can now possibly be represented by just one boolean instead of the two that were needed before. That is, we can make do with less storage space. How come?

Comparing the annotations of Version 2.0 and Version 2.1, we observe that the latter is the stronger one: it requires $d \leq 0$ as a pre-assertion to $d := d+1$, a requirement that is absent from Version 2.0. To understand what this signifies let us recall the operational interpretation of annotation, which is that when a component is "at" an assertion, the state of the system is supposed to satisfy that assertion. As a result, the stronger the annotation, the less computational freedom the system has, i.e. the fewer computations can be exhibited by the program, or — in case of multiprograms — the "less parallelism". It stands to reason that in case of such a reduction of computational freedom fewer states need to be distinguished, which might translate into a reduction of the storage space needed. And this is precisely what happened in the above transformation.

We can push the phenomenon to a limit by doing the same to B as we did to A, viz. we can satisfy B's queried assertion in Version 2.1 by transforming B into

$$B: \quad *[\, \{1 \leq d\}\, T$$
$$; \{?\, 2 \leq d\}$$
$$d := d-1$$
$$\{1 \leq d\}$$
$$]\quad .$$

Then invariant $1 \leq d \wedge d \leq 1$, i.e. $d = 1$, will be inevitable; assertions $d \leq 0$ in A and $2 \leq d$ in B are therefore equivalent to *false*, and total deadlock will be the result. And indeed: total deadlock is readily implemented with zero storage space.

*   *
*

Next, we wish to investigate whether the reduction of parallelism has affected the computation proper in that it may lead to some sort of degeneration, as, for instance, occurred in Solution 0. This time the potential parallelism for the computation proper is not affected: after completion of the phases $\{d \leq 1\}\, S$ and $\{1 \leq d\}\, T$, there is only one way in which the components can manoeuvre themselves through the synchronization protocol, viz. — the system state satisfying $d = 1$ — the only possible interleaving is

$d := d-1$ (in B)

if $d \leq 0 \rightarrow skip$ **fi** (in A)

$d := d+1$ (in A)

if $1 \leq d \rightarrow skip$ **fi** (in B)   ,

after which both components are free again to start their next phase. So in this solution the reduction of parallelism is confined to the protocol.

*   *
*

Finally, for the sake of completeness, we transform our solution — Version 2.2 — to the boolean domain through coordinate transformation

$$c \equiv (d=0) \quad \text{, and hence} - 0 \leq d \leq 1 -$$
$$\neg c \equiv (d=1) \quad .$$

Omitting all details, we obtain

Pre : $\neg c$	
A: $* [\, S$	B: $* [\, T$
; **if** $c \rightarrow skip$ **fi**	; $c := true$ (or: $\neg c$)
; $c := false$ (or: $\neg c$)	; **if** $\neg c \rightarrow skip$ **fi**
]	]

Version 2.3

And this completes our treatment of the problem of phase synchronization for two machines.

*   *
*

One of the purposes of this chapter has been to illustrate some elementary techniques by which we can influence the degree of parallelism that a multiprogram under execution can exhibit. We have seen that non-unique representation of data is one way to enhance computational freedom, and that choosing the annotation as weak as possible is another. As for the latter technique, we recall that in the very last remark of Chapter 6 on Strengthening the Annotation, we already mentioned one reason why choosing our annotation as weak as possible would be our overall strategy. And here we have seen another reason: by choosing the annotation as weak as possible we opt for designs with a maximal degree of computational freedom, which often results in a minimal amount of blocking of individual components, and thus enhances the likelihood of individual progress. And that is why we can travel a long way without a formalism for dealing with progress.

18

The Parallel Linear Search

The problem of the parallel linear search is a nice little paradigm that was first communicated to us in the mid 1980s by Ernst-Rüdiger Olderog. The problem can be used to illustrate a variety of phenomena that come with parallelism, and in this capacity it is one of the running examples in [AO91]. In [Kna92] we can find a first formal derivation of the algorithm, a derivation that is carried out in the UNITY formalism [CM88].

* *
*

The problem is as follows. We are given two boolean functions f and g, defined on the naturals. They are such that

(0) $\qquad \langle \exists i :: f.i \rangle \lor \langle \exists i :: g.i \rangle$

holds, and we are required to construct a program computing naturals x and y such that

R: $\qquad f.x \lor g.y$.

It so happens that we have at our disposal two machines, which are specially geared towards computing f and computing g, respectively. Now the idea is to establish R by means of a terminating two-component multiprogram, the one component searching for a position where f is *true* and the other one searching g. That is, we envisage a program of the following form

Pre : $x = 0 \ \wedge \ y = 0$	
CompF: **do** ... $\rightarrow$ $x := x + 1$ **od**	CompG: **do** ... $\rightarrow$ $y := y + 1$ **od**
Inv : $0 \leq x \ \wedge \ 0 \leq y$	
Post : ? $f.x \ \vee \ g.y$	

Specification

*   *
*

Let us, for the time being, forget about the postcondition and focus on termination first. If we were given $\langle \exists i :: f.i \rangle$, CompF could simply be

$\quad$ **do** $\neg f.x \rightarrow x := x + 1$ **od**$\qquad$,

and its termination would be no problem. However, from given (0) we cannot conclude the existence of a *true* f- value, so that such a CompF might fail to terminate. Therefore, we *must* strengthen the guard and consider a CompF of the form

$\quad$ **do** $\neg f.x \wedge \neg b \rightarrow x := x + 1$ **od**$\qquad$.

Because the problem is so symmetric in f and g , we choose CompG to have a similar shape; in particular, we propose CompG to be

$\quad$ **do** $\neg g.y \wedge \neg b \rightarrow y := y + 1$ **od**$\qquad$.

Remark$\quad$ As will become clear later, we can use exactly the same strengthening — with conjunct $\neg b$ — for CompG's guard as was used in CompF. **End** of Remark.

Now we first show in some detail that at least one of the components is guaranteed to terminate. To that end we note that CompF can be correctly annotated as follows:

$\quad$ **do** $\neg f.x \wedge \neg b \rightarrow \{\neg f.x\} \ x := x + 1$ **od**$\qquad$.

The assertion is correct because x is a private variable of CompF. As a result, the system maintains system invariant

$\quad$ $\langle \forall i : 0 \leq i < x : \neg f.i \rangle$

and, by symmetry, also

$\quad$ $\langle \forall i : 0 \leq i < y : \neg g.i \rangle$$\qquad$.

By (0), this implies that x is bounded from above or y is bounded from above. That is: at least one of the components terminates, this by our postulate of weak fairness.

*   *
*

Next we concentrate on queried postcondition $f.x \lor g.y$, and we consider the case that CompF, say, terminates. Upon termination it has established the local correctness of

$$f.x \lor b \quad ,$$

and if this condition is globally correct as well, the required postcondition $f.x \lor g.y$ is correct whenever

$$f.x \lor b \ \Rightarrow \ f.x \lor g.y$$

or, equivalently, whenever

$$P: \quad b \ \Rightarrow \ f.x \lor g.y \quad .$$

And, as we shall show, relation P is a system invariant (given that initially we have $\neg b$).

Summarizing, we have arrived at

Pre : $x=0 \ \land \ y=0 \ \land \ \neg b$
CompF: **do** $\neg f.x \land \neg b \rightarrow$ $\qquad\qquad \{\neg f.x\}$ $\qquad\qquad x := x+1$ **od** $\{? \ f.x \lor b\} \ \{f.x \lor g.y\}$
CompG: CompF   with (f,x) and (g,y) interchanged
Inv : $? \ P: \quad b \ \Rightarrow \ f.x \lor g.y$
Post : $f.x \lor g.y$

and what is left is to deal with the queried items and to see to the termination of CompG; all the rest follows from the symmetry.

- The (global) correctness of post-assertion $f.x \lor b$ of CompF is guaranteed whenever we see to it that CompG does not falsify b.

- Thanks to post-assertion $f.x \lor g.y$ of CompF, termination of CompG is permitted in this state, and it can be enforced by postfixing CompF with an assignment $b := true$, which makes CompG's guard stably *false*.

- Note that such an assignment clearly maintains P, since $\{f.x \lor g.y\}\ b := true\ \{P\}$ is a valid Hoare-triple. Our final task is to show the invariance of P under $x := x+1\ -\ y := y+1$ is symmetry. I.e. we have to investigate $(x := x+1).P$, which is $b \Rightarrow f.(x+1) \lor g.y$, and we shall show that it is implied:

$$f.(x+1) \lor g.y$$

$\Leftarrow$ $\{$nothing is known about $f.(x+1)\}$

$$g.y$$

$\Leftarrow$ $\{\ P,\ $ i.e. $b \land \neg f.x\ \Rightarrow\ g.y\}$

$$b \land \neg f.x$$

$\equiv$ $\{\neg f.x$ is pre-assertion of $x := x+1\}$

$$b\ .$$

And here is our final program for the problem of the parallel linear search — all annotation omitted —:

Pre : $x = 0 \land y = 0 \land \neg b$	
CompF: **do** $\neg f.x \land \neg b \rightarrow$ $\qquad x := x+1$ **od** $\quad ; b := true$	CompG: **do** $\neg g.y \land \neg b \rightarrow$ $\qquad y := y+1$ **od** $\quad ; b := true$
Post : $f.x \lor g.y$	

The Parallel Linear Search

*   *

*

There is a final transformation that may be worth carrying out, viz. the distribution of the operations on boolean b over the two components, with the aim of acquiring a fully distributed algorithm. Because the two components must, independently of each other, be able to set b equal to *true*, there is hardly any choice beyond representing b by

$$b \equiv c \lor d\quad ,$$

with c private to CompF and d private to CompG. With this change in coordinates we can replace

- $\neg b$ in Pre   by $\neg c \wedge \neg d$
- $b := true$ in CompF by $c := true$
- $\neg b$ in CompF by $\neg d$, because $\neg c$ is a loop invariant.

The program then becomes

Pre : $x = 0 \wedge y = 0 \wedge \neg c \wedge \neg d$	

CompF: **do** $\neg f.x \wedge \neg d \rightarrow$
      $x := x + 1$
 od
 ; $c := true$
	CompG: **do** $\neg g.y \wedge \neg c \rightarrow$
	      $y := y + 1$
	 od
	 ; $d := true$

Post : $f.x \vee g.y$	

A Distributed Parallel Linear Search

*   *
*

Of course, there are many variations on the theme "parallel searching", for instance searching in a bounded search space or searching with more than two components, but to all intents and purposes, they will all have the flavour of the above derivation and algorithm.

A postscript

In the very first chapter of this book we postulated that our computational model would adhere to the "weak fairness" property. What this boils down to is that in our model of interleaving no component is neglected forever. I.e. if a component is about to evaluate a guard or to execute the next assignment statement, it will do so within a finite number of steps of the system.

In studies about fairness we may also encounter the "minimal liveness" property. What this boils down to is that as long as something *can* happen something *will* happen; however, nothing is specified about *what* will happen: each time the same component could be selected in the interleaving.

The difference becomes manifest in the following little two-component multiprogram:

$$* [\, x := x + 1 \,] \quad \| \quad * [\, y := y + 1 \,] \quad .$$

Under the weak-fairness regime both x and y will eventually exceed any natural number, whereas under the minimal-liveness regime this can only be guaranteed for $x+y$: $x:=x+1$ could, for instance, be neglected forever.

In our solution of the parallel linear search we heavily rely on weak fairness: we used it in our proof that at least one component is guaranteed to terminate. Under minimal liveness, our solution is incorrect because termination is no longer guaranteed: if all g- values are *false*, CompG is always eligible for execution. To the best of our knowledge, the parallel linear search is the first algorithm in this monograph where minimal liveness does not suffice.

The question is: can we save our parallel linear search if the computing machinery available does not provide weak fairness? The answer is: yes, we can, viz. by means of a multibound. Let us require the additional invariance of, say,

Q: $x \leq y+1 \ \wedge \ y \leq x+1$.

A program implementing this is

Pre : $x=0 \ \wedge \ y=0 \ \wedge \ \neg b$	
CompF:	CompG:
do $\neg f.x \wedge \neg b$	**do** $\neg g.y \wedge \neg b$
$\rightarrow$ **if** $x \leq y \rightarrow x := x+1$	$\rightarrow$ **if** $y \leq x \rightarrow y := y+1$
$\| \ b \rightarrow skip$	$\| \ b \rightarrow skip$
fi	**fi**
od	**od**
; $b := true$	; $b := true$

The partial correctness of the original algorithm is not affected, because we only added skips, but termination might be. However, we observe that when both components are engaged in their repetition, $\neg b$ holds and, hence, $x+y$ will increase: the only way in which $x+y$ can remain constant is when the state satisfies b. Now Q all by itself admits the conclusion that both x and y will eventually increase when $x+y$ does, and thus we have recreated the original scenario, this time *without* postulating weak fairness, And here we see — in a nutshell — how the multibound technique can provide a simple means to bend minimal liveness into weak fairness.

19

The Initialization Protocol

Almost all of our multiprograms come with an initial state, as embodied by the precondition "Pre" in our schemes. In one way or another this initial state has to be established before any component can start executing its code. So here is a synchronization problem to be dealt with.

One idea — or rather: Jayadev Misra's idea [Mis91] — is to distribute the initialization task over the various components, and let the components start on their computation proper only after all initialization tasks have been completed. To put it more precisely, the canonical multiprogram

Pre :	pre-state
Comp.p:	$S.p$

will, for this purpose, be replaced with

Pre :	*true*
Comp.*p*:	*Init.p*
	; {? *R.p*}
	S.p

Specification

where

- *Init.p* is Comp.*p*'s contribution to establishing the original precondition "pre-state",

- for any *p*, *R.p* given by

  R.p: ⟨ ∀*q* : *q* ≠ *p* : *Init.q* has terminated ⟩   ,

  is to be established by proper synchronization of the components, subject to the constraint, however, that

- no assumption is to be made about the initial value of the variables used for achieving this synchronization (otherwise we would be begging the question).

*   *
*

At first sight, the problem very much looks like a simplified phase synchronization problem, with just two phases — *Init* and *S* — per component. However, due to the additional constraint, the situation has become rather more tricky. We first investigate the case of just two components, in order to get a feel for the difficulties involved.

A solution for two components

Let us call the two components X and Y respectively. Then target assertion *RX* in component X simplifies to

RX: *InitY* has terminated.

Because this is a stable condition — i.e. it is globally correct — we can establish its correctness via Modus Ponens (see Chapter 11). We, therefore, introduce two fresh booleans x and y , and transform our specification into

Pre :	*true*	
X:	*InitX*	Y: *InitY*
	; {? $y \Rightarrow RX$ }	; {? $x \Rightarrow RY$ }
	if $y \rightarrow skip$ fi	if $x \rightarrow skip$ fi
	; { RX }	; { RY }
	SX	SY

Version 0.0

Assertion $y \Rightarrow RX$ in component X would be *locally* correct if the pre-condition were to imply $\neg y$. However, we are not allowed to make any assumptions about y 's initial value. So the only possible solution is to make X create state $\neg y$ all by itself. This is realized by postfixing *InitX* with statement $y := false$.

In order for $y \Rightarrow RX$ to be *globally* correct, we will see to it that any assignment $y := true$ in further refinements of component Y has precondition RX , i.e. "*InitY* has terminated". In order not to forget this constraint, we explicitly record it in our next refinement.

Pre :	*true*	
X:	*InitX*	Y: *InitY*
	; $y := false$	; $x := false$
	; if $y \rightarrow skip$ fi	; if $x \rightarrow skip$ fi
	; SX	; SY
Constraints:	• $x := true$ in X only after *InitX*	
	• symmetrically for Y	

Version 0.1

* * *
*

Although partially correct, the above program lacks all progress properties whatsoever. (In particular, total deadlock is inevitable.) Fortunately, we still have the freedom to add statements $x := true$ and $y := true$. To begin with, we try to remove the deadlock, by prefixing the guarded skip

in X with $x := true$ and the guarded skip in Y with $y := true$, which
is in agreement with the Constraints. This, indeed, does away with total
deadlock, as we have shown in Example 5 of Chapter 8. We will not repeat
the construction of that proof here; we just give the resulting annotated
program, from which the absence of deadlock follows immediately. (In this
program, variable h is an auxiliary variable.)

Pre : $true$	
X: $InitX$	Y: $InitY$
; $y, h := false, $X	; $x, h := false, $Y
; $x := true$	; $y := true$
; $\{x \lor h = Y\}$	; $\{y \lor h = X\}$
if $y \to skip$ fi	if $x \to skip$ fi
; SX	; SY
Constraints: • $x := true$ in X only after $InitX$	
• symmetrically for Y	

Version 0.2

*   *
*

What about individual progress? At this point, the reader may construct
a scenario showing that individual progress is not guaranteed: one of the
components may get stuck in its guarded skip forever. In order to remove
this danger we argue as follows.

By the absence of total deadlock, at least one of the components terminates its protocol, i.e. can start its S . Let this be component X . If
we can now ensure — in one way or another — that x is a valid pre-
assertion to SX , then termination of component Y is guaranteed as well,
simply because then the guard in Y's guarded skip is stably $true$ [†]. A simple
way to ensure this is by prefixing SX with statement $x := true$ (which
agrees with the Constraints). The proof that then, indeed, x is a correct
pre-assertion to SX follows from the following annotated program (c. f.
Example 5, Chapter 8). Note that auxiliary variables like c are allowed
to have initial values.

[†]We owe this argument to Rob R. Hoogerwoord.

Pre : $\neg c$	
X: $InitX$	Y: $InitY$
$; y := false$	$; \{\neg c\}$
$; \{\neg y \lor c\}$	$x := false$
$x := true$	$; y, c := true, true$
$; \{\neg y \lor c\}$	$; $ **if** $x \to$ **skip fi**
if $y \to$ **skip fi**	$; y, c := true, true$
$; \{c\}$	$; SY$
$x := true$	
$; \{x\} \{c\}$	
SX	

Version 0.3

Eliminating all annotation, we thus obtain as our final solution.

Pre : $true$	
X: $InitX$	Y: $InitY$
$; y := false$	$; x := false$
$; x := true$	$; y := true$
$; $ **if** $y \to$ **skip fi**	$; $ **if** $x \to$ **skip fi**
$; x := true$	$; y := true$
$; SX$	$; SY$

Initialization Protocol for Two Components

*   *

*

We conclude this example with a few remarks, reflecting on how we managed to achieve individual progress.

(i)   The way in which we tried to achieve absence of total deadlock was not far-fetched at all: without the initial assignments $x := true$ in X and $y := true$ in Y , deadlock would be guaranteed to occur.

(ii) The way in which we tried to achieve individual progress by inserting the final assignments $x := true$ in X and $y := true$ in Y may seem more of a surprise. But on closer inspection it isn't. First, Hoogerwoord's suggestion to try to obtain x as a correct pre-assertion to SX is a legitimate one, because if it succeeds, the progress argument becomes extremely simple. (This is also true from an operational point of view, since by requiring x to be a correct pre-assertion of SX, all potential interest in the (invisible) program counter of component Y vanishes: component Y is guaranteed to terminate, whether it has "passed" its guarded skip or not.)

Second, Hoogerwoord's suggestion also is a viable one, because — as the annotation in version 0.3 shows — the *global* correctness of assertion x is already guaranteed. So the only thing that remains is to establish its *local* correctness, and that is where the final $x := true$ comes from.

Remark The correctness of x as a pre-assertion to SX will also form a vital ingredient in our subsequent derivation of an initialization protocol for more than two components.
End of Remark.

(iii) Finally we have to admit that, no matter how crisp the final solution turned out to be, its derivation seems to be driven by hope and a kind of opportunism. For instance, it was not clear at all at the outset that the required progress properties can be achieved via insertions of statements $x := true$ and $y := true$ — see the little experiment recorded at the very end of Chapter 8. The fact that things turned out well was probably just a matter of good luck[‡].

A general solution

In this section we deal with the initialization problem for an arbitrary number of components, and only now will it become clear how much luck we had in arriving at our solution for two components. In fact it was a narrow escape. We confine our attention to the case of three components, because it is general enough to reveal the trouble we are in but also general enough to show how we can get out of the trouble again. We invite and challenge the reader to stop here and first try to think of a solution for himself.

*   *
*

[‡]It is a common phenomenon that, in designing artefacts, one may have to retract a design decision, for instance because an induction hypothetis is too weak or a theorem has to be generalized to become amenable to proof.

We start our derivation in the same way as we did for two components. As a stepping stone we use the analogue of Version 0.1:

Pre :	*true*
X:	*InitX*
	; $y := false$
	; $z := false$
	; if $y \wedge z \rightarrow skip$ fi
	; *SX*
Y and Z:	symmetric versions of X
Constraints:	• $x := true$ in X only after *InitX*
	• symmetrically for Y and Z

A (hopeless) stepping stone

Remark   As an exercise, the reader may prove that the correctness of the above multiprogram is not affected if guarded skip if $y \wedge z \rightarrow skip$ fi is replaced by the sequential composition of if $y \rightarrow skip$ fi and if $z \rightarrow skip$ fi, in either order.
End of Remark.

In order to preclude deadlock we *have* to insert statements $x := true$ before the guarded skip in X. But no matter how many of these statements we insert, the situation cannot be saved, for we cannot preclude the following scenario:

Let X and Y execute their prelude up to their guarded skips. Then $\neg z$ holds, and both X and Y are blocked. Next, let Z execute its prelude, thus making two out of three booleans equal to *false*, i.e. leaving at most one boolean *true*. Because each guard is a conjunction of two booleans, all guards are *false*, and total deadlock is the result.

The diagnostics is becoming clear: in the deadlock state, when all three components are stuck in their guarded skips, the state no longer changes, whereas switching booleans from *false* to *true* is not only allowed but also badly needed. The mode of "waiting" in a guarded skip is just too "static". One way out is to resort to what is sometimes called "dynamic waiting", which refers to replacing

if $B \rightarrow skip$ fi   with   do $\neg B \rightarrow skip$ od   ,

and then replacing the latter with

> **do** $\neg B \to$ something useful for progress **od** .

In our example, the "something useful for progress" will be "$x := true$" in component X, and — exploiting the property referred to in the remark following the stepping-stone program — we will replace **if** $y \wedge z \to skip$ **fi** by

> **do** $\neg y \to x := true$
> ‖ $\neg z \to x := true$
> **od** .

Adding a final assignment $x := true$, just as we did in the two-component solution, we are thus led to consider a program of the form

Pre :	$true$
X:	$InitX$
	; $y := false$
	; $z := false$
	; **do** $\neg y \to x := true$
	‖ $\neg z \to x := true$
	od
	; $x := true$
	$\{x,$ see later$\}$
	; SX
Y and Z:	symmetric versions of X

Initialization Protocol for Three Components

and below we shall show that this program has all the desired progress properties.

Remark From Chapter 2, we recall the atomicity conventions regarding repetitive constructs: the evaluation of a guard is atomic, but the corresponding guarded statement is *not* part of it.
End of Remark.

Just as in the two-component solution, the correctness of the final assertion x in X — to be shown later — will play a vital rôle in the progress argument. And just as in the two-component solution, the final assignment $x := true$ is needed to establish it. (We invite the reader to construct a scenario showing that, if the final $x := true$ is omitted, individual progress is no longer guaranteed.)

*   *

*

In order to show individual progress, we have to show that each component will, within a finite number of steps of the system, start on the execution of its S. To that end, we first observe that, within a finite number of steps, all components will have completed their preludes, i.e. all their assignments "bool:=$false$". In such a state it holds that component X

- either has established the stable truth of x — this is the rôle of assertion x in X —
- or will do so within a finite number of steps — this on account of the structure of X.

Thus, all the booleans will eventually be stably $true$, so that all three repetitions are guaranteed to terminate. So much for progress.

Remark   As in the two-component solution, final assertion x has saved us from dragging the program counters into the argument, which in the current example would have complified the argument dramatically.
End of Remark.

*   *

*

Finally, we have to prove the correctness of assertion x in component X. It is locally correct (by construction!). In order to prove that it is globally correct, we address its global correctness under Y; then symmetry does the rest.

We introduce an auxiliary boolean variable c and the following annotation for component pair (X,Y) (cf. Version 0.3):

```
Pre :   ¬c
─────────────────────────────────────────────────────
X:                 InitX
   ;               y := false
   ; {¬y ∨ c} z := false
   ; {loop inv : ¬y ∨ c}
                      do ¬y → {¬y ∨ c} x := true {¬y ∨ c}
                      ▐   ¬z → {¬y ∨ c} x := true {¬y ∨ c}
                      od
   ;        {c} x := true
   ;   {x} {c} SX
─────────────────────────────────────────────────────
Y:        InitY
   ;        z := false
   ; {¬c} x := false
   ;        do ¬z → y, c := true, true
            ▐   ¬x → y, c := true, true
            od
   ;        y, c := true, true
   ;        SY
```

The global correctness of assertion x in X is ensured by the Rule of Disjointness. The local correctness of its co-assertion c follows from loop invariant $¬y ∨ c$ — or $y ⇒ c$ — by Modus Ponens. The global correctness of assertion $¬y ∨ c$ in component X is guaranteed by extending assignments $y := true$ — which occur in Y only! — with $c := true$. We trust that the reader can check the rest of the annotation for himself.

End of A general solution.

$$* \qquad *$$
$$*$$

This chapter has been the first one in which, at least to some extent, we had to resort to some sort of operational reasoning. Here we definitely pay a price for not having adopted a formalism for dealing with progress. Fortunately, the price is not too high, thanks to the special structure of the algorithm: from the (static) topology of the program text it is clear that the oscillating behaviour of the guards comes to an end after a finite number of steps of the system. (Recall from Chapter 8 that a necessary condition for progress is that oscillation of a guard's value does not continue forever.) In a later chapter, we will encounter an example in which this finiteness of oscillation is not automatically guaranteed and where we have to enforce it by incorporating it in the problem specification.

Finally, one may wonder whether we can make do with just the guarded skip as a synchronization primitive, for after all the above problem seemed to be unsolvable without using "dynamic waiting". To reassure the reader: guarded skips do suffice. Our resorting to dynamic waiting was just an ad-hoc solution. There is a fundamentally much better solution, which is based on the technique of introducing auxiliary components for special-purpose tasks. In the next chapter we will discuss the introduction of such auxiliary components as an isolated topic, and subsequently we will solve the Initialization problem once again, this time using auxiliary components for the task of truthifying the booleans.

20

Co-components

There is a rule that says: "Avoid duplication of volatile information."[†]
Disobedience of this rule may have disastrous consequences for an organization, whether it is just a computer system or a human society. Information — in the broadest sense of the word — that is widely diffused and then needs to be changed, may require a gigantic update operation, and — perhaps worse — may be unreliable or just wrong at all those places where the update operation has not been effectuated yet. (Changing all telephone numbers in the Netherlands, in the mid 1990s, was an enormous operation, which took a whole year. The transition of a lot of European currencies to the euro is an almost frightening prospect. The millennium problem, caused by an untraceable diffusion of an erroneous date field, will cost society billions and billions of dollars.)

Since the earliest days of computing, competent programmers have been aware of this rule and have recognized its importance. The concept of a subroutine and, in its wake, of a subroutine library is an early witness of this awareness. A little later, there was the independently running interrupt handler — an intermediary between a central processing unit and peripheral devices — in which all decisions concerning the handling of interrupts were concentrated. Later still, there was the concept of the monitor, an

---

[†]We learned this rule from Edsger W. Dijkstra in his lecture series "Aspects of Implementation" [Dij79].

independently running process in which all logical and strategical issues for the harmonious cooperation of sequential processes were embedded. Etcetera. (The current interest in object-oriented programming is an effort to do justice to the rule on a larger and more systematic scale.)

The subroutines, the interrupt handler, the monitor, they all are a kind of aids to computations proper, and they serve a particular purpose, here to isolate potentially changing data and other separable concerns. If those aids are independently running processes, we will refer to them as *co-components*.

Due to the advancement of electronic engineering, massive parallelism has become technically possible and economically feasible. This implies that, if for some reason or another, we wish to equip a computation with one or more co-components, we are always free to do so.

Co-components may be introduced for a variety of reasons, for instance to isolate potentially changing strategies in a dedicated piece of hardware or software — as in the monitors mentioned above —, or to speed up computations, or to accommodate communication obligations with an outside world that can hardly — or even impossibly — be combined with the computation proper (an alarm clock, for instance, is an indispensable co-component to enjoying a good night's rest). In some of the remaining chapters we will encounter opportunities to introduce co-components with advantage. The main purpose of this chapter is to show, through two examples, how we may handle co-components.

Speeding up a computation

In our first example, we consider a computation given by

$$X: \quad S_0$$
$$; \ S_1, S_2$$
$$; \ S_3 \quad ,$$

where S_1, S_2 is an ad-hoc notation, expressing that S_1 and S_2 can be executed in some, irrelevant, order or even interleaved, for instance because they operate on disjoint state spaces. Now, if S_1 and S_2 each embody lengthy computations, it pays to have them run in parallel. So let us farm out S_2 to a co-component Co-X of X. Then our programming task is specified by

Pre :	*true*	
X:	S_0	
	$; S_1$	
	$; \{? R_2 :$	S_2 has terminated$\}$
	S_3	
Co-X:	$\{? R_0 :$	S_0 has terminated$\}$
	S_2	

Now, because R_0 and R_2 are both stable, we resort to Modus Ponens, introducing two (fresh) booleans x and y, together with system invariants

$$x \Rightarrow R_0 \quad \text{and} \quad y \Rightarrow R_2 \quad .$$

Our solution then simply becomes

Pre :	$\neg x \wedge \neg y$		
X:	S_0	Co-X:	**if** $x \rightarrow skip$ **fi**
	$; x := true$		$; S_2$
	$; S_1$		$; y := true$
	$;$ **if** $y \rightarrow skip$ **fi**		
	$; S_3$		

The (simple) progress argument is left to the reader.

The above handshake-like communication pattern is so standard that at future occasions we shall use it without much ado: the guarded skips can be interpreted as "wait-for-completion signals" and the assignments $x := true$ and $y := true$ as the completion signals themselves.

$$* \qquad *$$
$$*$$

We can even save some storage space, since due to the rather sequential behaviour of the above system, we can implement the specification with just one boolean, say z. The solution is — verification left to the reader

Pre : $\neg z$	
X: S_0 ; $z := true$; S_1 ; if $\neg z \rightarrow skip$ fi ; S_3	Co-X: if $z \rightarrow skip$ fi ; S_2 ; $z := false$

(The reader may also prove that each of the two assignments to z can be replaced by $z := \neg z$.)

Now the similarity with the handshake protocol has become perfect. This communication scheme, too, will be used without much ado, should the need arise.

Alain J. Martin's Perpetuum Mobile

In our second example of the use of co-components, we consider the mutual exclusion problem for an arbitrary number of components that are arranged in a ring. The arrangement in the ring implies that a component can only communicate with its two neighbours in the ring.

As a means towards achieving mutual exclusion among the critical sections of the various components, we introduce a unique token that at any moment in time resides in one of the components. A component is allowed to execute its critical section if and only if it "owns" the token. More precisely, if $t = X$ captures that component X owns the token, then we are heading for an algorithm specified by: for each component X,

X: * [ncs
   ; {? $t = X$}
   cs
   ]   .

For the sake of progress, the token will be propagated through the ring in, say, clockwise order.

Token transmission by component A to component B will be described by

{$t = A$} $t := B$.

I.e. $t := B$ is the actual transfer to B, but A may only do so provided it owns the token, that is when $t = A$.

With this regime, assertion $t = X$ in component X above is stable under token transmission in different components — Rule of Disjointness. Therefore, we can satisfy $t = X$ by establishing its local correctness. Thus, we get

$$X: \quad * [\ ncs$$
$$; \text{if } t = X \rightarrow skip \text{ fl}$$
$$; \{t = X\}$$
$$cs$$
$$]\quad .$$

This settles mutual exclusion, and what remains is individual progress.

*   *
*

Individual progress means that the synchronization protocol does not hamper the computation proper indefinitely. Here the computation proper consists of ncs and cs , and in mutual exclusion problems the assumption has always been that cs terminates whereas ncs may or may not terminate. It is the potentially nonterminating ncs that causes a problem.

While in its ncs , component X will be "incommunicado"; more in particular, it will be unable to transmit the token. (Recall: a general rule of the game is that we are not allowed to change the computation proper in any way: cf. Chapter 10.) So, a component that owns the token while in its ncs may give rise to total deadlock, viz. if the ncs happens to fail to terminate. As a result, we have to see to it that for each component X

$$X \text{ in its } ncs \ \Rightarrow\ t \neq X \quad ,$$

which we shall make a system invariant.

In order to record whether X is in its ncs or not, we introduce boolean hX and change component X into

$$X: \quad \{hX\}$$

$$*\,[\; ncs$$

$$; hX := false$$

$$; \text{if } t = X \rightarrow skip \text{ fi } \{t = X\}$$

$$; cs \; \{t = X\}$$

$$; hX := true$$

$$]\quad ,$$

while requiring, for each X, the invariance of

$$PX: \qquad hX \;\Rightarrow\; t \neq X \qquad .$$

As a result, component X has to get rid of the token along with $hX := true$, i.e. before entering its ncs .

Let, for the remainder of this section, Y be the (clockwise) neighbour of X. Then X can get rid of the token by $hX, t := true, Y$. However, this is a hopeless proposal, because Y could be engaged in its ncs , so that token transmission would violate the corresponding PY . This is the place where — almost by necessity — co-components enter the picture.

*   *
*

We propose that each component X have its own co-component XX, and that the co-components are to take care of the token traffic along the ring. With the introduction of XX, component X can now get rid of the token by $t := XX$ (which does not violate any of the P's). For X we thus obtain

$$X: \quad \{hX\}$$

$$*\,[\; ncs$$

$$; hX := false$$

$$; \text{if } t = X \rightarrow skip \text{ fi } \{t = X\}$$

$$; cs \; \{t = X\}$$

$$; hX, t := true, XX$$

$$]\quad .$$

As for co-component XX, like any other component it can get hold of the token through a guarded skip **if** $t = XX \rightarrow skip$ **fi** . Once XX owns the token, it will propagate it — because this, we decided, is its task. There are only two components to propagate it to, viz. X and YY — the (clockwise) neighbour of XX . So XX gets the shape

XX: * [**if** $t = \text{XX} \rightarrow$ *skip* **fi**

    ; $\{t = \text{XX}\}$

    if *true* $\rightarrow t := \text{X}$

    ▌ *true* $\rightarrow t := \text{YY}$

    fi

    ]   ,

and what remains is to strengthen the guards, if necessary, in such a way that both partial correctness and individual progress for all components are guaranteed.

*   *
*

We will first deal with the partial correctness of component XX, i.e. with the correctness of XX with respect to the P's . Assignment $t := \text{YY}$ is harmless, but assignment $t := \text{X}$ may violate PX . Therefore, we require that it have precondition $\neg hX$, which we establish locally by plugging a condition G into the guard such that

(*) $G \Rightarrow \neg hX$.

Thus we arrive at

XX: * [**if** $t = \text{XX} \rightarrow$ *skip* **fi**

    ; $\{t = \text{XX}\}$

    if $G \quad \rightarrow \{t = \text{XX}\} \; \{\neg hX,\ \text{see below}\}$

                $t := \text{X}$

    ▌ *true* $\rightarrow \quad t := \text{YY}$

    fi

    ]   .

Assertion $\neg hX$ is locally correct by construction (property (*)). For its global correctness we need co-assertion $t = \text{XX}$: statement $hX := true$ in X has pre-assertion $t = \text{X}$, so that, by the Rule of Disjointness, it does not falsify $\neg hX$.

This settles the partial correctness of XX .

*   *
*

With regard to progress, we are left with two problems. The first one is that we cannot prevent XX from always choosing alternative $t := \text{YY}$.

This, however, is easily remedied by strengthening the second guard to $\neg G$. Thus we get

XX: $*\,[$ **if** $t = \text{XX} \rightarrow skip$ **fi**

    $;\,\{t = \text{XX}\}$

    if $G\;\;\; \rightarrow \{t = XX\}\,\{\neg hX\}$

          $t := \text{X}$

    $\|\;\neg G \rightarrow\;\; t := \text{YY}$

    fi

    $]$.

The second problem is more subtle. The weakest G satisfying $(*)$ is $\neg hX$, but this choice is not good enough: it does not prevent the token from commuting between X and XX indefinitely, viz. if all invocations of X's *ncs* terminate, hX keeps oscillating so that XX, upon receipt of the token, may all the time find hX equal to *false* and rebounce the token via $t := \text{X}$.

Therefore, we now constrain the freedom of XX in such a way that from the new text of XX alone we can see that such unbounded commuting will be impossible. We do so by imposing a (constant) upperbound uX, $1 \leq uX$, on the number of times that XX can consecutively send the token to X. We introduce a variable cX, local to XX, which will act as a variant function, we choose G equal to

    $\neg hX \;\wedge\; cX < uX\qquad,$

and we change XX into

XX: $\{cX = 0\}\;\{1 \leq uX\}$

    $*\,[$ **if** $t = XX \rightarrow skip$ **fi**

    $;$ **if** $\neg hX \;\wedge\; cX < uX\;\;\rightarrow\;\; cX := 1 + cX;\; t := \text{X}$

    $\|\;\;\; hX \;\vee\; uX \leq cX\;\;\rightarrow\;\; cX := 0;\; t := \text{YY}$

    fi

    $]$.

Thus we have, by construction, for any pair (X,XX) the invariance of

    $0 \leq cX \;\wedge\; cX \leq uX\qquad,$ and of

QX: $t \neq \text{X} \;\wedge\; t \neq \text{XX} \;\Rightarrow\; cX = 0$.

             $*$ $*$

               $*$

And now we are ready to provide the progress argument. For convenience, we first summarize what we have achieved so far, confining ourselves to one pair (X,XX) and the annotation relevant for it.

Pre :	$hX \;\wedge\; cX = 0 \;\wedge\; 1 \leq uX$
	$\langle\; \exists C :: t = CC \;\rangle$
X:	$* [\; ncs$
	$; hX := false$
	$; \mathbf{if}\; t = X \to skip\; \mathbf{fi}$
	$; cs$
	$; hX, t := true, XX$
	$\;]$
XX:	$* [\; \mathbf{if}\; t = XX \to skip\; \mathbf{fi}$
	$; \mathbf{if}\; \neg hX \;\wedge\; cX < uX \;\to\; cX := 1 + cX;\; t := X$
	$\qquad \parallel\; hX \;\vee\; uX \leq cX \;\to\; cX := 0;\; t := YY$
	$\quad \mathbf{fi}$
	$\;]$
Inv :	$0 \leq cX \;\wedge\; cX \leq uX$
$PX :$	$hX \;\Rightarrow\; t \neq X$
$QX :$	$t \neq X \;\wedge\; t \neq XX \;\Rightarrow\; cX = 0$

Alain J. Martin's Perpetuum Mobile

Our progress argument will use the lemma that

(**) Token propagation along the ring is guaranteed.

In other words: no co-component XX will be blocked forever in its guarded skip **if** $t = XX \to skip$ **fi** . We first prove this lemma.

Proof of (**) The token always resides in some (co-)component. Furthermore, every (co-)component that owns the token will propagate it within a finite number of terminating steps, i.e. the token keeps traveling. Now let the state be such that

$t = X \;\vee\; t = XX$.

This state is not a stable state, because the token keeps traveling and because by construction, it does not commute indefinitely between X and XX. As a result, the token will be propagated to YY, i.e. the token will be propagated along the ring.
End of Proof of (**).

Finally we show that component X will not be blocked forever in its guarded skip **if** $t = X \rightarrow skip$ **fi** — our target proof obligation. If X is stuck in its guarded skip, the state satisfies $\neg hX$ — see structure of X. We now distinguish two cases

(i) $t \neq X \wedge t \neq XX$ (the token is somewhere else)

Then, from QX, we have $cX = 0$ and hence, since $1 \leq uX$,

$$cX < uX \quad .$$

So from (∗∗) we conclude that, within a finite number of steps, XX will terminate its guarded skip and then select the first alternative of the subsequent alternative construct, thus making $t = X$ stably *true*. And X can proceed.

(ii) $t = X \vee t = XX$ (the token is somewhere here)

If $t = X$, component X can proceed. If $t = XX$, component XX will

(a) either select the first alternative and establish $t = X$

(b) or select the second alternative and establish $t \neq X \wedge t \neq XX$, which is covered by case (i). And this completes the progress argument.

*   *
*

The Perpetuum Mobile is the simplest of a trilogy of algorithms for achieving mutual exclusion along a ring [Mar85]. Alain Martin called it "Perpetuum Mobile" because of the ongoing traveling of the token along the ring. Later on Jan L. A. van de Snepscheut generalized Martin's algorithms to the case of an arbitrary graph. (See his impressive "Hands-in-the-pockets" presentation in [Sne90].)

End of Alain J. Martin's Perpetuum Mobile.

*   *
*

Herewith we conclude this introduction to co-components. In the literature we may find them under the name "slaves", which not only is an avoidable anthropomorphic nomenclature, but — worse — suggests a mathematical pecking order that just isn't there: co-components are fully-fledged components that partake in the cooperation on equal footing with the original components.

21

The Initialization Protocol Revisited

At the end of Chapter 19 we promised to return to the initialization problem after having dealt with co-components, and in this chapter we will do so. We do not repeat the problem statement here, but resume our development at what we called "A (hopeless) stepping stone"; this time, however, we omit the "hopeless":

Pre :	*true*
X:	*InitX*
	; $y := false$
	; $z := false$
	; if $y \wedge z \rightarrow skip$ fi
	; SX
Y and Z:	symmetric versions of X
Constraints:	• $x := true$ only after *InitX*
	• symmetrically for Y and Z

A stepping stone

Remark We recall that coarse-grained guarded skip **if** $y \wedge z \rightarrow skip$ **fi** can be split into the two fine-grained guarded skips **if** $y \rightarrow skip$ **fi** and

if $z \rightarrow skip$ **fi**, and that their order is irrelevant. At the end of the present chapter we will return to this possibility.
End of Remark.

*   *
*

As it stands, the algorithm lacks all progress properties whatsoever. In order to remedy this, it will be necessary to add statements $x := true$, to be performed after $InitX$ has terminated. In our earlier effort in Chapter 19 we saw that accommodating such statements in the text of component X itself is hopeless, that is to say, if we wish to retain the guarded skip as our only synchronization construct. In that earlier effort we escaped through "dynamic waiting", but here we will solve the problem via the introduction of special-purpose co-components: co-component XX of component X will be given the dedicated task of establishing the stable truth of x. We are therefore led to consider an XX of the form — comments below —

> XX: $sx := true$
>   ; {? $InitX$ has terminated}
>   **do** $sx \rightarrow x := true$ **od**

Version 0 for XX

• The assertion is there to do justice to the constraint that $x := true$ is only admitted after $InitX$ has terminated.

• When considered in isolation, the above program for XX is just equivalent to

> **do** $true \rightarrow x := true$ **od**   .

However, we are anticipating opportunities to terminate XX, which, for instance, is allowed when x has become stably $true$. That is why we introduced a *fresh* variable sx. Termination of XX can then be effectuated by

> $\{x\}$ $sx := false$.

*   *
*

Along with the introduction of XX, we adjust component X — explanation below —

```
X:    InitX
   ; y := false
   ; z := false
   ; {? sx}
     if y ∧ z → skip fi
   ; if x → skip fi
   ; {x}
     sx := false
   ; SX
```

Version 0 for X

• Compared with the previous version ("A stepping stone"), the above program text for X differs in two places, viz. two statements have been added: guarded skip **if** $x \rightarrow$ *skip* **fi** and statement $sx := false$. Neither of the two affects the partial correctness of the original multiprogram, simply because variable sx is fresh and because a guarded skip is just a skip as far as partial correctness is concerned.

• The global correctness of assertion x , under the operations of Y and Z, was discussed and proved in Chapter 19. This global correctness is not affected by the adjustments just made to Y and Z, since, again, these adjustments pertain to fresh variables. The same holds for the incorporation of the co-components: YY and ZZ do not change x , and XX only contains statement $x := true$.

As for the local correctness of assertion x , this time we prefixed it with guarded skip **if** $x \rightarrow$ *skip* **fi**, instead of with $x := true$, simply on the (esthetic) grounds that we wish to concentrate *all* assignments $x := true$ in XX.

• The text for X also contains queried assertion sx , which will be a vital ingredient for the progress argument, to be given in a moment.

So much for the explanation of our choice for component X.

*   *
*

What remains — besides proving progress — is to establish the queried assertions in X and XX, but we postpone this for a moment because, given these assertions, we can already now show individual progress for each of the components. So that is what we will do first, and we will do so by proving that, within a finite number of steps of the system, all three booleans x, y, and z become stably *true*. We concentrate on x.

First of all we observe that the *only* way in which component XX can terminate is through $sx := false$ in component X, and we will keep it that way. Now we consider a state of the system in which *all* components have completed their preludes. For component X this is fragment

$$InitX;\ y := false;\ z := false;\ \{?\ sx\}\qquad .$$

From the annotation in X we conclude that then the state of the system satisfies sx or x. We distinguish two cases:

- The state satisfies x. Then x is *stably true*, because all preludes containing $x := false$ have terminated.

- The state satisfies $\neg x$, and hence $\neg x \wedge sx$. In such a state, $sx := false$ will not be performed (Rule of Disjointness), so sx continues to hold and — see observation above — component XX has not terminated yet. As a result, XX will make x (stably) *true* within a finite number of steps of the system.

Thus, boolean x, and by symmetry booleans y and z as well, will become stably *true* and, as a result, individual progress for each of the components is guaranteed.

$$*\qquad\qquad *$$
$$*$$

Finally, we address the two queried assertions. We begin with sx in X. Since this assertion is globally correct, we only need to take care of its local correctness. This can be done in a variety of — standard — ways, but this time we establish it with the aid of component XX, by requiring that sx have as a co-assertion

"$sx := true$ in XX has terminated"   .

Then, on account of the topology of XX, sx indeed holds. Now the situation has become completely symmetric for the couple (X, XX): it now has the shape

```
X:      InitX
        ; y := false
        ; z := false
        ; IPX
        ; {? sx := true   in XX has terminated}
          if y ∧ z → skip fi
        ; if x → skip fi
        ; sx := false
        ; SX
XX:     sx := true
        ; IPXX
        ; {? InitX   has terminated}
          do sx → x := true od
```

Version 1 for (X, XX)

Here, *IPX* and *IPXX* are program fragments that are to establish their respective post-assertions. From the topology of the above components, from the structure of the assertions and the still pending obligation that nothing may be assumed about the initial values of the variables, we see that the problem to be solved is "just" the initialization problem for two components; so we can satisfy the queried assertions by choosing for the pair (*IPX*, *IPXX*) the initialization protocol for two components. With fresh variables fx and gx, we thus obtain (cf. Chapter 19)

$$
\begin{array}{ll}
IPX: & gx := false \\
     & ; fx := true \\
     & ; \text{if } gx \rightarrow skip \text{ fi} \\
     & ; fx := true
\end{array}
\qquad
\begin{array}{ll}
IPXX: & fx := false \\
      & ; gx := true \\
      & ; \text{if } fx \rightarrow skip \text{ fi} \\
      & ; gx := true
\end{array}
$$

Remarks

• In the above we superimposed one protocol, viz. the two-component initialization protocol, onto another, viz. the three-component protocol. Superimposing protocols is not uncommon, but not without danger either. It can easily lead to deadlock. The simplest example of this is when a consumer has to extract a portion from a buffer under mutual exclusion. One protocol then prevents the consumer from taking a portion from an empty buffer, and another protocol takes care of the mutual exclusion. The superposition, however, had better be such that the test for emptiness is not embedded in the critical section.

The superposition in the above does not cause any of these problems, since the *terminating* pair $(IPX, IPXX)$ is part of the "automatically" terminating preludes of the pair (X, XX) .

• The order, in X, of the three statements

$y := false$; $z := false$; IPX

is completely irrelevant. If we want $x := true$ to be performed "earlier", the order had better be

IPX; $y := false$; $z := false$.

In this text, however, quantitative behaviour is not a major concern — it is a legitimate but separable concern.

End of Remarks.

*   *
*

Here is the raw code of our solution, a rather inscrutable piece of text when viewed operationally:

Pre : *true*	
X: *InitX*	XX: $sx := true$
; $y := false$	; $fx := false$
; $z := false$	; $gx := true$
; $gx := false$	; **if** $fx \rightarrow skip$ **fi**
; $fx := true$	; $gx := true$
; **if** $gx \rightarrow skip$ **fi**	; **do** $sx \rightarrow x := true$ **od**
; $fx := true$	
; **if** $y \wedge z \rightarrow skip$ **fi**	
; **if** $x \rightarrow skip$ **fi**	
; $sx := false$	
; SX	
Symmetric versions for (Y, YY) and (Z, ZZ)	

Initialization Protocol for Three Components

And this completes our derivation of an initialization protocol for three components in which the only synchronization primitive used is the guarded skip. As in our earlier solution, the straightforward generalization to more than three components is left to the reader.

*   *

*

We conclude this chapter with two remarks and an observation. The remarks concern a "small" variation on the algorithm derived in the above and the confrontation of our algorithm with a model checker; the observation is made for later use.

• In a previous solution to this problem, we equipped X not only with the feature $sx := false$ to "switch off" co-component XX, but also with $sx := true$ to "switch XX on". The only — really small — difference with our current solution was that a statement $sx := true$ occurred at a judiciously chosen place in the code of X instead of in XX.

That algorithm was as correct as the current one, but its progress argument became more complex by at least an order of magnitude. The technical reason is that by the absence of statement $sx := true$ from XX , we could not easily draw conclusions from assertion sx in X as to how "far" XX had progressed in its protocol: it was considerably harder, for instance, to prove that the only way in which XX can terminate is through statement $sx := false$ in X. The danger of introducing the program counters was seriously lurking around the corner.

The most likely reason why we fell into this trap in the first place is that we have not yet freed ourselves sufficiently rigorously from the component/co-component or rather the master/slave metaphor. Of course a master must switch on a slave, that is what these words mean, don't they? The moral is clear: we must forget about these metaphors and obey what the neutral formulae demand. It is the formulae that come up in the development that ought to guide the way, not our often biased (mis)conception of how programs and program parts are to be arranged.

• As we mentioned in the beginning of this chapter, guarded skip
if $y \land z \to skip$ fi may be split into the two independent guarded skips
if $y \to skip$ fi and if $z \to skip$ fi , which may be executed in any order. In our program for component X there is also the final guarded skip
if $x \to skip$ fi , and in a moment of lightheartedness we thought that even the order of all three guarded skips would be irrelevant. It was this "patched-up" program that we submitted to a model checker through the help of our colleague Dennis Dams. The model checker reported: "Individual Starvation!". And then we sat back in our chairs and found out that the patched-up program was indeed wrong: guarded skip if $x \to skip$ fi must follow the other ones. One up for model checking! One down for us? Yes, indeed, because we changed a program without good reason; we should have known

better. Multiprograms are utterly vulnerable artefacts: *everything* has to be proved.

Of course we went back to the checker, this time with our original, correct program. The model checker reported: "Individual Starvation"! We were shocked, and on the verge of retracing our whole method of multiprogramming. But then the relieving message came that our program had unearthed an error in the model checker. After this error had been repaired, the checker accepted our program; but now this acceptance just meant a bit of information about which we could only shrug our shoulders.

• Our final observation concerns guarded skip **if** $x \rightarrow skip$ **fi** in component X. Its introduction, in Version 0 for X, did not affect partial correctness. The same would be true, had we used the weaker guard *true* instead of x. If, however, in our final version for component X, we replace guarded skip **if** $x \rightarrow skip$ **fi** by **if** *true* $\rightarrow skip$ **fi**, individual progress is no longer guaranteed. From this we observe, that

> weakening a guard may destroy progress.

We will return to this subject in the last technical chapter of this monograph.

22

The Non-Blocking Write Protocol

This example has been inspired by a problem from the field of real-time data processing. The rationale for that problem can be found in [Lam77, KR93]. Here we will only sketch it in brief. The problem concerns the following little two-component multiprogram

Pre :	*true*
Writer:	∗ [WRITE]
Reader:	**do** ...
	→ READ
	od

The computation proper

The Writer repeatedly writes (time-dependent) information into a data structure, which we have left anonymous. During the process of writing — i.e. during the execution of WRITE — the data structure may be inconsistent. In between two successive WRITEs the data structure is consistent. The Reader reads the data structure through READ. However, if the time interval over which a read activity extends overlaps with some write interval, the data read may be inconsistent and the Reader has to read the data structure again. The problem is to synchronize the Writer and the Reader in such a way that the Reader terminates its repetition when it has read a consistent data structure.

The problem is easily solved if we are allowed to embed writing and reading in critical sections, so that the two activities exclude each other in time. However, the specific nature of this problem is that the Writer should *not* be blocked. (For details, see [KR93].) One way to prevent the Writer from getting blocked on account of the state of the Reader is by disallowing the Writer to inspect any variable that can be changed by the Reader, and this is what we will do.

*   *
*

How can it be detected that during a READ no write activity has taken place? Since nothing is known about the speed ratio of Writer and Reader, the number of WRITEs that are initiated or completed during a READ can be anything. This observation prompts the introduction of two (fresh) integer variables to record these numbers. Thus the original multiprogram is changed into

Pre : $f=0 \,\wedge\, g=0$	
Writer: $* \,[\ f := f+1$ $;\ \{g < f\}$ WRITE $;\ g := g+1$ $]$	Reader: **do** ... $\rightarrow$ READ **od**
Inv : $g \le f$	

Version 0

The assertion and the invariant are correct by one of our Topology Lemmata.

The above annotation tells us that writing is characterized by the state $g < f$. We therefore conclude that no write activity takes place during a time interval whenever $f \le g$ holds during that entire interval. Now we observe

$f \le g$ during the entire interval

$\Leftarrow$ {algebra}

f's maximal value in the interval
$\qquad \le \quad g$'s minimal value in the interval,

and because both f and g ascend as time ascends, we now see that we are interested in f's value upon completion of a READ and in g's value upon initiation of the same READ. Let these values be x and y, respectively. We then have arrived at

$$x \leq y \ \Rightarrow \ \text{no write activity has taken place during READ},$$

which justifies the correctness of the following and final program

Pre: $f = 0 \ \wedge \ g = 0 \ \wedge \ y < x$	
Writer: $*[\ f := f + 1$	Reader: **do** $\neg(x \leq y) \rightarrow$
; WRITE	$y := g$
; $g := g + 1$	; READ
]	; $x := f$
	od

The Non-Blocking Write Protocol

Of course, there is no guarantee that the Reader will ever terminate. Whether it does depends on the distribution of WRITEs and READs over time, but if it does it has a consistent record of the data structure.

Remark We wish to mention that the above algorithm is a mini-example of a so-called snapshot algorithm. Snapshot algorithms are (mostly distributed) algorithms to detect whether a system has entered a stable state, in our example: whether the Reader has read a consistent data structure.

Several general snapshot algorithms exist [CL85], but we will not address any of them in this monograph. We will, however, address one special instance, to wit a general termination detection algorithm; it is special in the sense that it detects whether a (distributed) computation has terminated (which, indeed, is a stable state).

End of Remark.

* * *

An afterthought

The way we developed the above algorithm is completely different from what we have done so far in this monograph. No specification in terms of required annotation was given, no global or local correctness of assertions entered the game, and no use was made of the semantics of our program notation. What we did is *interpret* the computation proper as it evolves in time and translate the required result of the multiprogram into the requirement of certain non-overlapping time intervals. And then, by our analysis of the problem, we ran into the variables f, g, x, and y. End of development! And we said: "which *justifies* the correctness of the program".

However, we didn't say that this *proved* the correctness. Indeed, the question can be raised whether our presentation belongs to the domain of derivation or just to the domain of heuristics. People exposed to this presentation were invariably *convinced* of the correctness of the design, but when they were asked whether the correctness had been *proven*, hesitation crept in. And we think there is a point here. Therefore, we will now present a correctness proof according to the rules of our game, but before we can do so we must first cast the verbal problem statement into a form amenable to formal proof.

We propose to model our problem as follows — see explanation below —

Pre : $w \land \neg r$	
Writer: $* [\ w := false$	Reader: **do** $\ldots \to r := w$ **od**
$;\ w := true$	$\{?\ r\}$
$]$	

A formal specification

Variables w and r are auxiliary variables. Action WRITE happens in between $w := false$ and $w := true$. Thus the state $w \equiv true$ characterizes the consistency of the data structure. During each READ in the Reader, statement $r := w$ will be performed exactly once, and we introduce an aid, viz. a supervising daemon, which will see to it that $r := w$ is guaranteed to be performed at a moment that a simultaneous WRITE is going on, if any such moment exists. So upon termination of a READ, the state $r \equiv true$ signifies that a consistent data structure has been read. (Note that, because r is a genuine thought variable — owned by the daemon — it is not allowed to recur as a program variable in our solution.)

Once we have agreed that we thus correctly modeled and specified our problem, we can prove the correctness of the program developed in the previous section. We give the full annotation at once, leaving most of the verification to the reader.

Pre :	$w \;\wedge\; \neg r \;\wedge\; f=0 \;\wedge\; g=0 \;\wedge\; y \leq 0 \;\wedge\; y < x$	
Writer:	Reader:	
$*\,[\;\{y \leq f,\ \text{from Inv}\,\}$ $\quad f, w \;:=\; f+1, false$ $\;;\; \{g < f\}$ $\quad g, w \;:=\; g+1, true$ $\;]$	$\{y < x \;\vee\; r,\ \text{loop inv.}\}$ **do** $\neg(x \leq y) \;\rightarrow$ $\quad \{g < f \;\vee\; w,\ \text{from Inv}\}$ $\quad y := g$ $\;;\; \{y < f \;\vee\; w\}$ $\quad r := w$ $\;;\; \{y < f \;\vee\; r\}$ $\quad x := f$ $\;;\; \{y < x \;\vee\; r\}$ **od** $\{r\}$	
Inv : $\quad g < f \;\vee\; w \quad$, $\qquad\quad y \leq f \quad$, $\qquad\quad g \leq f$		

An assertional proof for the non-blocking write protocol

- The loop invariant for the Reader

  $x \leq y \;\Rightarrow\; r \qquad$, or equivalently

  $y < x \;\vee\; r \qquad$,

has been introduced in order to conclude r upon termination of the repetition. This loop invariant contains private variables (of the Reader) only.

- The assertions in the loop body of the Reader emerged from applications of the Rule of Assignment.

- Assertion $y \leq f$ in the Writer emerged from the requirement that assertion $y < f \;\vee\; w$ in the Reader be globally correct.

*   *
*

And herewith we conclude this Afterthought and this chapter.

23

Mutual Inclusion and Synchronous Communication

In the history of parallel computing, many synchronization primitives have been proposed, but only few have acquired a prominent position. A set of primitives that do have acquired such a position are C. A. R. Hoare's so-called CSP-constructs [Hoa78, Hoa85]. (CSP is an acronym for "Communicating Sequential Processes".) The constructs gracefully combine communication — i.e. information transfer — and synchronization. Below we describe them, briefly and informally.

To that end we consider a set of components connected by directed links — usually called uni-directional channels. There may be several distinct links between two components. On each link ch, two operations are defined, to wit

$ch!expr$, which is only allowed at the source side of link ch, and
$ch?v$, which is only allowed at the target side of link ch.

Argument $expr$ is an expression, and argument v is a variable of the type of $expr$.

The intention is that the component that performs $ch!expr$ — the sender —, sends the value of $expr$ along ch to the component that performs $ch?v$ — the receiver —, where this value is stored in variable v. This is the communication part of the primitives.

The synchronization part is that each of the individual operations on *ch* gives rise to blocking as long as the partner operation has not been initiated. As soon as the partner operation has been initiated as well, an activity takes place with the same effect as

$$v := expr \quad ,$$

after which both operations terminate. So the operations *ch!* and *ch?* have to "click": their executions have to "mutually include" each other in time.

There are always at least two aspects to a programming primitive: its use in program construction and its implementation. Because the use of the CSP-constructs falls outside the scope of this text — see the last section of this chapter —, we are left with their implementation, which constitutes a useful programming exercise in its own right. Before embarking on this exercise, however, we first try to construct a suitable specification for the CSP-constructs.

*   *
*

The most intriguing and interesting part of the cooperation between *ch!expr* and *ch?v* is the synchronization part, i.e. the mutual inclusion of their activities. Because this is what we shall focus on, we forget about the parameters and thus about the information transfer. Projected on the *ch* -operations, one component then has the form

$$* [\, ch! \,]$$

and the other has the form

$$* [\, ch? \,] \quad .$$

From our operational description we see that a component that is about to initiate a *ch* -operation is not allowed to proceed as long as the partner operation has not been initiated. We also see that if neither of the two components is engaged in a *ch* -operation, we have

the total number of completed *ch!*- operations

=

the total number of completed *ch?*- operations.

We can now specify the synchronization behaviour through two variables *x* and *y*, where $x := x + 1$ "announces" the initiation of the next *ch!*, and $y := y + 1$ the initiation of the next *ch?*.

Pre : $x = 0 \ \wedge \ y = 0$	
A: $* [\, x := x + 1$	B: $* [\, y := y + 1$
$; \{? \ x = y\}$	$; \{? \ y = x\}$
$ch!$	$ch?$
$]$	$]$

A specification for the CSP-constructs

The original fragments $ch!$ and $ch?$ have been extended with the (terminating) assignments to x and y , respectively, for reasons of specification. Now our task is to superimpose synchronization code on the above program so as to guarantee the correctness of the two queried assertions.

The Mutual Inclusion Problem

The CSP-constructs form an important incentive for our interest in what has been called the mutual inclusion problem. This problem can be specified as follows. (The specification slightly differs from the above specification for the CSP-constructs, for a minor reason to be dealt with shortly. The two problems can, however, be solved in exactly the same way, and we encourage the reader to do so after he has studied this chapter.)

Pre : $x = 0 \ \wedge \ y = 0$	
A: $* [\, \{? \ x = y\} \ S$	B: $* [\, \{? \ y = x\} \ T$
$; x := x + 1$	$; y := y + 1$
$]$	$]$

A specification for Mutual Inclusion

The reason for rendering the specification as we did is that in this way it very much resembles two problems we addressed earlier, viz. the Handshake Protocol and the problem of Phase Synchronization for two components. We recall their specifications.

Pre : $\quad x = 0 \ \wedge \ y = 0$	
A: $\ast [\, x := x + 1 \,]$	B: $\ast [\, \{? \ y = x\} \ T$
	$; \ y := y + 1$
	$]$

A specification for the Handshake Protocol

Pre : $\quad x = 0 \ \wedge \ y = 0$	
A: $\ast [\, \{? \ x \leq y\} \ S$	B: $\ast [\, \{? \ y \leq x\} \ T$
$; \ x := x + 1$	$; \ y := y + 1$
$]$	$]$

A specification for Phase Synchronization

These three problems form a weird family, and the solutions we ourselves know for them all look alike but differ in delicate, as yet nonunderstood details. Therefore we kindly invite the reader who feels challenged, to create order in this "mess" and to present us with a derivation of the Mutual Inclusion Algorithm that is far more beautiful than the one we are about to deliver.

There is, however, some order in the family. From the specifications we see that MI — the Mutual Inclusion problem — requires the strongest annotation, stronger than HP and stronger than PS. So each solution for MI is a solution for HP and PS as well, be it at the expense of a potential reduction of the parallelism (cf. Chapter 17).

One more result with regard to this family is known to us, namely that any solution to PS can be used to solve MI (roughly by doing the synchronization in PS twice in succession). It is Perry D. Moerland to whom we owe this theorem [Moe93]. The algorithms for MI resulting from the application of this theorem are, however, a little more complicated than we would hope for.

In Chapter 17 we explained how strengthening of the annotation may give rise to reduction of the storage space. In view of the circumstance that HP (and PS) can be solved at the expense of just one boolean variable, and that MI has the strongest annotation, the challenge is to derive a solution for MI that uses just a single, boolean variable. It was our student Frans W. van der Sommen who accepted this challenge and succeeded [Som94]. Here we present what is essentially his derivation.

Deriving a Mutual Inclusion Algorithm

We first copy the specification:

Pre : $x = 0 \wedge y = 0$	
A: $* [\{? \; x = y\} \; S$	B: $* [\; \{? \; y = x\} \; T$
$; x := x + 1$	$; y := y + 1$
$]$	$]$

This time, we wish to be very explicit about where we are allowed to superimpose synchronization code. We do so by the technique of using placeholders (cf. Chapter 10). Thus, our more explicit specification becomes

Pre : $x = 0 \wedge y = 0$	
A: $* [\; S_0$	B: $* [\; T_0$
$; \{? \; x = y\}$	$; \{? \; y = x\}$
S_1	T_1
$; x := x + 1$	$; y := y + 1$
$; S_2$	$; T_2$
$]$	$]$

Version 0

The only thing that matters about S and T is that they have precondition $x = y$, i.e. that S precedes S_1 and that T precedes T_1. Because they do not play any rôle in the derivation, we will from here onwards leave them out.

*   *
*

Right at the outset we can already see that it will be quite hopeless to strive for a symmetric solution, at least if we wish to arrive at a solution with just one boolean. Namely, from the specification we conclude that MB , given by

MB: $x \leq y + 1 \wedge y \leq x + 1$,

will be a system invariant — and a multibound! — of any solution we may come up with. A symmetric solution is quite likely to display all three possible values for the difference $x - y$, so that we can forget about the one-boolean solution. Within the freedom specified by MB , there is another symmetric possibility, viz.

$$x \leq y \ \land \ y \leq x \quad ,$$

or: $x = y$, but a solution obeying this invariant is bound to suffer from total deadlock: each of the individual assignments to x and y is guaranteed to falsify $x = y$. (See also our experiences with Phase Synchronization, Chapter 17.)

So let us break the symmetry and head for an algorithm with system invariant, say,

P: $\qquad x \leq y \ \land \ y \leq x+1$.

This requires $x+1 = y$ to be a correct pre-assertion of $x := x+1$ in component A, and $y = x$ to be a correct pre-assertion of $y := y+1$ in B. As a result, choosing a skip for S_1 is not an option, but choosing a skip for T_1 is, and this is what we will try to do. Thus we arrive at

Pre : $\quad x = 0 \ \land \ y = 0$	
A: $* \, [\, S_0$	B: $* \, [\, T_0$
$; \, \{? \ x = y, \ \text{Note}\}$	$; \, \{? \ y = x\}$
$\quad S_1$	$\quad y := y+1$
$; \, \{? \ x+1 = y\}$	$; \, T_2$
$\quad x := x+1$	$\quad]$
$; \, S_2$	
$\quad]$	
Inv : $\quad P$: $\quad x \leq y \ \land \ y \leq x+1$	

Version 1

*   *
*

According to our convention for dealing with queried items, we now deal with assertion $x = y$ in A, temporarily forgetting about the other queried items (cf. Chapter 10).

Note "$x = y$" in A
Since $x = y$ holds initially, we decide to make it an invariant of A's repetition, i.e. we choose S_0 to be a skip and we choose for A

A: $* [\{? \ x = y\}$

$\qquad S_1$

$\qquad ; \{? \ x+1=y\}$

$\qquad x := x+1$

$\qquad ; S_2$

$\qquad \{? \ x = y\}$

$\qquad]$.

We now handle the assertions $x = y$ in one go.

L: The first assertion $x = y$ follows from Pre and the post-assertion of the loop body; for the second assertion $x = y$ to be locally correct we choose S_2 to be a skip.

G: Since statement $y := y+1$ in component B will certainly falsify all three assertions in A, we resort to the Rule of Disjointness, giving the three assertions in A co-assertion c and providing $y := y+1$ in B with additional pre-assertion $\neg c$.

End of Note.

Thus we obtain

Pre : $x = 0 \ \wedge \ y = 0$	
A: $* [\{x = y\} \ \{? \ c, \text{Note } 0\}$ $\qquad S_1$ $\qquad ; \{? \ x+1 = y\} \ \{? \ c, \text{Note } 0\}$ $\qquad x := x+1$ $\qquad ; \{x = y\} \ \{? \ c, \text{Note } 0\}$ $\qquad]$	B: $* [\ T_0$ $\qquad ; \{? \ y = x\} \ \{? \ \neg c, \text{Note } 1\}$ $\qquad y := y+1$ $\qquad ; T_2$ $\qquad]$
Inv : P : $x \leq y \ \wedge \ y \leq x+1$	

Version 2

$*$ $*$

$\qquad *$

We handle the three assertions c in A simultaneously.

Note 0 "assertions c" in A

G: We handle the global correctness by the self-imposed constraint that statements $c := \mathit{false}$ are disallowed in B,   i.e. confined to A.

L: Apparently, c has to be an invariant of A's repetition. Therefore, we strengthen precondition Pre with c. As far as the assertions c in A are concerned, S_1 could now be chosen to be a skip. This, however, is not acceptable: in order to guarantee B's progress, we will have to add a statement $c := false$ somewhere. In view of our self-imposed constraint, such a statement can only be accommodated in A, i.e. in S_1. Thus, our only possible choice for S_1 is a fragment of the form

$\quad$ S_1

$\quad$; $c := false$

$\quad$; **if** $c \to skip$ **fi** .

And this settles the local correctness of the assertions c in A.

End of Note 0.

Note 1 "$\neg c$" in B

G: We see to it that statements $c := true$ will be confined to B.

L: We prefix the assertion with guarded skip **if** $\neg c \to skip$ **fi** , i.e. we choose T_0 to be of the shape

$\quad$ T_0

$\quad$; **if** $\neg c \to skip$ **fi** .

End of Note 1.

Assembling all our decisions, we get

Pre : $x = 0 \wedge y = 0 \wedge c$	
A: $*\,[\ \{x = y\}\ \{c\}$ $\quad$ S_1 $\quad$; $c := false$ $\quad$; **if** $c \to skip$ **fi** $\quad$; $\{?\ x + 1 = y,\ \text{Note 0}\}\ \{c\}$ $\quad$ $x := x + 1$ $\quad$ $\{x = y\}\ \{c\}$ $\quad]$	B: $*\,[\ T_0$ $\quad$; **if** $\neg c \to skip$ **fi** $\quad$; $\{?\ y = x,\ \text{Note 1}\}\ \{\neg c\}$ $\quad$ $y := y + 1$ $\quad$; T_2 $\quad]$
Inv : P : $x \le y \wedge y \le x + 1$	
Constraints: $\quad c := false$ confined to A $\qquad\qquad\quad c := true$ confined to B	

Version 3

* *
*

Note 0   "$x+1=y$" in A

L: Prefix guarded skip **if** $c \rightarrow$ *skip* **fi** with $\neg c \lor x+1=y$.

G: Correct by the Rule of Disjointness.

End of Note 0.

Note 1   "$y=x$" in B

L: Prefix guarded skip **if** $\neg c \rightarrow$ *skip* **fi** with $c \lor y=x$.

G: Correct by the Rule of Disjointness.

End of Note 1.

Thus, our next version becomes

Pre : $x=0 \land y=0 \land c$
A: $*[\{x=y\} \{c\}$ $\quad S_1$ $; c:= false$ $; \{? \neg c \lor x+1=y, \text{ Note } 0\}$ **if** $c \rightarrow$ *skip* **fi** $; \{x+1=y\} \{c\}$ $\quad x:=x+1$ $; \{x=y\} \{c\}$ $\quad]$
B: $*[T_0$ $; \{? c \lor y=x, \text{ Note } 1\}$ **if** $\neg c \rightarrow$ *skip* **fi** $; \{y=x\} \{\neg c\}$ $\quad y:=y+1$ $; T_2$ $\quad]$
Inv : P : $x \leq y \land y \leq x+1$
Constraints: $c:= false$ confined to A $\qquad\qquad\quad c:= true$ confined to B

Version 4

$$*   *$$
$$*$$

Note 0   "$\neg c \lor x+1=y$" in A

L: Correct by the preceding $c := false$.

G: $-$ $\{y=x \land \neg c\}$ $y:=y+1$ in B does not falsify the target assertion.

  $-$ $c := true$ in B will be constrained, viz. to

$$\{?\ x+1=y\}\ c := true   .$$

End of Note 0.

Note 1   "$c \lor y=x$" in B

Since $c \lor y=x$ holds initially, we choose skip for T_0 and make the target assertion an invariant of B's repetition, i.e. we consider

B: $*[\ \{?\ c \lor y=x\}$

  if $\neg c \to skip$ **fi**

  $;\ \{y=x\}\ \{\neg c\}$

  $y:=y+1$

  $;\ T_2$

  $\{?\ c \lor y=x\}$

  $]   ,$

and we handle the two queried assertions in one go.

L: Assertion $c \lor y=x$ holds initially and T_2 can establish it via $c := true$ — which accords with the Constraints as recorded in Version 4.

G: $-$ $\{c\}$ $x:=x+1$ in A does not falsify $c \lor y=x$.

  $-$ $c := false$ in A does not falsify $c \lor y=x$ either, provided it has pre-assertion $y=x$. Therefore, we choose a skip for S_1 .

End of Note 1.

The only remaining question is whether choice $c := true$ for T_2 satisfies the extra constraint introduced in Note 0, i.e. does T_2 have pre-assertion $x+1=y$? We leave to the reader the proof that, indeed, $x+1=y$ is a correct pre-assertion to T_2 — thanks to its having $\neg c$ as a co-assertion.

And this completes our derivation of a solution to the Mutual Inclusion problem. Assembling the choices made in Note 1 above, we arrive at the following, fully annotated algorithm, in which we have re-inserted the original S and T from the computation proper.

Pre : $\quad x = 0 \;\wedge\; y = 0 \;\wedge\; c$	
A: $\ast [\; \{x = y\}\; \{c\}\; S$	B: $\ast [\; \{c \vee\; y = x\}$
$\quad ;\; c := false$	$\qquad$ if $\neg c \rightarrow skip$ fi
$\quad ;\; \{\neg c \;\vee\; x + 1 = y\}$	$\qquad ;\; \{y = x\}\; \{\neg c\}\; T$
$\qquad$ if $c \rightarrow skip$ fi	$\qquad ;\; y := y + 1$
$\quad ;\; \{x + 1 = y\}\; \{c\}$	$\qquad ;\; \{x + 1 = y\}\; \{\neg c\}$
$\qquad x := x + 1$	$\qquad c := true$
$\qquad \{x = y\}\; \{c\}$	$\qquad \{c \vee\; y = x\}$
$\quad]$	$\qquad]$
Inv : $\quad P : \quad x \leq y \;\wedge\; y \leq x + 1$	

A (fully annotated) Mutual Inclusion Algorithm

Obviously, there is no danger of total deadlock, so that thanks to our multi-bound *MB* individual progress is guaranteed as well. And herewith we conclude our derivation.

Three (in)comparable algorithms

Earlier in this chapter, we confronted the specifications for Mutual Inclusion, the Handshake Protocol, and the problem of Phase Synchronization with each other, and we concluded that MI was the most demanding specification. The fact that MI is the hardest one becomes manifest in the derivation. In our earlier derivation for HP (cf. Chapter 16) and PS (cf. Chapter 17), we were able to carry out most of the development in terms of the variables x and y, only switching to the boolean domain at the very end, via a coordinate transformation. However, we did not succeed in replicating that pattern here (and we think we never will). The Mutual Inclusion algorithm is a very delicate one, and its derivation hardly allows any manoeuvring space; we are led to believe that it is almost uniquely determined in all its details. This latter observation does not pertain to the other two problems, which permit various solutions, for instance ... the Mutual Inclusion algorithm.

We conclude by displaying the raw code of the three algorithms as developed in the course of this monograph. They all maintain

$$x \leq y \;\wedge\; y \leq x + 1$$

and satisfy their specification. They all look similar, but differ in all details, such as the order of statements, the occurrence of negation symbols. It is a weird family indeed, and we suggest the reader never try to remember one of these algorithms by heart but to focus on their development instead.

Pre : $x = 0 \wedge y = 0 \wedge c$	
A: $*[\ \{x = y\}\ S$	B: $*[\ \textbf{if}\ \neg c \rightarrow skip\ \textbf{fi}$
$;\ c := false$	$;\ \{y = x\}\ T$
$;\ \textbf{if}\ c \rightarrow skip\ \textbf{fi}$	$;\ y := y + 1$
$;\ x := x + 1$	$;\ c := true$
$]$	$]$

Mutual Inclusion

Pre : $x = 0 \wedge y = 0 \wedge \neg c$	
A: $*[\ \textbf{if}\ c \rightarrow skip\ \textbf{fi}$	B: $*[\ \textbf{if}\ \neg c \rightarrow skip\ \textbf{fi}$
$;\ x := x + 1$	$;\ \{y = x\}\ T$
$;\ c := false$	$;\ y := y + 1$
$]$	$;\ c := true$
	$]$

Handshaking

Pre : $x = 0 \wedge y = 0 \wedge \neg c$	
A: $*[\ \{x \leq y\}\ S$	B: $*[\ \{y \leq x\}\ T$
$;\ \textbf{if}\ c \rightarrow skip\ \textbf{fi}$	$;\ y := y + 1$
$;\ x := x + 1$	$;\ c := true$
$;\ c := false$	$;\ \textbf{if}\ \neg c \rightarrow skip\ \textbf{fi}$
$]$	$]$

Phase Synchronization

A few words on CSP-programming

Just as has been the case with Dijkstra's P- and V-operations on semaphores, Hoare's CSP-constructs have, ever since their emergence, raised a lot of interest in the computing community. They — and variations on them — are discussed in almost any foundational text on synchronization primitives, and they have been supplied with a variety of semantic rules: [Mar81, Hoa85, CM88, Mil89, AO91, Sch97], to mention just a few. Also, we see them shown at work in programming, sometimes even impressively so [Hof94]. Unfortunately, however, and unlike with P- and V- operations, a *simple* and *uniform* discipline for program *derivation* based on these constructs has not been developed so far. And yet we believe that this should be possible. And we also believe that the Owicki/Gries theory can be an important formal ingredient of such a discipline. This may seem surprising.

The Owicki/Gries theory has, from the very moment of its emergence, held the stigma of only being good enough for the a-posteriori verification of shared-memory programs. (We hope that this monograph will help in strongly refuting this point of view.) At the same time, synchronous communication as embodied by the CSP-constructs, almost by design finds its main application in *distributed* computing. This, in combination with the stigma, may provide a historical explanation for the lack of influence that the theory of Owicki and Gries has had on program derivation based on synchronous communication. And this is a pity, but at the same time a challenge for future research.

Let us explain, in just a few words, where our optimism comes from. Many multiprograms, whether distributed or not, are to be mastered and understood through system invariants. System invariants usually induce required preconditions for statements. These preconditions have to be (made) locally and globally correct, and thus the whole Owicki/Gries theory enters the picture.

The CSP-constructs provide us with an additional, extremely simple way to establish the local correctness of an assertion: for instance, when $ch!expr$ and $ch?v$ click, we can infer the local correctness of the assertion in

$ch?v \ \{v = expr\}$.

Of course, as in any multiprogram, the issue of progress remains. Here one must see to it that the communication patterns that can be displayed by a component, can be adequately matched by the rest of the system. Mild forms of trace theory or regularity calculus, and, last but far from least, the application of variant functions, might turn out to be helpful here.

24

A Simple Election Algorithm

We consider a multiprogram with a positive and finite number of components. Component i has a private boolean variable $y.i$ and it does just one thing, namely it performs *one* as yet unknown assignment to this variable. The problem is to synchronize the components in such a way that they all terminate and leave the system in a final state satisfying[†]

$$(0) \qquad \langle\, \#j :: y.j \,\rangle = 1 \qquad .$$

However, the problem is to be solved subject to two more constraints, to wit

- that the final algorithm be entirely expressed in one-point atomic statements
- that the solution be symmetric in the components.

(This last constraint excludes that some components can get preference to others in finding their final y- value equal to *true*.)

This is not such a difficult problem, and the reader may try to invent or construct a solution for himself. We will give a derivation from scratch, completely according to the rules of the game and without pulling rabbits out of the hat.

[†]Dummies range over the component names and $\#$ stands for "the number of".

*   *
*

The first thing we do is render the problem a little more formal in order to make it amenable to manipulation and calculation. To begin with, there is the assignment to $y.i$. Let it be

$$y.i := B.i$$

for some expression $B.i$ still to be determined. Whether or not postcondition (0) is established by the assignments $y.i := B.i$ will depend on our choice of the expressions $B.i$. If we insist that component i have post-assertion $y.i \equiv B.i$, we will be able to tackle (0) in terms of the expressions B, which grant us more manipulative freedom. We thus propose to consider

Pre :	$true$
Comp.i:	$y.i := B.i$
	$\{?\ y.i \equiv B.i\}$
Post :	$?\ \langle\, \#j :: y.j \,\rangle = 1$

Version 0:   A formal specification

*   *
*

From the post-assertions of the individual components we conclude that a postcondition of the multiprogram is

$$\langle\, \forall j :: y.j \equiv B.j \,\rangle   ,$$

so that required postcondition (0) can be rewritten into the equivalent

(1) $\langle\, \#j :: B.j \,\rangle = 1$.

Remark At this point many a reader might just "see" a simple and elegant choice for the B's that satisfies (1). With full respect for these readers, we will nevertheless derive a suitable shape for the B's , for the benefit of the readers who don't "see".
End of Remark.

Formula (1) is rather a packed formula. It is equivalent to the conjunction of

(2a) $\langle\, \exists j :: B.j \,\rangle$ and

(2b) $\langle\, \forall i,j :: B.i \wedge B.j \Rightarrow i = j \,\rangle$.

Viewed as an equation in B, (2a) doesn't provide much of a clue. So let us focus on (2b).

Choosing *false* for the B's solves (2b) irrespective of the consequent $i = j$. But this choice is no good for (2a). So the clue is in the consequent $i = j$. Both i and j are (arbitrary) component names, and the question is how one can conclude the equality of two things taken from an arbitrary domain. To the best of our knowledge, the only mathematical law that can do this for us is the transitivity of the equality operator. This requires that a third element, v say, enter the picture; and this settles our choice for the B's :

$$B.i \equiv v = i \, .$$

Thus, (2b) is satisfied by construction. As for (2a), component i can establish it by the assignment $v := i$, which, in view of the required symmetry between the components, is the only choice possible. Once established, (2a) will not be falsified again.

Thus, (2a) and (2b), and therefore (1), and therefore (0), have become correct postconditions to the multiprogram, and this takes us to the next version, in which for caution's sake we include placeholders S and T:

Pre :	*true*
Comp.i:	$S.i$
	$; v := i$
	$; T.i$
	$; y.i := v = i$
	$\{? \ y.i \equiv v = i\}$
Post :	$\langle \#j :: y.j \rangle = 1$

Version 1

*   *

*

We are left with assertion $y.i \equiv v = i$, which is locally correct by construction. Its global correctness is endangered by statement $v := j$ in Comp.j, $j \neq i$. We therefore investigate:

$$(y.i \equiv v = i) \ \Rightarrow \ (v := j).(y.i \equiv v = i)$$

$\equiv \qquad$ {substitution, using $i \neq j$}

$$(y.i \equiv v = i) \ \Rightarrow \ \neg y.i$$

$\equiv$ {predicate calculus}

   $\neg y.i \ \lor \ v \neq i$.

As a result, the global correctness of assertion $y.i \equiv v = i$ in Comp.i is not for free. We therefore strengthen the annotation (cf. Chapter 6) by

- giving target assertion $y.i \equiv v = i$ co-assertion $f.i$,
- giving $v := j$ pre-assertion $g.j$, for each j, $j \neq i$, and
- requiring that, for all i

(3) $\langle \forall j : j \neq i : f.i \land g.j \Rightarrow \neg y.i \lor v \neq i \rangle$

be a system invariant.
We will thus be considering a multiprogram of the form

Pre :	*true*
Comp.i:	$S.i$
	; {? $g.i$}
	$v := i$
	; $T.i$
	; $y.i := v = i$
	$\{y.i \equiv v = i\} \ \{? \ f.i\}$
Inv :	? (3) for all i
Post :	$\langle \#j :: y.j \rangle = 1$

Version 2

*   *

*

The most convenient way to make the rather awkward looking (3) into a system invariant is to bend it into a mathematical theorem, i.e. to make it just *true*. This is quite possible, because we can solve (3) for $f.i$:

   (3)

$\equiv$ {predicate calculus}

   $\langle \forall j : j \neq i : f.i \Rightarrow \neg g.j \lor \neg y.i \lor v \neq i \rangle$

$\equiv$ {predicate calculus}

   $f.i \Rightarrow \langle \forall j : j \neq i : \neg g.j \lor \neg y.i \lor v \neq i \rangle$.

Because $f.i$ was introduced as an assertion, we follow our standard rule of thumb and choose it as weak as possible, i.e. we opt for an $f.i$ defined by

$$\langle\, \forall j : j \neq i : \neg g.j \lor \neg y.i \lor v \neq i \,\rangle \quad .$$

Taking furthermore into account that $f.i$ has co-assertion $y.i \equiv v = i$, we can simplify it to

$f.i$: $\langle\, \forall j : j \neq i : \neg g.j \lor v \neq i \,\rangle$

(thus eliminating its dependence on $y.i$). Having thus satisfied (3), we obtain

Pre :	$true$
Comp.i:	$S.i$
	$; \{?\ g.i\}\ v := i$
	$;\ T.i$
	$;\ y.i := v = i$
	$\{y.i \ \equiv\ v = i\}\ \{?\ f.i\}$
Post :	$\langle\, \#j :: y.j \,\rangle = 1$

Version 3

*   *
*

Now we are close to the end. We represent $g.i$ by a boolean variable private to Comp.i and give it initial value $true$. Then a skip for $S.i$ suffices for the correctness of assertion $g.i$. As for $f.i$, i.e. $\langle\, \forall j : j \neq i : \neg g.j \lor v \neq i \,\rangle$, its local correctness will be realized by a guarded skip in $T.i$, and its global correctness is for free, both under statements $v := j$ and under statements $g.j := false$ — to be included in $T.j$ for reasons of progress. The final, fully annotated program thus reads:

Pre : $\langle \forall j :: g.j \rangle$

Comp.i: $\{g.i\}$

$v := i$

; $g.i := false$

; **if** $\langle \forall j : j \neq i : \neg g.j \lor v \neq i \rangle$

$\rightarrow$ *skip* **fi**

; $\{\langle \forall j : j \neq i : \neg g.j \lor v \neq i \rangle\}$

$y.i := v = i$

$\{y.i \equiv v = i\} \{\langle \forall j : j \neq i : \neg g.j \lor v \neq i \rangle\}$

Post : $\langle \#j :: y.j \rangle = 1$

A Simple Election Algorithm

*   *

*

Two issues remain, viz. progress and the grain of atomicity. We consider atomicity first. The only atomic statements in our solution that are not one-point are the guarded skips. However, since each of the individual conjuncts in the guards is globally correct, the Guard Conjunction Lemma tells us that the conjunction can be evaluated conjunctwise. So the guarded skip in Comp.i can be replaced with, for instance,

for $j : j \neq i$ **do**

if $\neg g.j \lor v \neq i \rightarrow$ *skip* **fi**

od   .

Now the individual guarded skips are the only statements that are not one-point yet: their guards refer to both $g.j$ and v. There is a theorem, however, that we owe to Mohamed G. Gouda and that has not been mentioned in this monograph yet (Peccavimus!), which says that a disjunction may be evaluated disjunct-wise without impairing the total correctness of the algorithm, whenever one of the disjuncts is globally correct. Gouda's theorem clearly applies in this case. Thus our algorithm can be expressed in one-point atomic statements.

Because these program transformations preserve progress properties, we can carry out the progress argument in terms of the coarse-grained algorithm — which is easier. We will prove that each individual component terminates. To that end we first observe that at most one component can be blocked in its guarded skip (this due to disjunct $v \neq i$). Now let Comp.i be blocked indefinitely. Then all other components terminate and together establish the — stable — correctness of $\langle\, \forall j : j \neq i : \neg g.j \,\rangle$, thus making Comp.i's guard stably *true*. As a result, Comp.i will terminate.

Herewith we conclude the treatment of this algorithm.

*   *
*

There is one final remark we wish to make on our choice for $f.i$, which was

$$\langle\, \forall j : j \neq i : \neg g.j \,\vee\, v \neq i \,\rangle \quad .$$

Because $f.i$ occurred as an assertion, we chose it as weak as possible. Had we not insisted on adhering to this rule of thumb, we could have selected the stronger

$$\langle\, \forall j : j \neq i : \neg g.j \,\rangle \quad ,$$

or the other stronger

$$\langle\, \forall j : j \neq i : v \neq i \,\rangle \quad .$$

The first choice would have given rise to a guarded skip

(*)   **if** $\langle\, \forall j : j \neq i : \neg g.j \,\rangle \rightarrow$ *skip* **fi**

and the second to

(**)   **if** $\langle\, \forall j : j \neq i : v \neq i \,\rangle \rightarrow$ *skip* **fi**   ,

instead of the one in our current algorithm. With (*) the algorithm would still enjoy all progress properties, albeit that the amount of parallelism would reduce drastically: guarded skip (*) acts as a barrier that can only be passed when all components are about to execute it. With (**), however, the program would become incorrect in its progress properties, since one component would fail to terminate.

So here we have another example illustrating why assertions should not lightheartedly be chosen too strong. During the development of the algorithm we were therefore keen on finding the *weakest* $f.i$ satisfying (3), and it goes without saying that in playing this game, well-versedness in the predicate calculus is of decisive importance.

25

Peterson's General Mutual Exclusion Algorithm

As we already pointed out earlier, the concept of mutual exclusion historically was one of the first concepts for dealing with the enormous complexity brought about by the concurrent execution of cooperating sequential programs. Along with the emergence of the concept, the quest for mutual exclusion algorithms began, and a continuous stream of such algorithms has seen the light, ever since the first general mutual exclusion algorithm was conceived [Dij65]. (For an overview, the reader may consult [Ray86].)

It can be safely stated that all those designs embodied a great intellectual achievement. One reason for their complexity is that they invariably had to be expressed in terms of one-point statements only, simply because that was required by the underlying machine architecture. (A mitigating circumstance is that, in this kind of game, one has always required solutions to be symmetric in the components, which helps bridling the complexity.)

In composing a monograph like this, we feel it both a challenge and a bounden duty to address the general mutual exclusion problem at least once, simply to test our proposed method of multiprogramming on an apparently larger scale. In this chapter we take up the challenge by presenting a formal derivation of the simplest mutual exclusion algorithm that we know of, viz. Peterson's algorithm for N $(2 \leq N)$ components [Pet81]. We should mention right at the start, however, that while Peterson's algorithm for two components has conquered the world, this does not hold for his general solution. This general solution is outperformed in almost every quantitative respect by many of its predecessors, but that is irrelevant here.

*   *
*

Thus far, most of our derivations have been rather "flat", taking place at one and the same level of abstraction. In our current example this is no longer convenient: it is the occurrence of the number N that may call for a more macroscopic investigation of the problem first, most notably for some sort of inductive argument. Of course, there is a huge variety of ways in which one may tackle the mutual exclusion problem via mathematical induction, but we will confine ourselves to just one very simple way.

In each mutual exclusion algorithm, the components will have shape

$$* [\ ncs$$
$$; In$$
$$; cs$$
$$; Out$$
$$]\ .$$

Here, In and Out are placeholders for the protocol by which mutually exclusive access to the critical section cs is to be realized. We observe that

the number of components engaged in
program fragment "$In;\ cs;\ Out$"

$$(*)\qquad \leq$$

$$N\qquad ,$$

whereas it is required that

the number of components engaged in
program fragment "cs"

$$(**)\qquad \leq$$

$$1\ .$$

Relation $(*)$ is given and relation $(**)$ is demanded. The important differences between the two are in the upperbounds N and 1, and in the program fragments specified. So why not replace these by variables k and $Section.k$ respectively, and set ourselves the goal of decreasing k under invariance of

the number of components engaged in
program fragment "$Section.k$"

$$\leq$$

k .

Thanks to (*), this relation holds for

k, $Section.k = N$, "In; cs; Out",

whereas it yields the desired result (**) for

k, $Section.k = 1$, "cs".

With $nc.k$ short for "the number of components engaged in program fragment $Section.k$ ", the induction step is readily specified by

$Section.(k+1)$: $entry.k$
; $Section.k$
; $exit.k$
Inv : $nc.(k+1) \leq k+1$,
? $nc.k \leq k$

Specification of $Section.(k+1)$, for $1 \leq k$

Here, $entry.k$ and $exit.k$ are placeholders for the protocol by which the required invariant $nc.k \leq k$ is to be realized.

In this terminology, our mutual exclusion algorithm can now be described by

    Comp.p: * [ncs

           ; $Section.N$

         ]   ,

with for $Section$ a recursive routine of the form

    $Section.(k+1)$:

            if $k+1=1 \rightarrow cs$

           [] $k+1>1 \rightarrow$

                $entry.k$

                ; $Section.k$

                ; $exit.k$

         fi   .

In order to stay closer to Peterson's original encoding of the algorithm, we eliminate $Section$ from the program text by repeated unfolding and thus arrive at

```
Pre :    true

Comp.p:  * [ ncs
            ; |[ var k : int;
               k := N − 1
            ; do k ≠ 0 →
                  entry.k
                ; k := k − 1
              od
            ; cs
            ; do k ≠ N − 1 →
                  k := k + 1
                ; exit.k
              od
              ]|
          ]
```

Macroscopic view on Peterson's algorithm

*   *

*

The only thing we are left with is the design of the *entry-* and *exit-* protocols as specified by *Section*, but before doing so we first discuss some notational issues.

We did not bother to write *ncs.p* and *cs.p* in Comp.p, although these fragments may very well vary from component to component. Neither did we write *entry.k.p* and *exit.k.p*, although these pieces of code may vary from component to component as well — be it only in a symmetrical fashion. We should keep in mind, though, that we shall be developing the *entry-* and *exit-* protocols as they will manifest themselves for arbitrary Comp.p. (With this strategy, symmetry will be guaranteed!)

Also, we will design *entry.k* and *exit.k* for one particular, but arbitrary value of k in the range $1 \leq k < N$. Since it is not clear whether the required synchronization can be achieved independent of k's value, we must be prepared to let *entry.k* and *exit.k* depend on k. In particular we will, therefore, introduce *distinct* sets of — fresh — synchronization variables for distinct values of k. The advantage of this choice is that assertions pertaining to the set for k are globally correct under manipulations on the variables of the set for i, $i \neq k$. This creates the freedom to notationally suppress the dependence on k. Thus we will, for instance, write "f", but we have to bear in mind that "$f.k$" is meant.

With these notational conventions, we can now formalize the specification of $Section.(k+1)$ as follows — explanation below —

Pre : $f = 0$	
$Section.(k+1)$:	$f := f + 1$
(in Comp.p)	; $Section.k$
	; $f := f - 1$
Inv : $nc.(k+1) \leq k+1$,	
? $f \leq k$	

Version 0

Variable f is introduced to record the value of $nc.k$, i.e. the number of components engaged in $Section.k$. Statements $f := f + 1$ and $f := f - 1$ also serve as our first approximation to $entry.k$ and $exit.k$, respectively.

*   *   *

The invariance of $f \leq k$ is taken care of right away by the following program

Pre : $f = 0$	
$Section.(k+1)$:	if $f < k \rightarrow f := f + 1$ fi
(in Comp.p)	; $Section.k$
	; $f := f - 1$
Inv : $nc.(k+1) \leq k+1$,	
$f \leq k$	

Version 1

(Note that nothing of the given $nc.(k+1) \leq k+1$ has been taken into account yet.)

The above program, however, suffers two shortcomings:

- One — easily seen —: the statements are far from one-point. In particular the guarded statement is far too coarse-grained.

- Two — less easily seen —: the algorithm lacks the desired progress properties. In particular, individual starvation of a component is not excluded. This can be seen as follows. Since $f \leq k$ is an invariant, this is a correct pre-assertion to the guarded skip as well, but nothing stronger than that can be inferred about this precondition. So the system state may satisfy $f = k$, in which case some component may become blocked in the guarded statement and then remain so, because by the cyclic character of the components it may be overtaken infinitely often by other components.

We now focus on the first shortcoming, i.e. on unraveling the guarded statement, and address progress issues later.

Remark This order of coping with the two shortcomings is not random at all. As we have seen a couple of times before, unraveling too coarse-grained statements is realized by Guard Strengthening. If in our current situation, we would try to remedy the lack of progress first — most likely by guard weakening! — we would still be left with the too coarse-grained guarded statement, the unraveling of which — via Guard Strengthening! — might undo the accomplished progress properties again, and thus necessitate yet another guard weakening. Our general strategy therefore is to focus on progress only after everything else has been done. Gathering from experience we know that this usually works out well. We will, however, return to this issue in the very last technical chapter of this monograph. **End** of Remark.

For the purpose of unraveling the guarded statement, we introduce a fresh variable g ($g.k$) to take over the rôle of f; it is related to f by $f \leq g$ — inspired by the shape of the guard.   Our topology lemmata then dictate the next version.

Pre : $\quad f = 0 \ \wedge \ g = 0$
$\quad$ *Section.*$(k+1)$: $\quad g := g+1$ $\quad\quad$ (in Comp.p) $\quad$; $\{f < g\}$ $\quad\quad\quad\quad\quad\quad$ **if** $g \leq k \rightarrow f := f+1$ **fi** $\quad\quad\quad\quad\quad\quad$; *Section.k* $\quad\quad\quad\quad\quad\quad$; $f,g := f-1, g-1$
Inv : $\quad nc.(k+1) \ \leq \ k+1,$ $\quad\quad\quad f \leq k,$ $\quad\quad\quad f \leq g$

Version 2

(Note that, still, nothing of the given $nc.(k+1) \leq k+1$ has been taken into account yet, but this will change shortly.)

Assertion $f < g$ follows from the program topology, and because it is a correct pre-assertion for the guarded statement we have

$$f < k \;\Leftarrow\; g \leq k \quad,$$

so that the transition from Version 1 to Version 2 indeed comprises a guard-strengthening, but only a cautiously designed minimal one[†]. We could now eliminate f, but we leave it in a little longer for further discussion.

$$* \qquad *$$
$$*$$

By the above guard strengthening, progress has been damaged even more severely: now total deadlock is possible (viz. when all $k+1$ components that can initiate $Section.(k+1)$ first perform $g := g+1$). So now the time has come to weaken the guard. We propose to replace the current guarded statement with

if $g \leq k \;\lor\; H.p \;\rightarrow\; f := f+1$ **fi**   .

Here $H.p$ is an as yet unknown condition, which, however, we insist must *not* depend on f (because f is going to vanish from the program text).

By this weakening of the guard, the partial correctness, i.e. the invariance of

$$f \leq k \quad,$$

is no longer guaranteed, and here is the place where we finally use the given invariance of $nc.(k+1) \leq k+1$. From the structure of the program we conclude the invariance of $g \leq nc.(k+1)$ and, hence, of $g \leq k+1$. By our last Topology Lemma in Chapter 7, $g \leq k$ therefore is a correct pre- and post-assertion to $Section.(k+1)$. This causes us to consider the following version:

[†]We just mention that had we lightheartedly replaced guard $f < k$ by $g < k$ instead of the weaker $g \leq k$, the whole design would have failed miserably.

Pre : $f = 0 \land g = 0$

Section.$(k+1)$: $\{g \leq k\}$
(in Comp.p) $g := g+1$
; $\{f < g,$ hence $f \leq k\}$
if $g \leq k \lor H.p \rightarrow f := f+1$ **fi**
; $\{? \ g \leq k \lor H.p,$ see below$\}$
Section.k
; $\{g \leq k \lor H.p\}$
$f, g := f-1, g-1$
$\{g \leq k\}$

Inv : $g \leq k+1,$
       $f \leq g,$
     $? \ f \leq k$

Version 3

Assertion $g \leq k \lor H.p$ is the strongest relation we can assert as a post-condition of the guarded statement. (Recall: $H.p$ does not depend on f.) Since we wish the current annotation to be helpful in concluding the potentially damaged invariant $f \leq k$, we want the annotation to be as strong as possible, and that is why we will require that assertion $g \leq k \lor H.p$ be globally correct as well. Thus we insist that

(i)   Each Comp.q, $q \neq p$, will truthify $H.p$ along with $g := g+1$.

Next we analyze for which choice of $H.p$ the invariance of $f \leq k$ can be inferred. From the annotation of *Section*.$(k+1)$ we conclude that the system as a whole maintains

P: $\langle \forall p :: f \leq k \lor g \leq k \lor H.p \rangle$,

which is the strongest statement we can make about the system state. Now the question is when and how we can infer

   $P \Rightarrow f \leq k$?

To that end we calculate:

   P

$\equiv$ {definition of P}

   $\langle \forall p :: f \leq k \lor g \leq k \lor H.p \rangle$

$\equiv$ {$f \leq g$ is a system invariant, hence $g \leq k \Rightarrow f \leq k$}

$\langle \forall p :: f \leq k \lor H.p \rangle$

$\equiv$ {predicate calculus}

$\langle \forall p : \neg H.p : f \leq k \rangle$

$\Rightarrow$ {(ii) below}

$f \leq k$,

where

(ii) $\neg H.p$ does not describe an empty range.

Remark Requirement (ii) on H is sharp: the implication in the above calculation just doesn't hold for an empty range.
End of Remark.

So provided (i) and (ii) are satisfied, we have saved the invariance of $f \leq k$.

Now, because $H.p$ occurs as a disjunct in the guard, progress is served best by choosing $H.p$ as as weak as possible, or, equivalently, by choosing $\neg H.p$ as strong as possible. The strongest $\neg H.p$ satisfying (ii) definitely is a one-point predicate[‡], and this causes us to introduce a fresh variable v $(v.k)$ and choose

$\neg H.p$: $v = p$, or
$H.p$: $v \neq p$.

Thus (ii) is met, and in order to satisfy requirement (i) on $H.p$ we shall expand $g := g+1$ in Comp.q, $q \neq p$, into

$g, v := g+1, q$.

This analysis, which constitutes the heart of the design, takes us to the following approximation, from which f has now been eliminated:

Pre : $g = 0$	
Section.$(k+1)$: $g, v := g+1, p$	
(in Comp.p) ; if $g \leq k \lor v \neq p \rightarrow$ *skip* fi	
; *Section.k*	
; $g := g-1$	

Version 4

*   *

*

[‡]This is a predicate that yields value *true* in one point only.

We are getting close to our final solution, albeit that we still have to eliminate the too coarse-grained assignments and guard. The unraveling of the multiple assignment is quite simple: we have seen it a few times before (cf. Chapters 11 and 14), but we first tackle the assignments to g, which are "two-point" — they inspect the old value and assign a new one.

We shall eliminate g by coupling it to a set of N private booleans, $x.p$ ($(x.p).k$!) for Comp.p, as follows:

$$g = \langle\, \#q :: x.q \,\rangle \quad .$$

Then $g := g+1$ in Comp.p gets expanded into

$$\{\neg x.p\}\ g,\ x.p := g+1,\ \textit{true} \quad ,$$

and $g := g-1$ into

$$\{x.p\}\ g,\ x.p := g-1,\ \textit{false} \quad .$$

The translation of the guard has a little surprise in store:

$$g \leq k \ \lor\ v \neq p$$

$\equiv \qquad$ {coupling for g}

$$\langle\, \#q :: x.q \,\rangle \leq k \ \lor\ v \neq p$$

$\Leftarrow \qquad$ {surprise, using $1 \leq k$}

$$\langle\, \#q :: x.q \,\rangle \leq 1 \ \lor\ v \neq p$$

$\equiv \qquad$ {relation $\#/\forall$ and using that $x.p$ is a pre-assertion of the guarded skip}

$$\langle\, \forall q : q \neq p : \neg x.q \,\rangle \ \lor\ v \neq p$$

$\equiv \qquad$ {predicate calculus}

$$\langle\, \forall q : q \neq p : \neg x.q \ \lor\ v \neq p \,\rangle \quad .$$

Remark (on the surprise)
It is absolutely against our general strategy to apply a strengthening as huge as in the above calculation, because it may cause great problems for progress. In this case the damage is not too big, because on closer scrutiny our guarded skip is very "permeable", thanks to disjunct $v \neq p$: at most one component can be blocked at it, irrespective of what the other disjunct is. As we shall see shortly, progress itself is not endangered. It is only the progress argument that will become just a little more complicated.
End of Remark.

So, thanks to the strengthening step in the above calculation, our guard has become

$$\langle \forall q : q \neq p : \neg x.q \lor v \neq p \rangle \quad ,$$

and since the individual conjuncts are globally correct (under $x.q := false$ and $x.q, v := true, q$ in Comp.q, $q \neq p$), the conjunction may be evaluated conjunct-wise and in any order (cf. the Guard Conjunction Lemma). Hence

if $\langle \forall q : q \neq p : \neg x.q \lor v \neq p \rangle \rightarrow skip$ **fi**

can be replaced with, for instance,

for $q : q \neq p$ **do**

    if $\neg x.q \lor v \neq p \rightarrow skip$ **fi**

od   .

Finally, because $v \neq p$ is globally correct, Gouda's Guard Disjunction Lemma (see Chapter 24) tells us that the disjunction $\neg x.q \lor v \neq p$ may also be evaluated disjunct-wise. We will keep all this in mind, but we will not do notational justice to it. Thus having eliminated g, we get as our next approximation

Pre : $\langle \forall q :: \neg x.q \rangle$
$Section.(k+1)$: $x.p, v := true, p$ (in Comp.p)   ; **if** $\langle \forall q : q \neq p : \neg x.q \lor v \neq p \rangle$ $\rightarrow skip$ **fi**   ; $Section.k$; $x.p := false$

Version 5

*   *

*

In our final massaging, we replace multiple assignment

$x.p, v := true, p$

by

$x.p := true$

$; v := p$.

and do not even bother to rename x. This transformation leads us to the final code for $Section.(k+1)$:

Pre : $\langle \forall q :: \neg x.q \rangle$

Section.$(k+1)$:	*entry.k* :	$x.p := true$
(in *Comp.p*)		; $v := p$
		; **if** $\langle \forall q : q \neq p : \neg x.q \lor v \neq p \rangle$
		$\rightarrow skip$
		fi
	; *Section.k*	
	; *exit.k* :	$x.p := false$

Version 6: final code for Section.$(k+1)$

*   *
*

Before addressing progress, we first present the raw code for Peterson's algorithm. This time we do supply the indices k coming with *Section.k* .

```
Pre :   ⟨ ∀k : 1 ≤ k < N : ⟨ ∀q :: ¬x.q.k ⟩ ⟩

Comp.p:  *[ ncs
          ; |[ var k : int;
              k := N − 1
            ; do k ≠ 0 →
                  x.p.k := true
                ; v.k := p
                ; if ⟨ ∀q : q ≠ p : ¬x.q.k ∨ v.k ≠ p ⟩ → skip fi
                ; k := k − 1
              od
            ; cs
            ; do k ≠ N − 1 →
                  k := k + 1
                ; x.p.k := false
              od
            ]|
          ]
```

G. L. Peterson's Mutual Exclusion Algorithm for N components

For completeness' sake we mention that in Peterson's original publication, the $N * (N-1)$ booleans are coded in a different more compact way. This is possible because of the monotonicities in $x.p.k$ as a function of k. However, we do not carry out this last coordinate transformation here, because it no longer contributes to our purpose: the formal derivation of a non-trivial algorithm.

*   *
*

Finally we address progress, which means that we will show that a component that has terminated its *ncs* will, within a finite number of steps of the system, enter its *cs* (and vice versa, which is obvious from the program text).

By (our) lack of a formalism for addressing progress, our argument will, of necessity, be informal. Fortunately that doesn't harm in our current example, because our informal argument, we believe, will be found to be simple and totally convincing. To the best of our knowledge, no formal progress argument has ever been published* (nor an informal one). The reason for this is unclear. Maybe computing scientists didn't care (because they didn't care about the algorithm?), or they didn't succeed because it was too difficult. We just don't know.

As for the structure of our progress argument, it need not come as a surprise that the argument is as inductive as the development of the algorithm. We return to Version 6 to which we add two obviously correct assertions about private variable $x.p$:

Pre : $\langle \forall q :: \neg x.q \rangle$
$Section.(k+1)$: $\{\neg x.p\}$
(in Comp.p) $x.p := true$
; $v := p$
; **if** $\langle \forall q : q \neq p : \neg x.q \lor v \neq p \rangle \rightarrow skip$ **fi**
; $Section.k$
; $x.p := false$
$\{\neg x.p\}$

Version 6

---

*After this text had been written, we found one in [Lyn96]

*   *
*

Recalling that each component has the form * [*ncs*; *Section.N*] , where *Section*.1 is the *cs* , we have met our demonstrandum whenever we have shown that for each *k* such that $1 \le k \le N$, *Section.k* terminates for each component engaged in it. We do so by mathematical induction, with induction hypothesis

(*)   *Section.k* terminates for each component engaged in it.

- Condition (*) certainly holds for $k = 1$, since *Section*.1 is *cs* and, therefore, is supposed to terminate (for each component engaged in it).

- At most one component can be blocked in the guarded skip of *Section*.$(k+1)$, thanks to disjunct $v \ne p$. Now let Comp.p be blocked indefinitely in this guarded skip. We show that within a finite number of steps the guard will become stably *true*, after which Comp.p can engage in *Section.k* , which by (*) terminates, so that *Section*.$(k+1)$ terminates for Comp.p . We distinguish two different computations that can be generated by the system:

  (i) Some Comp.q , $q \ne p$, initiates *Section*.$(k+1)$ while Comp.p is blocked. It will make $v \ne p$ stably *true* through $v := q$ — and hence Comp.p's guard as well.

  (ii) No Comp.q , $q \ne p$, initiates *Section*.$(k+1)$ while Comp.p is blocked. We show that in this case the system will generate the stable truth of $\langle \forall q : q \ne p : \neg x.q \rangle$, so that, again, Comp.p's guard becomes stably *true*. The argument is as follows. For components Comp.q , $q \ne p$, that are outside *Section*.$(k+1)$, we have the stable truth of $\neg x.q$ (see annotation). For components Comp.q , $q \ne p$, inside *Section*.$(k+1)$, we conclude from (*) that *Section.k* terminates. These components will also finish *Section*.$(k+1)$ through $x.q := \textit{false}$ and thus generate state $\neg x.q$.

This concludes our progress argument and our treatment of Peterson's general mutual exclusion algorithm.

*   *
*

When, many years ago, Lex Bijlsma and one of the authors (WF) managed to give an a-posteriori correctness proof for (the partial correctness of) Peterson's algorithm, they arrived at essentially the same two-level structure as presented here [Fei90]. But that is the only similarity. That former treatise was completely upside down. It started at the raw code given by Peterson and tried to extract from it meaningful pieces of code that perhaps could be dealt with in isolation. Those were what we now identified as the entries and the exits of the "*Section*"s. The "*Section*"s themselves could not be found there, and consequently the induction was only present in the background of that treatment instead of in the foreground.

It was during a classroom session that a student observed that we were doing things completely bottom up, and threw down the gauntlet. Then Perry D. Moerland immediately picked it up, and it is essentially his derivation that we have presented here. It was the experimentation with this algorithm that irrevocably taught us that verifying multiprograms is one or two orders of magnitude more complicated than developing them.

26

Monitored Phase Synchronization

In Chapter 17 we addressed the problem of phase synchronization — also known as "barrier synchronization" — for the case of two components. The main purpose of that chapter was to show program derivation at work in a simple setting and to discuss various methodological issues. It should not be surprising that, as this text progresses, we become interested in more "scaled-up" problems, problems closer to everyday practice so to speak. Therefore in this chapter we will tackle, as an example, the problem of barrier synchronization for an arbitrary but fixed number of components, and show how it can be solved through an intermediary in the shape of a monitor or a bus. In the next chapter we will then develop an algorithm for barrier synchronization that is fully distributed, i.e. that is intended for an architecture where the components are located in the nodes of a — sparsely connected — network. The overall intention of these examples is to show program derivation at work in a less simple setting and on a variety of potential machine architectures. In addition, the problem of barrier synchronization all by itself has proved to be important enough, because of its applications in areas where components are to proceed in a "lock-step-like" fashion.

*   *
*

The specification of our problem is a straightforward generalization of the formal specification developed for two components in Chapter 17:

$$
\begin{array}{|l|}
\hline
\text{Pre:} \quad \langle\, \forall q :: x.q = 0 \,\rangle \\
\hline
\text{Comp.}p: \quad *\,[\; \{?\; Z.p\}\; S.p \\
\qquad\qquad ;\; x.p := 1 + x.p \\
\qquad\qquad] \\
\hline
\end{array}
$$

Specification of Barrier Synchronization

where $Z.p$ is given by

$Z.p$: $\langle\, \forall q :: x.p \leq x.q \,\rangle$.

The computation proper for Comp.p is $*\,[\, S.p\,]$. The x's have been introduced for specification purposes only. Assertion $Z.p$ is the required precondition for $S.p$. It goes without saying that, in solving the problem, we are not to change the x's in any way.

*   *
*

Because $Z.p$ is globally correct — Widening — we only need to see to its local correctness, which is readily established by guarded skip

   if $Z.p \rightarrow$ *skip* **fi**   .

And here the example would end if we were to implement the algorithm on a shared-memory installation. For the sake of the argument, however, let us assume that the components cannot directly communicate with one another, but that their information exchange has to take place via one dedicated additional component to be called the Monitor. In order to do justice to this constraint, we have to investigate how the local correctness of $Z.p$ can be concluded without referring to the $x.q$'s . Because $Z.p$ states an upper bound on $x.p$ (viz. $\langle\, \downarrow q :: x.q \,\rangle$), we ask ourselves under which condition

   $x.p \leq m \;\Rightarrow\; Z.p$

holds, where m is a fresh variable private to the Monitor. To that end we calculate

   $x.p \leq m \;\Rightarrow\; Z.p$

$\equiv$ {definition of $Z.p$}

   $x.p \leq m \;\Rightarrow\; \langle\, \forall q :: x.p \leq x.q \,\rangle$

$\equiv$ {predicate calculus}

   $\langle\, \forall q :: x.p \leq m \;\Rightarrow\; x.p \leq x.q \,\rangle$

$\Leftarrow$ {transitivity of $\leq$}

$$\langle\, \forall q :: m \leq x.q \,\rangle \qquad ,$$

and now we see that by adoption of system invariant

P_0: $\qquad \langle\, \forall q :: m \leq x.q \,\rangle \qquad ,$

the correctness of assertion $Z.p$ — recall the Modus Ponens — can be established through guarded skip

> if $x.p \leq m \rightarrow$ *skip* fi $\{Z.p\}$.

Aside The above analysis can also be carried out by observing that $Z.p$ can be rewritten as $x.p \leq \langle\, \downarrow q :: x.q \,\rangle$. This would result in the emergence of invariant $m \leq \langle\, \downarrow q :: x.q \,\rangle$, which is equivalent to P_0, but we prefer the above, more homogeneous symbol manipulation, simply because there is no compelling reason to introduce $\downarrow$. This is a kind of "mannerism", invoked by one of our calculational rules of thumb, which says: "Avoid manipulating a formula, unless there are good reasons to do so.". **End** of Aside.

Herewith we arrive at our first approximation to the Monitored Barrier Synchronization:

Pre :	$\langle\, \forall q :: x.q = 0 \,\rangle$
Comp.p:	$*\,[\,$ if $x.p \leq m \rightarrow$ *skip* fi
	; $\{Z.p\}\ S.p$
	; $x.p := 1 + x.p$
	$]$
Monitor:	$*\,[\,manipulate\ m\,]$
Inv :	? P_0 : $\quad \langle\, \forall q :: m \leq x.q \,\rangle$

Version 0

*   *
*

By the shape of the components, a steady increase of m will be necessary, lest total deadlock is bound to occur. Therefore we investigate a Monitor of the form $*\,[\,m := m+1\,]$. For $m := m+1$ to maintain P_0, its precondition should imply

$$\langle\, \forall q :: m+1 \leq x.q \,\rangle \qquad .$$

Since this condition is globally correct under the increments of the x's , establishing its local correctness suffices. Thus we arrive at the next (and final) version, in which we add assertion $x.p \leq m$ in Comp.p for later use.

Pre :	$\langle \forall q :: x.q = 0 \rangle \ \wedge \ m = 0$
Comp.p:	$* [$ **if** $x.p \leq m \rightarrow$ *skip* **fi**
	$; \{Z.p\} \ \{x.p \leq m\} \ S.p$
	$; \ x.p := 1 + x.p$
	$]$
Monitor:	$* [$ **if** $\langle \forall q :: m + 1 \leq x.q \rangle \rightarrow$ *skip* **fi**
	$; \ m := m + 1$
	$]$
Inv :	$P_0 : \quad \langle \forall q :: m \leq x.q \rangle$

Version 1

*   *
*

What remains is the progress proof. The added assertion $x.p \leq m$ in Comp.p is obviously correct, and from it we conclude the system invariance of

P_1: $\qquad \langle \forall q :: x.q \leq m + 1 \rangle$.

The conjunction of P_0 and P_1 then forms an adequate multibound for our multiprogram, so that individual progress is guaranteed if there is no total deadlock. And there is no total deadlock, because the disjunction of all the guards, viz.

$$\langle \exists q :: x.q \leq m \rangle \ \vee \ \langle \forall q :: m + 1 \leq x.q \rangle \quad ,$$

is just *true*. Finally, we observe that — by the Guard Conjunction Lemma — the Monitor's guard may be evaluated conjunct-wise. In principle, this concludes our derivation of the Monitored Barrier Synchronization.

*   *
*

However, in many practical situations it may be advantageous or even necessary to eliminate the ever-growing integers x, which, after all, were introduced for specification purposes only, and along with them the induced m. This is possible because the multibound, i.e. the conjunction of P_0 and P_1,

$$\langle \forall q :: m \leq x.q \ \wedge \ x.q \leq m + 1 \rangle \quad ,$$

tells us that all differences $x.q - m$ are two-valued, and it is only these differences that matter for the control of the algorithm — see the guards.

So let us apply a coordinate transformation to the boolean domain. We introduce booleans $b.p$, one for each p, coupled to the original coordinates by

$$b.p \;\equiv\; x.p \leq m \qquad, \text{or} - \text{equivalently} -$$

$$\neg b.p \;\equiv\; m+1 \leq x.p \quad.$$

Because this kind of coordinate transformation has been discussed before (cf. Chapters 10 and 17), we now give the resulting program at once:

Pre : $\langle \forall q :: b.q \rangle$
Comp.p: $\ast\,[$ **if** $b.p \rightarrow$ *skip* **fi** $\quad;\ S.p$ $\quad;\ b.p := false \qquad$ (or: $b.p := \neg b.p$) $\quad]$
Monitor: $\ast\,[$ **if** $\langle \forall q :: \neg b.q \rangle \rightarrow$ *skip* **fi** $\quad;\ \langle$ **for** $q ::$ **do** $b.q := true$ $\qquad\qquad\qquad$ (or: $b.q := \neg b.q$) $\qquad\qquad$ **od** $\rangle$ $\quad]$

Version 2

Here the atomic $m := m+1$ from Version 1 is translated, using an ad-hoc notation, into one big atomic flipping operation of all booleans $b.q$. And thus we have removed the ever-growing integers m and $x.p$.

If the big atomic flipping is felt to be too coarse-grained, it can be eliminated by a next coordinate transformation, viz. by introducing booleans $c.p$ — $c.p$ private to Comp.p — and boolean d — private to the Monitor —, coupled to the b's by

$$b.p \;\equiv\; c.p \;\equiv\; d \quad.$$

Then the Monitor can flip all booleans $b.q$ in one fell swoop by assignment $d := \neg d$. The corresponding program thus becomes

Pre : $\langle \forall q :: c.q \equiv d \rangle$
Comp.p: $*\lceil$ **if** $c.p \equiv d \rightarrow skip$ **fi** $; S.p$ $; c.p := \neg c.p$ $\rfloor$
Monitor: $*\lceil$ **if** $\langle \forall q :: c.q \not\equiv d \rangle \rightarrow skip$ **fi** $; d := \neg d$ $\rfloor$

Monitored Barrier Synchronization with private booleans

$$* \qquad *$$
$$*$$

Many more variations and divergences are possible; for instance there is the question of how to transform the algorithm into a "four-phase" one, as we did with the handshake protocol, or how to realize the communication of d's value via a common bus. However, we rather leave these elaborations to the engineers, who are better trained in these issues than we are. Our goal was to neatly derive a rather fine-grained algorithm for this kind of problem and this kind of architecture, and we think that by now we have reached that goal.

27

Distributed Liberal Phase Synchronization

There is a rather wide-spread belief that the design of distributed algorithms requires methods that are quite different from those used for the design of shared-variable algorithms. This is an unfortunate misunderstanding. In previous chapters we already showed the development of a number of small distributed algorithms, and in this chapter we will try to dispel the misunderstanding more rigorously by presenting the design of a nontrivial, fully distributed algorithm for phase synchronization (an algorithm which most likely is beyond what can operationally be conceived and comprehended).

*　　*
*

The kind of phase synchronization we have in mind is more liberal than we discussed before, in that for each component a "slack" is given, which specifies how far the component is allowed to run ahead of the other components, measured in terms of the number of completed phases. More precisely, we are given natural numbers $M.p$, one for each Comp.p, and we are requested to solve the following problem, subject to the architectural constraints described below:

Pre : $\langle \forall q :: x.q = 0 \rangle$
Comp.p: $* [\{? \ Z.p : \langle \forall q :: x.p \leq M.p + x.q \rangle \}$ $\quad\quad S.p$ $\quad\quad ; x.p := 1 + x.p$ $\quad\quad]$

Specification of Liberal Phase Synchronization

What the architectural constraints boil down to is that the components are located in the nodes of a — sparsely connected — network, and that a component can only communicate with its immediate neighbours. It goes without saying that our problem is unsolvable if the network is not connected. The sparsest connected network, in terms of the number of edges, is a tree, and we shall solve our problem for such an, a-priori given, rooted tree. We do not add this aspect of the problem to our formal specification, but rather take it into account as we go along.

Remark If we choose $M.p = 0$ for all p, the above formal specification reduces to a specification of barrier synchronization. When taking the architectural constraints into account, we then obtain an algorithm for *distributed* barrier synchronization. We will return to this special case at the very end of this chapter.
End of Remark.

*　　*
*

Even before starting our development, we can already conclude from the specification, that any solution that we may end up with will inevitably have system invariant

MB:　　　$\langle \forall p :: \langle \forall q :: x.p \leq 1 + M.p + x.q \rangle \rangle$　　　,

which is a multibound for our multiprogram, so that individual progress of the components follows from the absence of total deadlock. We wish to stress this right at the start, because the algorithm that we will ultimately arrive at is (operationally) so complicated that arguing about progress from the program text alone is all but undoable, let alone attractive.

*　　*
*

The first step in our development is quite similar to what we did in the previous chapter on Monitored Barrier Synchronization. Because, due to the restricted communication facilities, we cannot simply establish the local correctness of $Z.p$ by means of guarded skip

> **if** $Z.p \rightarrow$ *skip* **fi**   ,

we must find a way to eliminate all references to the $x.q$'s in $Z.p$.

One advantage of a rooted tree is that it contains one special node, namely the root. Let us call it R. Then we can eliminate almost all of the $x.q$'s in $Z.p$ by observing that

$$(*) \qquad \begin{array}{l} Z.p \\ \Leftarrow \\ x.p \leq M.p + x.R \;\wedge\; \langle\, \forall q :: x.R \leq x.q \,\rangle \end{array}$$

Now, the correctness of $Z.p$ is guaranteed if we strengthen the annotation into the antecedent of $(*)$. Because conjunct $\langle\, \forall q :: x.R \leq x.q \,\rangle$ is highly independent of p, it is bound to become a system invariant. We thus obtain

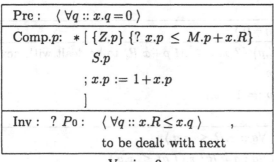

Pre : $\langle\, \forall q :: x.q = 0 \,\rangle$
Comp.p: $*\,[\,\{Z.p\}\,\{?\; x.p \leq M.p + x.R\}$ $\qquad\quad S.p$ $\qquad\; ;\, x.p := 1 + x.p$ $\qquad\;]$
Inv : $?\, P_0$: $\langle\, \forall q :: x.R \leq x.q \,\rangle$, $\qquad\qquad$ to be dealt with next

Version 0

*   *
*

If our tree were star-shaped with the root in the center of the star, we would obtain a monitor-like solution, with Comp.R besides being a component also acting as the monitor. The reader may wish to carry out this development, by way of exercise. However, our tree is supposed to be quite arbitrary.

Of the two queried items that remain, assertion $x.p \leq M.p + x.R$ is the harder one: it isn't straightly clear how we can deal with the occurrence of $x.R$. The required invariance of P_0 does, however, leave little room for choice, and for lack of the better we therefore concentrate on this item first.

Relation P_0 demands that the minimal x-value reside at the root, and we immediately comply with this demand by requiring that each path from a node to the root exhibit a descending sequence of x-values. More formally, with $f.q$ denoting the father node of node q, $q \neq R$, we require the invariance of

P_1: $\langle \forall q : q \neq R : x.(f.q) \leq x.q \rangle$.

Thus, projected on the x-values, the tree forms a so-called *downheap*.

Remark   As an aside, let us see why, in meeting P_0, there is little choice beyond adopting P_1. Comp.R will have to increase its x-value but can only communicate with its children. A necessary condition for this increment to maintain P_0 is that $x.R$ is smaller than the x-values of R's children, and for it to be sufficient it had better be the case that the x-values of these children are, in their turn, the minimum x-values in their respective subtrees. By unfolding this recursion we exactly arrive at P_1. **End** of Remark.

The next version of our program thus becomes

Pre : $\langle \forall q :: x.q = 0 \rangle$
Comp.p: $\ast [\; \{Z.p\} \; \{? \; x.p \leq M.p + x.R, \text{ to be dealt with next}\}$ $S.p$ $; x.p := 1 + x.p$ $]$
Inv : P_0: $\langle \forall q :: x.R \leq x.q \rangle$ $\quad ? \; P_1$: $\langle \forall q : q \neq R : x.(f.q) \leq x.q \rangle$

Version 1

*   *

*

Realizing the invariance of P_1 will be a matter of routine, and therefore we first focus on handling assertion $x.p \leq M.p + x.R$. This will turn out to be the heart of the design. The only way in which we can eliminate $x.R$ is by having an expression of the form

something $\leq x.R$,

where, preferably, the "something" is expressed in terms of the states of Comp.p's immediate neighbourhood in the tree. Unfortunately, there isn't a formula as yet that provides a lower bound on $x.R$: P_0 doesn't and P_1 doesn't either because it excludes $q = R$.

Therefore, an essentially new ingredient has to enter the picture, and this new ingredient will consist in a set of fresh variables $y.p$, $y.p$ private to Comp.p. We can then separate the $x.p$ and the $x.R$ in our target assertion by observing that

$$x.p \leq M.p + x.R$$

(∗∗) $\Leftarrow$

$$x.p \leq M.p + y.p \ \wedge \ y.p \leq y.R \ \wedge \ y.R \leq x.R \quad .$$

Now the correctness of $x.p \leq M.p + x.R$ is guaranteed if we strengthen the annotation into the antecedent of (∗∗). Because the two final conjuncts in this antecedent are rather independent of p and p's neighbours in the tree, we will require them to become system invariants. As for $y.p \leq y.R$, we will satisfy this condition for all p by demanding that, projected on the y- values, the tree forms a so-called *upheap*, i.e.

$$\langle \ \forall q : q \neq R : \ y.q \leq y.(f.q) \ \rangle \quad .$$

Because for Comp.p with $p = R$, target assertion $x.p \leq M.p + x.R$ is automatically fulfilled — $0 \leq M.p$ —, the above strengthening needs to be carried out for $p \neq R$ only. Thus the program for the non-roots diverges from that of the root.

Pre :	$\langle \ \forall q :: x.q = 0 \ \rangle \ \wedge \ \langle \ \forall q :: y.q = 0 \ \rangle$
Comp.p:	∗ [$\{Z.p\} \ \{x.p \leq M.p + x.R\}$
$(p \neq R)$	$\{? \ x.p \leq M.p + y.p\} \ S.p$
	; $x.p := 1 + x.p$
	]
Comp.R:	∗ [$\{Z.R\} \ S.R$
	; $x.R := 1 + x.R$
	]
Inv :	P_0 : $\langle \ \forall q :: x.R \leq x.q \ \rangle$
	? P_1 : $\langle \ \forall q : q \neq R : x.(f.q) \leq x.q \ \rangle$
	? P_2 : $\langle \ \forall q : q \neq R : y.q \leq y.(f.q) \ \rangle$
	? P_3 : $y.R \leq x.R$

Version 2

*   *
  *

As far as P_1 through P_3 are concerned, the y's are allowed to be constant, but assertion $x.p \leq M.p + y.p$ demands increments of $y.p$, lest the assertion becomes stably *false* — with total deadlock as a result. We now decide to equip each component with an independent co-component to take care of the orderly increments of the y's . Thus we introduce for each p

Co.p: $* [\, y.p := 1 + y.p \,]$,

to reside, just like Comp.p, in node p of the tree. With this arrangement, all four queried items in Version 2 are readily implemented.

Re $x.p \leq M.p + y.p$ in Comp.p, $p \neq R$

L: Prefix the assertion with guarded skip **if** $x.p \leq M.p + y.p \rightarrow$ *skip* **fi**

G: Widening.

Re P_3: $y.R \leq x.R$

Init: Follows from Pre

- $y.R := 1 + y.R$ in Co.R:

  Prefix this statement with guarded skip **if** $1 + y.R \leq x.R \rightarrow$ *skip* **fi** , the guard of which is globally correct — Widening.

Re P_1: $\langle \forall q : q \neq R : x.(f.q) \leq x.q \rangle$

Init: Follows from Pre

- $x.p := 1 + x.p$ in Comp.p

  This statement requires additional precondition

  $$\langle \forall q : q \neq R \wedge p = f.q : 1 + x.(f.q) \leq x.q \rangle \quad .$$

  Since $p = f.q \Rightarrow q \neq R$, this can be simplified to

  $$\langle \forall q : p = f.q : 1 + x.p \leq x.q \rangle \quad .$$

Because this condition is globally correct — Widening —, we only need to take care of its local correctness. This time we can do so with impunity by means of a guarded skip, viz.

$$\textbf{if } \langle \forall q : p = f.q : 1 + x.p \leq x.q \rangle \rightarrow \textit{skip} \textbf{ fi} \quad ,$$

since the evaluation of its guard in Comp.p requires communication with Comp.p's children only.

Re P_2: $\langle \forall q : q \neq R : y.q \leq y.(f.q) \rangle$

Init: Follows from Pre

- $y.p := 1 + y.p$ in Co.p, for $p \neq R$

  This statement requires additional precondition

  $$\langle \forall q : q \neq R \wedge p = q : 1 + y.q \leq y.(f.q) \rangle \quad ,$$

which equivales (since $p \neq R$)

$$1 + y.p \leq y.(f.p) \quad .$$

This condition is readily established by a guarded skip as well.

End of Re's.

Assembling all the above, we obtain

Pre :	$\langle \forall q :: x.q = 0 \rangle \wedge \langle \forall q :: y.q = 0 \rangle$
Comp.p: $(p \neq R)$	$* [$ **if** $x.p \leq M.p + y.p \rightarrow skip$ **fi** $; \{Z.p\} \{x.p \leq M.p + x.R\} \{x.p \leq M.p + y.p\}$ $\quad S.p$ $;$ **if** $\langle \forall q : p = f.q : 1 + x.p \leq x.q \rangle \rightarrow skip$ **fi** $; x.p := 1 + x.p$ $]$
Co.p: $(p \neq R)$	$* [$ **if** $1 + y.p \leq y.(f.p) \rightarrow skip$ **fi** $; y.p := 1 + y.p$ $]$
Comp.R:	$* [\{Z.R\} \ S.R$ $;$ **if** $\langle \forall q : R = f.q : 1 + x.R \leq x.q \rangle \rightarrow skip$ **fi** $; x.R := 1 + x.R$ $]$
Co.R:	$* [$ **if** $1 + y.R \leq x.R \rightarrow skip$ **fi** $; y.R := 1 + y.R$ $]$
Inv : P_0 : P_1 : P_2 : P_3 :	$\langle \forall q :: x.R \leq x.q \rangle \quad ,$ $\langle \forall q : q \neq R : x.(f.q) \leq x.q \rangle \quad ,$ $\langle \forall q : q \neq R : y.q \leq y.(f.q) \rangle \quad ,$ $y.R \leq x.R$

Distributed Liberal Phase Synchronization, fully annotated.

By the Guard Conjunction Lemma, the conjunctive guards in the above may be evaluated conjunct-wise, and with this remark we conclude the development of our program.

$$* \qquad *$$
$$*$$

Of course a number of issues remain, the most important one of which is our obligation to prove individual progress. Because we want to do so by means of our multibound technique, we first prove the absence of total deadlock.

We do so by assuming that *all* components are blocked in a guarded skip and then proving the validity of *false*. Because most of the components Comp.p have two guarded skips, we have to be a little careful. Let us concentrate on the co-components first, which have one guarded skip only. From their being blocked in the total-deadlock state, we infer (the stable truth of)

(i) $\langle \forall q : q \neq R : y.(f.q) \leq y.q \rangle$ — the Co.q —, $q \neq R$, are blocked

(ii) $x.R \leq y.R$ — Co.R is blocked.

Now we turn to the components Comp.p. Generalizing property (ii), we introduce notion *black.p* , defined by

$$black.p \equiv x.p \leq y.p \quad .$$

Thus we have that

(iii)   the root is black.

We shall derive the validity of *false* by showing that there is an infinite number of black nodes in the given, finite network. In particular, we shall prove that in the deadlock state we have

(iv)   each black node has a black child,

so that (iii) and (iv) together do the job.

As for a proof of (iv), we first observe that no black Comp.p is blocked in its first guarded skip **if** $x.p \leq M.p + y.p \to$ *skip* **fi** (which is absent in the root):

$\qquad x.p$

$\leq \qquad$ {Comp.p is black}

$\qquad y.p$

$\leq \qquad$ {$0 \leq M.p$}

$\qquad M.p + y.p \quad .$

So, a black component is blocked in its second guarded skip, which means — see the program text — that a black Comp.p has a child q for which

(v) $p = f.q$ and

(vi) $x.q \leq x.p \quad .$

We now derive $black.q$, i.e. $x.q \leq y.q$:

$x.q$

$\leq$ $\{(vi)\}$

$x.p$

$\leq$ $\{black.p\}$

$y.p$

$=$ $\{(v)\}$

$y.(f.q)$

$\leq$ $\{(i), \text{ using } q \neq R \text{ (from (v))}\}$

$y.q$.

And this completes our proof of the absence of total deadlock, a proof which we owe to Frans W. van der Sommen.

Remark If all slacks $M.p$ are equal, a simpler proof for the absence of total deadlock is possible [FvG97].
End of Remark.

*   *
*

Finally we address individual progress. We recall that we already have — from the specification — the invariance of

MB: $\langle\, \forall p :: \langle\, \forall q :: x.p \leq 1 + M.p + x.q \,\rangle \,\rangle$,

which is a perfect multibound for the components Comp.p. However, meanwhile we have introduced the co-components, and for our multibound technique to be applicable we need a multibound for the entire system. It is very well possible to construct such a universal multibound, which then guarantees individual progress for all components and all co-components, but we may also proceed in a different way, viz. we may confine ourselves to showing individual progress for just the Comp.p's which after all make up the computation proper. To that end we observe

some Comp.p gets stuck

$\Rightarrow$ $\{MB\}$

each Comp.p gets stuck $(*)$

$\Rightarrow$ $\{\text{instantiate } p = R\}$

Comp.R gets stuck

$\Rightarrow$ $\{\text{inv } P3:\quad y.R \leq x.R\}$

    Co.R gets stuck

$\Rightarrow$ {inv P_2: the y's form an upheap}

    each Co.p gets stuck   , $(*)$

and from the lines marked $(*)$ we conclude

    some Comp.p gets stuck

$\Rightarrow$

    total deadlock   .

However, since we have shown the absence of the danger of total deadlock, we conclude that no Comp.p gets stuck — as demanded. And this concludes our treatment of the Distributed Liberal Phase Synchronization.

Final Remarks

• Without realizing it, we have developed an algorithm that belongs to the family of so-called wave algorithms [Tel94, Lyn96]. Here, waves of permission signals diffuse — starting at the leaf nodes — through the tree to the root, where they are reflected leafwards to grant new permissions to the components to execute their next phases. The waves come and go and interfere with each other in an almost chaotic fashion, and we had better not try to understand our algorithm using this metaphor.

• There is one degree of freedom that we have not explored, namely the mapping of the components to the nodes of the tree. From our development we conclude that it is irrelevant from a correctness point of view. However, from a performance point of view it might matter, due to the different values of the slack $M.p$. Viable as such considerations may be in practice, they are beyond the scope of this monograph.

• In practice, one might also wish to eliminate the ever-growing integers x and y. This is very well doable, because the entire program runs under control of differences between various x- and y-values, and because we can prove that all those differences are bounded. We do not carry out this coordinate transformation here, because it does not really contribute to our prime reason for dealing with this example: to give a formal derivation of a not too trivial distributed algorithm.

• There is one special case that is very important in the everyday practice of building large-scale distributed systems, namely the case that $M.p = 0$ for all p. Then the algorithm reduces to a distributed handshake-like protocol, called "barrier synchronization", to be used for simulating/implementing clocked systems by means of asynchronous building blocks. In this case the algorithm can also be simplified so as to run under control of a few private booleans per component, and the co-components can be eliminated altogether [BF96]. We believe that, at this point, developing an algorithm for this special case, right from scratch, would be an instructive, illuminating, and rewarding exercise for the reader.

28

Distributed Computation of a Spanning Tree

A typical architecture that one encounters is that of a number of computers located in the nodes of a sparsely connected, but otherwise arbitrary network. One of the difficulties with such an architecture is that the flow of control and the information exchange between the various computers are not always easily orchestrated, simply because the network is so arbitrary. This brings about the so-called routing problem. There are, however, at least two general ways to reduce these difficulties.

One way is to simply avoid such arbitrariness and confine oneself to more regularly shaped networks such as linear, cyclic, or tree-shaped arrangements of the machines, or regular grids, tori, hypercubes, etcetera. Such configurations have been studied extensively (and they still are), and they have shown to be very useful in many special-purpose applications. However, one cannot always make do with such special networks, and, in addition, the existence of arbitrary networks of computers is just a fact of life.

For such arbitrary nets, the difficulties in managing the information exchange can be reduced considerably by selecting a manageable subnetwork to which all information exchange is to be confined. One of the easiest to handle — because sparsest — such subnetworks is a spanning tree. Also, of all the manageable subnetworks that one can think of, the spanning tree is the only one that is guaranteed to exist, given that the original network is connected. And, finally, a tree has the advantage that it provides a unique connection between any pair of nodes, and that the length of these connections is relatively small — if at least the tree is not too unbalanced.

It is the distributed computation of such a spanning tree that we will be occupied with in this chapter. We will present two types of algorithm, but before doing so we first study the "mathematics" of a tree.

$$*\qquad*$$
$$*$$

As a stepping stone, we consider the following highly nondeterministic sequential program for constructing a spanning tree in a connected network:

> {all nodes and edges of the network are white}
>
> "select an arbitrary node R and redden it"
>
> ; **do**   "there exists an edge (p,q) with white p and red q "
>
> $\rightarrow$ "redden node p and edge (p,q) "
>
> **od**   .

An invariant of this repetition is that the red graph is a tree (and a subgraph of the given network), i.e. it is connected and contains no cycles. The connectedness is maintained by the body of the repetition because q is red, and the absence of cycles follows from p being white. Also, the program surely terminates, because the number of red nodes increases while the network is finite. And upon termination, the red tree is indeed a spanning tree, since the network is connected.

In many applications it is advantageous to have a *rooted* spanning tree. The above algorithm grants us such a rooted tree at a bargain; the initially selected node R will be the root, and in the body of the repetition node q will be nominated p 's father.

Clearly, the freedom in selecting a white-red edge is so big and the order in which such edges are selected is so irrelevant, that it becomes tempting to distribute these activities over the components of the network. And this is what we shall do, in two different ways.

In distributing these activities we encounter a snag. Let A and B be red nodes, each connected via a white edge to a white node C . If now A and B decide, independently of each other, to adopt C as a child, by reddening AC and BC , respectively, then a cycle is created in the red graph and the tree shape is destroyed. We preclude this danger by seeing to it that it will be C that nominates exactly one of the candidate fathers as its actual one.

Solution I

In our first distributed solution, every component Comp.p different from the root has a shared variable $v.p$ of type component name, accessible to its neighbours. Ignoring root component R for a while, the first version of our algorithm becomes

Pre : all nodes and edges are white
Comp.p: { p is white }
$(p \neq R)$ {? $v.p$ is a red neighbour of p }
"redden p and edge $(p, v.p)$,
selecting $v.p$ as p's father"

And, indeed, the tree shape is maintained, thanks to the preconditions of the colouring act.

*   *

*

We are left with the queried assertion. Since neighbourhood is constant and colours (will) only turn red, its global correctness is guaranteed if each assignment $v.p := q$ takes place in a state where q is a red neighbour of p. For the assertion's local correctness, we introduce guarded skip

   if $B.p \rightarrow$ *skip* fi   ,

which suffices if we can make

P: $\langle\, \forall q :: B.q \;\Rightarrow\; v.q$ is a red neighbour of $q \,\rangle$

a system invariant.

In order to find out what we can choose for the B's , let us now turn our attention to progress, which — by definition — requires that each of the B's becomes stably *true*. To that end, we must first investigate opportunities for truthifying P's consequents. Comp.p contains only one statement changing the state, namely the colouring. As a postcondition of that statement we have

   p is red   ,

which implies that for each neighbour q of p

   p is a red neighbour of q .

A result is that in this state an assignment

   $v.q := p$

truthifies the consequent in P, so that here we have an opportunity par excellence to make the corresponding $B.q$ *true* without violating P. Nicest of all would be if statement $v.q := p$ all by itself would make $B.q$ stably *true*. And this is possible indeed, if we introduce a *fresh* constant, $\perp$ say, different from all component names, and define B by

$$B.q \equiv v.q \neq \perp \quad .$$

We thus arrive at our next version of the program, which reads

Pre : all nodes and edges are white,
$\langle \, \forall q :: v.q = \perp \, \rangle$
Comp.p: { p is white }
$(p \neq R)$ **if** $v.p \neq \perp \rightarrow$ *skip* **fi**
; { p is white }
{ $v.p$ is a red neighbour of p }
"redden p and edge $(p, v.p)$,
selecting $v.p$ as p's father"
; **for** q: q is a neighbour of p **do**
{p is red} $v.q := p$
od
Inv : $P : \langle \, \forall q :: v.q \neq \perp$
$\Rightarrow$ $v.q$ is a red neighbour of $q \, \rangle$

*   *
*

The above design was partly prompted by progress requirements, but that doesn't mean we have shown progress. To do so, we have to show that each node will become red, and this we do by insisting that

(i)   some node becomes red

and showing that

(ii)   some node becomes red $\Rightarrow$ each node will become red.

It is for the accomplishment of (i) that we need the root component R; it will be similar to the regular components except that it is coloured red unconditionally and is not assigned a father:

Comp.R: "redden R"

       ; **for** q : q is a neighbour of R **do**

           $\{R$ is red$\}$ $v.q := R$

      od .

This settles (i). We show (ii) by showing that for each p

(iii) node p becomes red

$\Rightarrow$

     each neighbour of p will become red.

Then (ii) follows, because the network is connected. As for (iii), we observe from the program text that a node p upon turning red will, within a finite number of steps, perform $v.q := p$ for each neighbour q, thus making the guards of these neighbours stably *true*. As a result, they will become red as well. And this completes our progress argument.

*   *
*

Finally, we can clean up the above program text, since control does not depend on colours. The colouring serves to record the computed tree (but has also been introduced for the purpose of reasoning). As for the administration, it suffices to record the father relation. When doing so, we can dispense with the colours, so as to arrive at the following raw code, in which $f.p$ records the father of p :

Pre :	$\langle \forall q :: v.q = \bot \rangle$
Comp.p:	**if** $v.p \neq \bot \rightarrow$ *skip* **fi**
$(p \neq R)$	; $f.p := v.p$
	; **for** q : q is a neighbour of p
	do $v.q := p$ **od**
Comp.R:	**for** q : q is a neighbour of R
	do $v.q := R$ **od**

Distributed Computation of a (rooted) Spanning Tree

*   *
*

We conclude the treatment of Solution I with a number of assorted remarks.

• If it is inconvenient to have one component — the root — differ from all the others, we can make all components equal to each other by introducing an additional — dummy — component D that fires the algorithm by performing

    for some (genuine) node q **do** $v.q := D$ **od**   ,

and thus makes itself the dummy root of the tree.

• The choice of R is completely arbitrary. In particular applications and particular networks, some nodes might be preferred to others to become the root. Also, it may sometimes be beneficial to have a number of different spanning trees. Then one might run a number of instances of the above algorithm in parallel, of course each with its own v's , f's , and R .

• If we retain the colours of the nodes, the efficiency of our algorithm might perhaps be improved by constraining the range of q in the for-clause to the white neighbours of p . (Whether this actually is an improvement very much depends on the kind of communication lines between two neighbours.)

• The shape of the tree constructed by the algorithm is completely outside our control. For reasons of performance, however, one may prefer a tree that, for instance, is rather balanced or has nodes of rather small degree. If admitted by the original network at all, one may try to obtain such a tree by, for instance, pruning the permissible computations or by equipping nodes with the means to redefine their father so as to obtain a "better" tree. We will explore the latter in our next solution, which will be more amenable to such a treatment.

• In common parlance, our algorithm is said to be based on a "broadcasting" regime: a node that has become red "broadcasts" this event to all its neighbours via the assignments to the v's . Also, variable $v.p$ is sometimes identified as a "mailbox" in which a candidate father drops its identity. Common as such metaphors may be, we prefer to avoid them whenever possible. We rather view the v's as variables, and nothing else.

• In our algorithm, the reddening spreads over the network like a "wave". And indeed, our algorithm is about the simplest instance from a huge class of so-called "wave algorithms" [Tel94, Lyn96].

End of Solution I.

Solution II

Our next solution will be quite different from the previous one, although at first sight the difference may seem minor. In our previous solution, the extension of the tree is triggered by the nodes in the tree (through the assignments to the v's), whereas in our next solution the extension will take place "on the initiative" of the nodes outside the tree. Re-introducing the colour metaphor for the nodes, we can now state this solution without much ado. After what has been said before, the reader can easily check its correctness. In the subsequent text, $q \in \mathcal{N}.p$ is used as a shorthand for "q is a network neighbour of p".

Pre :	all nodes are white
Comp.p:	[†] **if** $q :: q \in \mathcal{N}.p \ \wedge \ q$ is red $\rightarrow$ *skip* **fi**
$(p \neq R)$	; $\{p$ is white$\}$
	$\{q \in \mathcal{N}.p \ \wedge \ q$ is red$\}$
	$f.p := q$
	; redden p
Comp.R:	redden R

$$* \qquad *$$
$$*$$

The above algorithm nicely computes a spanning tree, but again the shape of that tree is completely beyond our control. This time, however, we aim at an algorithm that can compute a "better" tree. To that end we must be prepared to extend our components with an as yet unknown number of opportunities to redefine their father. This leads us to consider a program of the form

---

[†]A guard of the form $q :: B.q$ is short for $\langle \exists q :: B.q \rangle$. When *true* it — on the fly — yields a witness q for $B.q$.

Pre :   all nodes are white

Comp.p: **if** $q :: q \in \mathcal{N}.p \;\wedge\; q$ is red $\rightarrow$ *skip* **fi**

$(p \neq R)$; $f.p := q$

; redden p

; $\{p$ is red$\}$

$* \,[\, $ **if** $q :: q \in \mathcal{N}.p \;\wedge\; q$ is red $\wedge$

q is a "better" father

$\rightarrow$ *skip* **fi**

; $f.p := q$

$]$

Comp.R: redden R

The prelude of the repetition in Comp.p is as before and serves to compute *some* father for p. In the repetition the father is repeatedly replaced by a "better" one. (What is meant by "better" may depend on the particular application one has in mind.) Unfortunately, there are two severe problems with this algorithm.

One problem is that, already now, we may wonder how these components are going to terminate. They clearly cannot terminate their repetition. All we can hope for is that our notion of "better" is such that the choice of a "better father" cannot go on forever. Then the components ($\neq R$) are guaranteed to get stuck indefinitely in their guarded skips: the multiprogram as a whole is bound to "terminate" in a state of total deadlock! We shall return to this problem at the end of this chapter.

The second problem is that statement $f.p := q$ in the body of the repetition no longer has precondition "p is white". So how are we going to guarantee that the structure as recorded by f continues to be a tree? Here we interrupt our treatment with a very short intermezzo on the mathematics of trees.

Intermezzo We previously characterized a tree as a connected graph without cycles. An alternative characterization is that it is an acyclic graph on $N+1$ nodes that has N edges. The reader may show, using mathematical induction on N, that the two characterizations are equivalent.
End of Intermezzo.

By the redefinition of p's father through $f.p := q$, one edge of the tree is replaced by another, so that the number of edges recorded by f does not change. According to the intermezzo, the tree shape will then be preserved if we can see to it that the redefinition of the father does not introduce cycles. We know of only one simple way to avoid cycles, viz. by requiring that each f-chain exhibit a decreasing sequence of values coming with it; more specifically and more precisely, we introduce variables x, one per component, such that

$$Q.p: \qquad \langle\, \forall r : r \in \mathcal{N}.p : f.p = r \,\Rightarrow\, x.r < x.p \,\rangle$$

will be a system invariant for all p.

Relation Q will play a central rôle in any further refinements of our algorithm, whatever the "better" trees they will be aiming at. We establish its initial validity by assuming that the f-values are so (un)defined that $f.p \neq r$ for all nodes p, r.

On the fly, we use the x-values for the minor purpose of removing the colours, viz. we adopt the convention that

$$p \text{ is white} \quad\equiv\quad x.p = inf \quad , \text{ and}$$
$$p \text{ is red} \quad\equiv\quad x.p < inf \quad ,$$

where inf is a very large number, e.g. 6.02×10^{23}. The other values to be assumed by the x's depend on the particular applications. We shall deal with two applications, one giving rise to the computation of a so-called "Breadth-First" spanning tree, and another one yielding "Shortest (root) paths". Both types of tree are very popular in practice.

A Breadth-First Algorithm

For a connected network with predetermined node R, the *distance* of a node is defined as the length of a shortest connection of that node to R, measured in terms of the number of edges on that connection. A Breadth-First spanning tree for this network is a tree in which for each node the distance in the tree equals the distance in the network.

In our algorithm we will see to it that the value of $x.p$, which starts at inf, steadily shrinks towards p's distance $dist.p$ in the network, which implies that, among other things, we will see to it that

$$H: \qquad \langle\, \forall r :: dist.r \leq x.r \,\rangle$$

is a system invariant; and then we will show that, in the final state, $x.p$ not only equals $dist.p$, i.e. p's distance to R in the network, but also equals p's distance to R in the tree.

In view of our target, viz. accomplishing $x.p = dist.p$, we investigate decrements of $x.p$ (that maintain H and Q). In this particular problem, where distances are measured in terms of the *number* of edges, we propose for "q is a better father (for p)" condition

$$1 + x.q < x.p \quad ,$$

and we shall be heading for assignment

$$x.p := 1 + x.q \quad .$$

For guard

$$q \in \mathcal{N}.p \ \wedge \ q \text{ is red} \ \wedge \ q \text{ is a better father}$$

we now choose

$$q \in \mathcal{N}.p \ \wedge \ 1 + x.q < x.p \quad .$$

Note that, by our convention, the redness of q is implied since $x.q < inf$ is implied by $x.q < -1 + x.p$. For the same reason, guard

$$q \in \mathcal{N}.p \ \wedge \ q \text{ is red}$$

in the prelude can be replaced by (the stronger)

$$q \in \mathcal{N}.p \ \wedge \ 1 + x.q < x.p$$

as well. Thus, the colours having been removed and the two guards identified, we can gracefully combine (=fold) the prelude and the repetition in Comp.p's text, so as to arrive at the following multiprogram (annotation discussed below):

Pre :	$\langle \forall p, r :: f.p \neq r \rangle$
	$\langle \forall r :: x.r = inf \rangle$
Comp.p:	$*\,[\,\mathbf{if}\ q :: q \in \mathcal{N}.p \ \wedge \ 1 + x.q < x.p$
$(p \neq R)$	$\quad \rightarrow skip \ \mathbf{fi}$
	$;\ \{1 + x.q < x.p\}$
	$\quad f.p := q$
	$;\ \{1 + x.q < x.p\}\ \{f.p = q\}$
	$\quad x.p := 1 + x.q$
	$\,]$
Comp.R:	$\{x.R = inf\}\ x.R := 0$
Inv : H :	$\langle \forall r :: dist.r \leq x.r \rangle$
$Q.p$:	$\langle \forall r : r \in \mathcal{N}.p : f.p = r \ \Rightarrow \ x.r < x.p \rangle$

Distributed Computation of a Breadth-First Spanning Tree

- From the annotation it follows that each individual x decreases, and that is why the annotation in Comp.p is correct.

- For the invariance of H under $x.p := 1 + x.q$ we need

$$dist.p \leq 1 + x.q$$

as a precondition, the validity of which follows from $dist.p \leq 1 + dist.q$ — because p and q are neighbours — and $dist.q \leq x.q$ — from H.

- The invariance of $Q.p$ may be endangered by assignments $f.p := q$ and $x.p := 1 + x.q$ (but changes to other variables $x.r$ are harmless, thanks to Widening). Assignment $f.p := q$ maintains $Q.p$, because its pre-assertion $1 + x.q < x.p$ implies required precondition $x.q < x.p$; and, finally, assignment $x.p := 1 + x.q$ has pre-assertion $f.p = q$ and, as a result, maintaining $Q.p$ only requires the trivially correct pre-assertion $x.q < 1 + x.q$.

Because each x-value decreases and is bounded from below — see H — the system will indeed come to a halt, viz. in the aforementioned total-deadlock state. In that state we have

(i) $x.R = 0$ — Comp.R has terminated —

(ii) $\langle \forall q : q \in \mathcal{N}.p : x.p \leq 1 + x.q \rangle$,   for $p \neq R$
    — Comp.p is blocked in its guarded skip.

We now prove that in this state it holds that, for any component q and for any k,

$$dist.q = k \Rightarrow x.q = k \quad.$$

This we do by mathematical induction with respect to k.

- *Base* $k = 0$:
There is only one node at distance 0 in the network, viz. R, and by (i) we indeed have $x.R = 0$.

- *Step*
Let p be at distance $1 + k$, i.e. $dist.p = 1 + k$. Then there exists a neighbour qq of p at distance k, for which — by induction — we have $x.qq = k$. Now we observe

$$x.p = 1 + k$$

$$\equiv \quad \{1 + k \leq x.p, \quad \text{see } H \text{ for } r := p\}$$

$$x.p \leq 1 + k$$

$$\equiv \quad \{x.qq = k\}$$

$$x.p \leq 1 + x.qq$$

$\equiv$ {(ii) for $q := qq$}

true   .

And this completes our proof that $x.p = dist.p$ for all p.

*   *

*

Finally we have to show that the tree computed is a Breadth-First tree — which was our overall target. That is, we have to prove that, in the final state, $x.q$ equals the distance of q in the tree. Since $x.R = 0$, the result follows if, in the final state, with each single step along an f-chain the value decreases by exactly 1. Now, let p and q be such that $f.p = q$. Then $p \neq R$, and we conclude

from (ii): $x.p \leq 1 + x.q$

from Q: $x.q < x.p$ or, equivalently $1 + x.q \leq x.p$

so that $1 + x.q = x.p^{\ddagger}$.

This settles our final proof obligation and our treatment of the Breadth-First algorithm.

A Shortest-Path Algorithm

In a monograph like this, one cannot afford to include a chapter on the distributed computation of spanning trees without making mention of the Shortest-Path problem. It is as follows. Given a connected network of computers with one predetermined node R and with each edge having a positive integer length — $len.p.q$ for neighbours p and q —, the problem is to design a distributed algorithm that computes for each node a shortest connection to R.

We shall not deal with this design in any detail, because it is so very similar to the Breadth-First problem, which is, in fact, just a Shortest-Path problem where all edges have length 1. We simply state our solution, but not before having mentioned that it has very much of the flavour of Dijkstra's sequential shortest-path algorithm [Dij59], while, remarkably enough, the algorithm is conceptually simpler when rendered as a multiprogram.

$\ddagger$We owe this extremely simple argument to our colleague Gerard Zwaan.

Pre :	$\langle\, \forall p,r :: f.p \neq r\,\rangle$
	$\langle\, \forall r :: x.r = inf\,\rangle$
Comp.p:	$*\,[\,\text{if } q :: q \in \mathcal{N}.p \;\wedge\; len.p.q + x.q < x.p$
$(p \neq R)$	$\rightarrow skip$ **fi**
	$;\ f.p := q$
	$;\ x.p := len.p.q + x.q$
	$]$
Comp.R:	$x.R := 0$

Distributed Computation of Shortest Paths

The computed spanning tree provides a shortest path towards R, for each node. We leave all the details to the reader.

End of Solution II.

*   *

*

We are left with one issue, viz. the unusual termination of a multiprogram in, for instance, the form of a total deadlock, as encountered above in the Breadth-First algorithm. In all our examples so far, deadlock was unwanted. It referred to a state in which the computation had come to a grinding halt, whereas it should have continued. Here the situation is quite different, because here the deadlock state signifies that the computation need not continue any longer: the desired work has been done, the tree has been computed. How do we deal with this phenomenon?

In one way or another, the components have to be extended with facilities to signal that they have terminated, whether in a usual or an unusual way. When via this signalling the conclusion can be drawn that all components have terminated, we may — through proper adjustment of the component programs — see to it that then each component will terminate in the regular and usual way. (For a mini-example of this, see our treatise of the co-components in Chapter 21.) In general, the orderly processing of the signals in order to justly draw the conclusion of termination is delegated to a special-purpose algorithm, a so-called Termination Detection Algorithm, which operates concurrently with the computation proper whose termination has to be detected. The design of one such Termination Detection Algorithm is the topic of our next chapter.

29

Shmuel Safra's Termination Detection Algorithm

Along with the rise of large-scale distributed systems, a number of new problems and algorithmic paradigms saw the light. One of these was the problem of so-called quiescence detection, which led to the wider class of so-called distributed snapshot algorithms. Roughly speaking, distributed snapshot algorithms have to detect, in a distributed fashion, whether a system has entered a state in which no relevant things will happen any more. What is relevant very much depends on the specifics of the problem. For instance, in a self-stabilizing system, i.e. a system that stabilizes towards some pre-specified state, one might be interested in whether that state has been reached. The so-called termination detection algorithms, which were the first algorithms of this class to attract the attention of computing scientists, are to detect whether a distributed computation proper has arrived at a final state, i.e. has terminated.

Since the emergence of the first termination detection algorithms [DS80, Fra80], computing science has produced dozens, perhaps even grosses of such algorithms. For an overview, the reader might consult [Tel94]. And, indeed, the problem has always been fascinating, intriguing and challenging, and it still is. This chapter is devoted to one such algorithm, viz. Shmuel Safra's, which is a beautiful and practical extension of the algorithm that was first reported in [DFvG83].

* *
*

Before describing our problem, we first have to face a fact of life. Suppose we go to a shop where we buy a machine that generates an infinite sequence of bits that, as we are told by the shopkeeper, will be such that eventually only '1's will be produced. So eventually no relevant things will happen anymore. We go home, plug our machine into the power supply, switch it on, wait until it has reached the final state in which only '1's are produced, and then switch it off.

Now the reader may, in whatever way he likes, conclude that this experiment makes no sense at all: there is no moment in time at which we can safely conclude that the machine has entered its final state and will never produce a zero anymore. In short: not all termination detection problems are solvable. The fact of life is that we have to know something more about the computation proper than just that it terminates (if at all). An investigation into what in general is needed in addition falls outside the scope of this text. We will consider only one, fairly general, kind of computation proper.

Problem Description

The kind of computation proper that we will address has the following characteristics:

(i) The individual components are located in the nodes of a finite, connected network;

(ii) Each component can be in just two, mutually exclusive states, viz. neutral and active;

(iii) An active component can send a message to a neighbour in the network. Neutral components *cannot* send messages. Sending a message is a separate atomic event;

(iv) A neutral component will only become active upon receipt of a message. Receiving a message together with becoming active is a separate atomic event;

(v) An active component may unconditionally turn neutral; this also is a separate atomic event;

(vi) Each message in transit was sent by some component.

Now, with M equal to the number of messages in transit, the final state of the computation proper is characterized by

$$Z: \qquad \langle\, \forall i :: neutr.i \,\rangle \ \wedge\ M = 0 \ .$$

The reader may verify that condition Z is stable indeed. In passing we note that $M0$, given by

$$M0: \qquad 0 \leq M$$

is a system invariant.

Remark No matter how obvious property (vi) above may seem, it will play an essential rôle in the design of our algorithm: if the system were capable of creating traveling messages out of the blue, the stability of Z would no longer be guaranteed.
End of Remark.

The problem now is to design an algorithm that reports, within a finite number of steps, the validity of Z, once the computation proper has established Z. Such an algorithm, to be superimposed on the computation proper, will be referred to as "the termination detection algorithm".

The global structure

The termination detection algorithm has to explore the state of the entire system, and it will do so by means of a sequence of one or more *probes*. After initiation, a probe is propagated through the system to collect information about the state of the system. An important event in the algorithm is the termination of a probe. If the information collected permits the conclusion that Z holds, the termination detection algorithm can terminate; otherwise a next probe is started. For the termination detection algorithm to be effective, we will require that

the detection algorithm terminates within a finite number of steps, once Z holds.

Given this global structure of the algorithm, the next question is how to propagate a probe. It should be clear that for the conclusion that Z holds, the state of the entire system — components and links alike — matters: a message in transit can re-activate the entire system ((vi) and (iii)), and so can each single active component ((iii)). So, our probe will have to diffuse through the *entire* network; all components will have to partake in it.

To that end, we assume available a graph that spans all the nodes of the network. For our considerations it is immaterial where this graph comes from, i.e. whether its edges coincide with links of the original network or whether they are specially installed for the purpose. Of course there is a variety of spanning graphs that we can think of, but here we opt for a (unidirectional) cycle.

Remark Choosing a cycle for the spanning graph is just a design decision. A subspanning tree would be another possibility. Different choices lead to different algorithms. One advantage of a cycle is that it provides a simple topology (and a simple algorithm in its wake).
End of Remark.

We choose the cycle to be directed in order to have a fixed direction in which to propagate the probe. Probe initiation will take place at one designated component. "Return" of the probe at this component marks the termination of this probe. We will describe the propagation of the probe by means of a traveling token.

The token

We identify the components along the cycle with the natural numbers $N-1$ through 0, in the directed cyclic order. Variable t records the place of the token. The designated component from which probes start is Comp.0. It initiates a probe by sending the token to Comp.$(N-1)$, which is symbolized by $t := N-1$. Token propagation to the next component on the cycle is symbolized by $t := t-1$. Arrival of the token at Comp.0 marks the end of a probe. It goes without saying that only the component that owns the token can send it. Token Initiation and Token Propagation are separate atomic events.

Remark The choice of Comp.0 as the designated component is as arbitrary as the numbering of the components and the direction in which the token travels. The above choices just happen to yield the nicer formulae.
End of Remark.

Detecting termination

The main goal to be achieved is that our algorithm will detect the validity of

Z: $\langle\, \forall i :: neutr.i \,\rangle\ \land\ M = 0$,

once this state has been established (by the computation proper). Therefore, let us first investigate what is involved in concluding Z upon return of the token to Comp.0.

Upon the token's return, it should be possible for Comp.0 to determine the validity of Z on account of information locally available to it. Because there is very little local information available, the bulk of the information had better be carried by a system invariant. In finding out what invariants are appropriate, let us consider the two conjuncts of Z separately.

As for the first conjunct, Comp.0 can only contribute to it by its value of $neutr.0$. So upon arrival of the token (i.e. $t = 0$), the invariant had better imply $\langle\, \forall i : 0 < i < N : neutr.i \,\rangle$. This leads to the adoption of system invariant

PoA: $\langle\, \forall i : t < i < N : neutr.i \,\rangle$.

Then, indeed, we have

$(0A)$ $t = 0\ \land\ PoA\ \land\ neutr.0\ \Rightarrow\ \langle\, \forall i :: neutr.i \,\rangle$.

As for the second conjunct of Z, the value of M cannot be evaluated by any component. As is not unusual in distributed systems, global data had better be represented in a distributed fashion. Because — see (vi) —

$M\ =\ (\#\text{messages sent}) - (\#\text{messages received})$,

we can now easily distribute this "deficit" by recording for each Comp.i value $d.i$ defined by

$d.i\ =\ (\#\text{messages sent by Comp.}i)$
$\qquad - (\#\text{messages received by Comp.}i)$.

Then, by construction, $M1$ given by

$M1$: $M = \langle\, \Sigma i :: d.i \,\rangle$,

is a system invariant.

How can Comp.0 determine the validity of $M = 0$ upon return of the token? Comp.0 can only contribute its own value of $d.0$. Therefore the rest of M, i.e. the value of $\langle \Sigma i : 0 < i < N : d.i \rangle$, had better be carried by a system invariant. To that end we embellish the token with an integer attribute q, for which we propose system invariant

P_0B: $q = \langle \Sigma i : t < i < N : d.i \rangle$.

Then, indeed, we have

(0B) $t = 0 \ \wedge \ P_0B \ \wedge \ q + d.0 = 0 \ \Rightarrow \ M = 0$.

Summarizing, we will try to see to the invariance of

P_0: $P_0A \ \wedge \ P_0B$,

because then — combining (0A) and (0B) — we have

(0) $t = 0 \ \wedge \ P_0 \ \wedge \ neutr.0 \ \wedge \ q + d.0 = 0 \ \Rightarrow \ Z$.

> And here we emphasize that (0) will constitute the one and only way in which the validity of Z can be inferred.

Figure Star

It stands to reason that, if upon return of the token at Comp.0 the antecedent of (0) is not fulfilled, nothing can be concluded about Z and nothing else can be done but to initiate another probe.

Token traffic and P_0

After having decided how Z is to be detected, we now turn our attention to the invariance of P_0, and we start by investigating the token traffic.

Initiation of the probe is realized by Comp.0 injecting the token into the ring via $t := N - 1$, which establishes P_0A. Along with it, statement $q := 0$ establishes P_0B. We record this fact in the following guarded command

Token Initiation:
    Comp.0: $\{true\}$
$$t = 0 \rightarrow t, q := N - 1, 0$$
$$\{P_0\}$$

It can be read as an *atomic* statement that is eligible for execution if the guard is *true* and which then establishes (the local correctness of) P_0.

Propagation of the probe, i.e. $t := t - 1$, is not unconditional. We have

$$(t := t - 1).P_0A$$

$\equiv$ {substitution and predicate calculus}

$$P_0A \wedge neutr.t \quad ,$$

and

$$(t := t - 1).P_0B$$

$\equiv$ {substitution and calculus}

$$q = \langle \Sigma i : t < i < N : d.i \rangle + d.t \quad ,$$

which tells us that q needs to be increased by $d.t$ along with $t := t - 1$. Thus we get

Token Propagation:
    Comp.i: $\{P_0\}$
    $(i \neq 0)$ $t = i \wedge neutr.i$
$$\rightarrow t, q := t - 1, q + d.i$$
$$\{P_0\}$$

The computation proper and P_0

Besides the atomic token operations, our system contains three more atomic statements, viz. Message Sending, Message Receipt and a component Turning Neutral, and we have to investigate the effect of each of them on P_0. We recall

P_0A: $\langle \forall i : t < i < N : neutr.i \rangle$

P_0B: $q = \langle \Sigma i : t < i < N : d.i \rangle \quad .$

- Turning Neutral does not violate P_0A or P_0B (Widening).

- Sending a message by Comp.j is described by — see (iii) —

    $\{act.j\}\ d.j := 1 + d.j$.

  This statement does not violate P_0A, and it can only violate P_0B if j is in the range $t < j < N$. By pre-assertion $act.j$ and P_0A, however, we conclude that j isn't. So Message Sending is safe with respect to P_0. We obtain

---

Message Sending:

  Comp.i: $\{P_0\}\ \{act.i\}$

   $true \rightarrow d.i := 1 + d.i$

   $\{P_0\}$

- Message Receipt by Comp.j is described by — see (iv) —

    $d.j := -1 + d.j\ \{act.j\}$,

  which, unfortunately, has a disastrous effect on both P_0A and P_0B, for each j in the range $t < j < N$. What can we do about it?

*   *
*

In this monograph we have seen two general techniques of how to proceed if the correctness of an assertion or invariant is endangered by some atomic statement. One technique was to strengthen the annotation so as to prevent the violation — mostly by an appeal to the Rule of Disjointness. The other technique was to weaken the threatened assertion or invariant (e.g. cf. Chapter 14 and Example 5 of Chapter 8). In the current example the first technique is ruled out because we cannot possibly impose a pre-assertion on Message Receipt: (a) messages arrive outside our and the recipient's control and   (b) Comp.j has no means of detecting whether $t < j < N$ holds.

As a result, we will have to resort to weakening the invariant, i.e. to finding a P_1 such that

    $P_0 \lor P_1$

will be an invariant. However, this requires that we reconsider the termination detection possibilities of Comp.0.

Saving the detection mechanism

Because of the decision laid down in Figure Star, the possibility to detect termination completely depends on the possibility to conclude the validity of P_0 upon return of the token in Comp.0. Since our new invariant is the weaker $P_0 \lor P_1$, we can only hope to ensure the validity of P_0 if by local information of Comp.0 we can conclude the *falsity* of P_1. This severely limits the potential shapes for P_1.

In our example, $d.j := -1 + d.j$ may falsify $P_0 B$, i.e.

$P_0 B$: $\qquad q = \langle \Sigma i : t < i < N : d.i \rangle$,

namely it does so for j in the range $t < j < N$. Thereby it then definitely establishes

$$q \geq \langle \Sigma i : t < i < N : d.i \rangle \quad ,$$

and we might think that this condition is a good candidate for P_1, but it is *not*! For $t = 0$, Comp.0 has no means of establishing its falsity. The only quantified expressions that can be nominated for P_1 are expressions over — roughly — the complementary range, say $0 \leq i \leq t$.

Finding P_1

With the above in mind, what can we choose for P_1? It was a message *receipt* that caused the problem. Now we have to remember that our system does not spontaneously — out of the blue — create messages, but that each message in transit was sent by a component — see (vi). Recalling invariants

M_0: $\qquad 0 \leq M$

M_1: $\qquad M = \langle \Sigma i :: d.i \rangle$,

we conclude that the precondition of a receipt implies $0 < M$.

Now let us study the falsification of P_0, in particular of $P_0 B$, by statement

$$\{0 < M \land P_0 \land t < j < N\} \; d.j := -1 + d.j \quad .$$

We have, from this statement's precondition,

0

$<$ $\qquad$ {first conjunct}

M

$=$ $\{M_1\}$

$\langle\, \Sigma i : 0 \leq i < N : d.i \,\rangle$

$=$ $\{$splitting the range$\}$

$\langle\, \Sigma i : t < i < N : d.i \,\rangle + \langle\, \Sigma i : 0 \leq i \leq t : d.i \,\rangle$

$=$ $\{P_0B\}$

$q + \langle\, \Sigma i : 0 \leq i \leq t : d.i \,\rangle$.

So, $0 < q + \langle\, \Sigma i : 0 \leq i \leq t : d.i \,\rangle$

– is a precondition of the damaging statement, and
– the damaging statement does not affect it — $t < j < N$ —, and
– it has the right shape.

Therefore we try to get away with

P_1: $0 < q + \langle\, \Sigma i : 0 \leq i \leq t : d.i \,\rangle$.

Upon return of the token at Comp.0, its falsity can be concluded via

(1) $t = 0 \,\wedge\, q + d.0 \leq 0 \,\Rightarrow\, \neg P_1$.

Remark   The fact that the system cannot generate messages out of the
blue is an essential given. If it could, termination detection would be im-
possible. The explicit exploitation of this fact, as we did in the above, is
Shmuel Safra's great and impressive addition to the algorithm reported in
[DFvG83].
End of Remark.

With the above, Message Receipt is described by

> Message Receipt:
>   Comp.i: $\{P_0\}$
> $true \rightarrow d.i := -1 + d.i$
> $\{P_0 \vee P_1\}$

But how do we know that $P_0 \vee P_1$ cannot be falsified?

An intermezzo

As it stands, Token Initiation, Token Propagation and Message Sending are examples of statements S satisfying

(*) $[\, P_0 \wedge B \;\Rightarrow\; wlp.S.P_0 \,]$,

each with its own B. Message Receipt satisfies a rule of the form

(**) $[\, P_0 \wedge B \;\Rightarrow\; wlp.S.(P_0 \vee P_1) \,]$.

After having weakened the invariant into $P_0 \vee P_1$, however, we are no longer interested in (*) and (**), but rather in whether our atomic statements S, for some B, satisfy

(***) $[\, (P_0 \vee P_1) \wedge B \;\Rightarrow\; wlp.S.(P_0 \vee P_1) \,]$.

Fortunately, our knowledge of (*) and (**) can help us in dealing with (***). To that end we calculate

    (***)

=   {predicate calculus}

    $[\, P_0 \wedge B \;\Rightarrow\; wlp.S.(P_0 \vee P_1) \,]$

        $\wedge\; [\, P_1 \wedge B \;\Rightarrow\; wlp.S.(P_0 \vee P_1) \,]$,

and we see that the first conjunct has already been catered for: for an S satisfying (**), the first conjunct just equals (**), and for an S satisfying (*), it is implied by (*) (by the monotonicity of wlp). So our only care concerns the second conjunct:

    $[\, P_1 \wedge B \;\Rightarrow\; wlp.S.(P_0 \vee P_1) \,]$.

The result is that for the invariance of $P_0 \vee P_1$ it suffices to focus on the effect that our statements have on P_1 all by itself.

Sometimes we can even go one step further in our simplification: because we have that

    $[\, P_1 \wedge B \;\Rightarrow\; wlp.S.(P_0 \vee P_1) \,]$

follows from

    $[\, P_1 \wedge B \;\Rightarrow\; wlp.S.P_1 \,]$,

we may try to establish the latter; in that case we only have to worry about the invariance of P_1. And if, for the benefit of maintaining P_1, the precondition B of S needs to be strengthened, this is fine because harmless to (***).

We thus obtain a layered, disentangled pattern of reasoning: first deal with P_0 in isolation, then with P_1 in isolation, then with P_2 should the need arise, etcetera. And the need for P_2 will arise, as we shall see shortly.

Introduction of P_2 (or: dealing with P_1)

Before proceeding, let us summarize what we have got. The envisaged invariant is $P_0 \lor P_1$, with

P_0: $P_0A \land P_0B$,

P_0A: $\langle\, \forall i : t < i < N : neutr.i \,\rangle$,

P_0B: $q = \langle\, \Sigma i : t < i < N : d.i \,\rangle$, and

P_1: $0 < q + \langle\, \Sigma i : 0 \leq i \leq t : d.i \,\rangle$.

The components so far are

Token Initiation:
  Comp.0: $\{true\}$
      $t = 0 \rightarrow t, q := N - 1, 0$
      $\{P_0\}$

Token Propagation:
  Comp.i: $\{P_0\}$
  $(i \neq 0)$ $t = i \land neutr.i$
      $\rightarrow t, q := t - 1, q + d.i$
      $\{P_0\}$

Message Sending:
  Comp.i: $\{P_0\}$ $\{act.i\}$
      $true \rightarrow d.i := 1 + d.i$
      $\{P_0\}$

Message Receipt:
  Comp.i: $\{P_0\}$
      $true \rightarrow d.i := -1 + d.i$ $\{act.i\}$
      $\{P_0 \lor P_1\}$

Turning Neutral:
  Comp.i: $\{P_0\}$
      $true \rightarrow neutr.i := true$
      $\{P_0\}$

Version 0

Now we investigate the effect of these statements on $P_0 \lor P_1$, where, following the intermezzo, we just focus on P_1.

- Token Initiation correctly establishes P_0, hence also $P_0 \lor P_1$.

- Token Propagation maintains P_1: just apply the axiom of assignment, taking $t = i$ into account.

- Message Sending maintains P_1: Widening.

- Unfortunately, Message Receipt by a Comp.i with i in the range $0 \leq i \leq t$ may falsify P_1. If along with this potential violation of P_1 relation P_0 were (re-)established, we would be done. But it isn't, and therefore we have to weaken our invariant once more, with a disjunct P_2 to be established along with any damaging Message Receipt.

- Turning Neutral maintains P_1: Orthogonality.

In order to record that something nasty may happen by a Message Receipt, we introduce the notion of a coloured component, viz. a component will be black or white. The receipt of a message will be recorded by blackening the component. With P_2 defined by

P_2: $\langle\, \exists i : 0 \leq i \leq t : black.i \,\rangle$,

the above damaging receipt establishes P_2 by the following program adjustment — see Remark below —

```
Message Receipt:
   Comp.i:  {P0 ∨ P1}
               true →   black.i := true
               ; d.i := −1 + d.i
            {P0 ∨ P1 ∨ P2}
```

Termination detection is still possible upon return of the token, because we have

(2) $t = 0 \land white.0 \;\Rightarrow\; \lnot P_2$

(where $white \equiv \lnot black$).

Remark   In more detail, the massaging we carried out to obtain the above extended Message Receipt is, in fact, a sequence of steps:

- first, we extended our previous Message Receipt with statement
  $black.i := true$, yielding

  $\{P_0\}$

  Message Receipt

  $\{P_0 \lor P_1\}$,

  which is correct because P_0 doesn't mention colours;

- second, our extended Message Receipt was constructed so as to satisfy

  $\{P_1\}$

  Message Receipt

  $\{P_1 \lor P_2\}$;

- third, we combined these two Hoare triples into the one in the box above.

For the other atomic events, similar combinations can be given. We will,
however, omit these detailed manipulations.
End of Remark.

In summary, we have for our next version

Token Initiation:

    Comp.0: $\{true\}$

            $t = 0 \rightarrow t, q := N - 1, 0$

            $\{P_0\}$

Token Propagation:

    Comp.i: $\{P_0 \lor P_1\}$

    $(i \neq 0)$ $t = i \land neutr.i$

            $\rightarrow t, q := t - 1, q + d.i$

            $\{P_0 \lor P_1\}$

Message Sending:

    Comp.i: $\{P_0 \lor P_1\} \{act.i\}$

            $true \rightarrow d.i := 1 + d.i$

            $\{P_0 \lor P_1\}$

Message Receipt:

   Comp.i: $\{P_0 \lor P_1\}$

          $true \rightarrow black.i := true$

               $; d.i := -1 + d.i$

          $\{P_0 \lor P_1 \lor P_2\}$

Turning Neutral:

   Comp.i: $\{P_0 \lor P_1\}$

          $true \rightarrow neutr.i := true$

          $\{P_0 \lor P_1\}$

Version 1

where

P_0:	$P_0A \land P_0B$,
P_0A:	$\langle \forall i : t < i < N : neutr.i \rangle$,
P_0B:	$q = \langle \Sigma i : t < i < N : d.i \rangle$,
P_1:	$0 < q + \langle \Sigma i : 0 \le i \le t : d.i \rangle$, and
P_2:	$\langle \exists i : 0 \le i \le t : black.i \rangle$.

Finally: introducing P_3 (or dealing with P_2)

Next we investigate the effect of our statements on $P_0 \lor P_1 \lor P_2$, where, according to the intermezzo, it suffices to focus on just P_2:

P_2: $\langle \exists i : 0 \le i \le t : black.i \rangle$.

- Neither Turning Neutral nor Message Sending affects colours, so both are harmless to P_2.

- Message Receipt blackens a component, so that is Widening.

- Token Initiation establishes P_0, hence also $P_0 \lor P_1 \lor P_2$.

- However, Token Propagation may violate P_2: Comp.t could be the only black component in the range $0 \le i \le t$. We therefore weaken our invariant once more, with a disjunct P_3 to be established along with token transmission.

For this purpose, we introduce the notion of a coloured token. If the token is propagated by a black component, it will be propagated black. With ct a variable to record the colour of the token, we introduce

P_3: $ct = black$,

and adjust token transmission so as to establish P_3 when P_2 may be violated. (Note that, like q, ct is an attribute of the token.)

Token Propagation:

Comp.i: $\{P_0 \lor P_1 \lor P_2\}$

$(i \neq 0)$ $t = i \land neutr.i \rightarrow$

        if $white.i \rightarrow$ $t, q := t - 1, q + d.i$

        ▌ $black.i \rightarrow$ $t, q, ct := t - 1, q + d.i, black$

        fi

$\{P_0 \lor P_1 \lor P_2 \lor P_3\}$

Termination detection has remained possible upon return of the token, because

(3) $ct = white \Rightarrow \neg P_3$.

*   *

*

Because P_3 is not falsified by any of our statements, we are done. Our system maintains invariant

$P_0 \lor P_1 \lor P_2 \lor P_3$,

and termination detection by Comp.0 is still possible because, combining (0) through (3), we have

$$t = 0 \land (P_0 \lor P_1 \lor P_2 \lor P_3) \land neutr.0$$
$$\land q + d.0 = 0 \land white.0 \land ct = white$$
$$\Rightarrow$$
$$Z \quad .$$

The only question that remains is whether Comp.0 will actually report termination, once Z has been established, i.e. whether — after termination — the state

$$t = 0 \land neutr.0 \land q + d.0 = 0 \land white.0 \land ct = white$$

will indeed be reached, in a finite number of steps.

Progress

As its stands, the token is only blackened and never whitened. The same holds for the components. Without whitening operations, we cannot hope that termination will ever be reported by Comp.0. So we had better explore our program for whitening opportunities, of course without violating the invariant.

The opportunity par excellence to whiten the token is Token Initiation, because that establishes P_0 (which does not mention colours at all). For the same reason, Comp.0 may also whiten itself. So we propose to extend Token Initiation into

> Token Initiation:
> Comp.0: $t = 0 \rightarrow$ $t, q, ct := N - 1, 0, white$
> ; $white.0 := true$

The opportunity par excellence for a black Comp.i, $i \neq 0$, to whiten itself is Token Propagation, because for a black Comp.i, Token Propagation establishes P_3.

Incorporating this whitening, and collecting the pieces, we arrive at

> Token Initiation:
> Comp.0: $t = 0 \rightarrow$ $t, q, ct := N - 1, 0, white$
> ; $white.0 := true$
> $\{P_0, \text{ hence } PP\}$
>
> Token Propagation:
> Comp.i: $\{PP\}$
> $(i \neq 0)$ $t = i \wedge neutr.i$
> $\rightarrow$ **if** $white.i \rightarrow$ $t, q := t - 1, q + d.i$
> $\|$ $black.i \rightarrow$ $t, q, ct := t - 1, q + d.i, black$
> ; $white.i := true$
> **fi**
> $\{PP\}$

Message Sending:
Comp.i: $\{PP\}$ $\{act.i\}$
$\quad\quad\quad true \rightarrow d.i := 1 + d.i$
$\quad\quad\quad \{PP\}$
Message Receipt:
Comp.i: $\{PP\}$
$\quad\quad\quad true \rightarrow\ black.i := true$
$\quad\quad\quad\quad ; d.i := -1 + d.i$
$\quad\quad\quad \{PP\}$
Turning Neutral:
Comp.i: $\{PP\}$
$\quad\quad\quad true \rightarrow neutr.i := true$
$\quad\quad\quad \{PP\}$
Inv : PP : $P_0 \vee P_1 \vee P_2 \vee P_3$

Shmuel Safra's Termination Detection Algorithm

*   *
*

Now we finally show that termination will be reported (by Comp.0) within a finite number of steps after Z has been established. We recall

$$Z: \quad\quad\quad \langle\, \forall i :: neutr.i \,\rangle \ \wedge\ \langle\, \Sigma i :: d.i \,\rangle = 0 \quad .$$

In a state satisfying Z, Message Sending and Receipt are no longer possible, and as a result

(a) the d's are constant, and

(b) components don't turn black.

Furthermore, since all components are neutral, the token will travel along the ring unhampered and return to Comp.0. So, if necessary, Comp.0 will initiate a next probe. By the program text, that next probe will proceed under invariance of

(c) $\langle\, \forall i : t < i < N : white.i \,\rangle \ \wedge\ white.0 \quad$, and

(d) $q = \langle\, \Sigma i : t < i < N : d.i \,\rangle \quad$,

relations that cannot be falsified thanks to (a) and (b). So upon return of the token in Comp.0 we have

$neutr.0$ — from first conjunct of Z —,

$q + d.0 = 0$ — from (d) and the second conjunct of Z —,

$white.0$ — from (c).

The only conjunct that may be lacking for the conclusion of termination is $ct = white$. If it is, yet a next probe is to be initiated, which now proceeds under the additional invariance of

$\langle \, \forall i :: white.i \, \rangle$ — thanks to (c) and (b).

As a consequence — see the program text —

the token doesn't turn black,

and because it is injected with colour white into the ring, it will return white as well.

And herewith we conclude our progress argument and our treatment of Shmuel Safra's termination detection algorithm.

Final Remarks

We end this chapter with a number of loosely connected remarks.

- We learned about Shmuel Safra's algorithm through [Dij87].

- Since in our derivation we made no assumptions about the initial colours of the components and the token, they may be anything, be it black or white.

- We have all the time assumed that the five guarded commands were atomic. But they can be made more fine-grained in many ways. We leave such explorations to the reader.

- An important and not too easy aspect of the problem is the description of the precise interplay between a component's participation in the computation proper and in the termination detection algorithm. This interplay is arranged most smoothly by splitting the various activities of a component over a number of well-chosen subcomponents. Important and interesting though this problem may be, we consider it a separate concern.

- The technique we used in designing our solution, viz. the steady weakening of our target relation $(P0)$ into a relation (PP) that is closed under the system operations, is not an uncommon one. We can already see it, in a very rudimentary form, in the development of sequential programs, where target relation R is established by finding a weaker P and a condition B such that $[\,P \wedge \neg B \Rightarrow R\,]$, and by aiming at a program of the form

> {*loop inv* : P}
>
> **do** $B \rightarrow S$ {P} **od**
>
> {R}   .

- In Shmuel Safra's design, the successive disjuncts added to the invariant were designed such that they could be dealt with in isolation, according to the rules of our Intermezzo. They thus allowed a "layered" design, a contribution to simplicity that is not to be ignored lightly.

30

The Alternating Bit Protocol

The Alternating Bit Protocol is an algorithm for the correct transmission of a data stream from one place to another via so-called "faulty channels". Here, a faulty channel is a kind of medium that can garble, duplicate or lose data in some well-specified ways. This protocol has raised a lot of interest ever since its emergence [BSW69]. It is discussed, specified, and provided with correctness proofs abundantly in the established literature. However, in spite of this reputation, the general understanding of the algorithm is at an extremely low level: most computing scientists "know" the Alternating Bit Protocol in the sense that they have heard of it, but only a few can explain it. This is a pity for such a fundamental algorithm.[†]

One reason for this state of affairs is, we believe, that the algorithm is mostly explained with too many irrelevant details, i.e. it is not reduced to its most rudimentary form. Another, more important, reason might be that the algorithm is usually postulated rather than derived, and then — at best — provided with an a-posteriori proof of correctness.

The main purpose of this chapter is to try to remedy the situation, by removing from the traditional specification everything that seems irrelevant,

---

[†]The ABP shares this fate with many other elementary algorithms, e.g. the Binary Search and the Depth-First Search, and with some highly respectable mathematical theorems, e.g. Ramsey's Theorem from Combinatorial Mathematics.

and then deriving the algorithm from scratch. It will then turn out that the Alternating Bit Protocol is as simple as the handshake protocol, with just some minor adjustments to take the presence of "faulty channels" into account. We hope that thus we provide the reader with a new appreciation of this fundamental algorithm.

Describing the problem

At the most macroscopic level, the problem can be described by means of the following picture, in which the contents of the rectangular box are not revealed as yet.

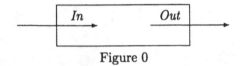

Figure 0

An infinite stream of data is injected at the *In*-side of the box and ejected from the *Out*-side. The intention is that the stream ejected be equal to the stream injected, possibly with some delay. If *In* and *Out* were (perfect) synchronous CSP-links (cf. Chapter 23), the intended behaviour of the box could be described by the little program

(0) $* [\ In?x;\ Out!x\ ]$.

And if there were no constraints on the interior of the box, this program would even be a simple and elegant implementation for our problem.

Unfortunately, we are not free to choose the interior of the box. It so happens that when we open it a little bit, we see two completely independent components, specially designed to take care of the input and the output traffic, respectively. Their behaviour is described by the two-component multiprogram

(1) $A:\quad * [\ In?x\ ]$
          $B:\quad * [\ Out!y\ ]$.

Fortunately, we are entitled to adjust the components, for instance we might synchronize them in such a way that their combined behaviour is as demanded, i.e. like (0). Now we seem to be on familiar ground, because if we were able to identify y and x, program (1) would simplify to

          $A:\quad * [\ In?x\ ]$
          $B:\quad * [\ Out!x\ ]$,

and superposition of a simple handshake protocol would do the job (cf. Chapter 16).

Unfortunately, we are not free to identify y and x, because we are not free to choose how A and B communicate. It so happens that A is equipped with a perfect synchronous link to some interior box F, some sort of channel, to which it can deliver a data item. And, symmetrically, B is equipped with such a link as well, by which it can extract a data item from F. So the situation inside the box of Figure 0 can be sketched by the following picture.

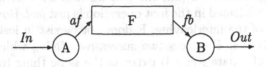

Figure 1

Component A may be modified so as to inject a data item into F via $af!x$. Similarly, B can extract such an item via $fb?y$. That is how the x and y in (1) are coupled, but to understand this fully we must now open F.

Inside F we discover the following two-component multiprogram:

$$(2) \qquad \begin{aligned} &\text{AF}: \ * \, [\, af?p\,] \\ &\text{FB}: \ * \, [\, fb!p\,] \quad, \end{aligned}$$

and it so happens that we are *not* allowed to modify this multiprogram in any sense whatsoever.

$$* \qquad *$$
$$*$$

Now let us analyze the situation we are in. It is the intention that, via A, an infinite stream of data is transmitted to B. Because the only communication line available is via F, the implementation has to see to it that

(3a)   A performs operations $af!$ with positive frequency,

and, symmetrically, that

(3b)   B performs operations $fb?$ with positive frequency.

And what about F in this respect? Because we will not intervene in (2), — because that is not allowed! —, F will produce some fair interleaving of operations $af?$ and $fb!$, and it can choose the interleaving autonomously. By "fair" we mean that at any moment during operation of F a next $af?$ and a next $fb!$ are guaranteed to occur. As a result, F will perform operations *af?* and *fb!* each with positive frequency, which nicely matches the requirements laid down in (3a) and (3b).

*   *
*

Now, F can behave nicely,   like

$$* [\, af?p; \; fb!p \,]   ,$$

and then it is a perfect one-place channel, but it need not. It can misbehave in two different ways. One way is that it selects two successive *af?*'s in the interleaving. Thanks to (3a) these operations both terminate, but the data item communicated in the first operation is just *lost*. However, because of the fairness of the interleaving, F does not persist in losing. The other misbehaviour is that F selects two successive *fb!*'s , which corresponds to *duplication* of a data item: B extracts the same thing from F twice in succession. But again, F does not persist in duplicating.

A piece of machinery like F is called a *faulty channel*. It is a realistic model for communication "facilities" as we may encounter them in practice, and the problem is how to correctly transmit a stream of data from one place to another when faulty channels are our only devices for information transfer.

In the rest of this chapter we shall derive programs for A and B so that the correct transmission be achieved. But before doing so, we first simplify the problem statement by reducing it to its bare essentials.

Simplifying the problem

As yet, the input stream to be consumed by component A through statements *In?x* is completely arbitrary. Without losing the essence of the problem, we assume that it is the sequence of natural numbers, which is the simplest sequence that enables us to distinguish between the individual items in the stream (cf. the Handshake Protocol, Chapter 16). With this assumption, statement *In?x* is just $x := x + 1$, so that the basic structure of component A now simplifies to

$$A: * [\, x := x + 1 \,]   .$$

Likewise, we are not really interested in where B sends its output to via *Out!y* . Let us assume that it just prints it via command *print(y)*. Furthermore, a value y printed by B is always extracted from F via the clicking pair $(fb?y, \; fb!p)$, which to all intents and purposes amounts to $y := p$.

Thus, B always prints a value p to be read from F, so that the basic structure of component B now becomes

B: $* [\, print(p) \,]$.

At the other end of the channel, A and F communicate via the clicking pair $(af!x,\ af?p)$, which amounts to $p := x$. Thus the structure of F can now be described as

F: $* [\, p := x \,]$.

What about constraints (3a) and (3b)? The former says that the transfer of value x to p is to occur with positive frequency, and this is okay in our simplified version, since the F above proceeds with positive speed (cf. Chapter 1). The latter constraint demands that B inspect p with a positive frequency, and this will follow from the final progress argument — to be given anyway —, which guarantees that B continues printing, and hence inspecting, p.

So much for our simplified model of the problem, which in summary can now be phrased as follows. Given three-component multi-program

Pre: $x = 0$

A: $* [\, x := x + 1 \,]$

F: $* [\, p := x \,]$

B: $* [\, print(p) \,]$,

we are to synchronize the components in such a way that B prints the sequence of natural numbers, under the additional constraint that *no* synchronization code (i.e. blocking constructs) may be added to faulty channel F. Moreover, if "feedback" is required in A from B, such information exchange may only be realized through the intermediary of another faulty channel (recall: no other communication media are allowed between A and B).

Deriving a solution

We will develop a solution in three steps. First we formally specify the problem and give a solution under the assumption that direct communication between A and B is allowed. Then we plug in the faulty channel(s) and adjust the solution accordingly, and, finally, we transform the resulting program into one that uses boolean variables only, thereby arriving at the Alternating Bit Protocol.

A solution using direct communication

Our starting point is multiprogram

Pre :	$x = 0$	
A:	$*[\, x := x + 1\,]$	B: $*[\, print(x)\,]$

and our task is to synchronize the components in such a way that B prints the sequence of natural numbers. This is exactly the problem that led us to the Handshake Protocol (cf. Chapter 16), and we do not repeat that development here, but rather give an annotated solution at once. The reader can easily check the correctness of the annotation in place.

Pre :	$x = 0 \,\wedge\, y = 0$	
A:	$*[\,$ **if** $x + 1 \leq y \rightarrow$ *skip* **fi** $\quad ; \{x + 1 \leq y\}$ $\qquad x := x + 1$ $\quad]$	B: $*[\, \{x = y\}$ $\qquad print(x)$ $\quad ; y := y + 1$ $\quad ;$ **if** $y \leq x \rightarrow$ *skip* **fi** $\quad]$
Inv :	$P_0 :\ x \leq y$ $P_1 :\ y \leq x + 1$	

Version 0

From the text of B alone together with precondition $y = 0$ we can conclude that B prints as demanded. But recall from Chapter 16 that y is a (clairvoyance) variable mimicking the behaviour of x in A, and that it has to be eliminated from the program text in the end. Also notice that $P_0 \wedge P_1$ is a proper multibound for the multiprogram.

Introducing the faulty channels

If we now disallow the direct communication between A and B, component B can no longer inspect variable x, and A is denied access to y. So, we plug in two faulty channels, viz.

$$\text{F:}\quad *[\, p := x\,]\quad,$$

for transmitting the value of x from A to B, and

$$\text{G:}\quad *[\, q := y\,]\quad,$$

for transmitting the value of y from B to A. Along with this change in architecture, *all* occurrences of x in B have to be replaced by p, and *all* occurrences of y in A by q. So we have to change guard $y \leq x$ and statement $print(x)$ in B, and guard $x + 1 \leq y$ in A. However, in doing so we wish to retain the correctness of our solution.

We deal with the replacement of the guards first. By the Rule of Guard Strengthening, (partial) correctness is preserved under guard strengthening. So we can replace guard $y \leq x$ in B with $y \leq p$, whenever we can rely on the validity of

P_2: $p \leq x$,

and we will see to P_2 by making it a system invariant. And this is for free: both $p := x$ in F and $x := x + 1$ in A maintain P_2, and we make it hold initially by adding $p = 0$ to the precondition.

Similarly, we can replace guard $x + 1 \leq y$ in A by $x + 1 \leq q$, because with $q = 0$ initially,

P_3: $q \leq y$

is a system invariant as well.

Thus we arrive at the next version, in which $print(x)$ still appears unchanged. On the fly, we introduce a number of queried items to be used later on to transform the algorithm to the boolean domain:

Pre :	$x=0 \;\wedge\; y=0 \;\wedge\; p=0 \;\wedge\; q=0$

A: $*\,[\,$ **if** $x+1\le q \to$ *skip* **fi**
$\quad ;\;\{?\; x+1\le q\}$
$\quad x:=x+1$
$\,]$

F: $*\,[\,p:=x\,]$

B: $*\,[\,\{x=y\}\;\{?\; y\le p\}$
$\quad print(x)$
$\quad ;\; y:=y+1$
$\quad ;\;$ **if** $y\le p \to$ *skip* **fi**
$\,]$

G: $*\,[\,q:=y\,]$

Inv :
$\qquad P_0:\quad x \le y$
$\qquad P_1:\quad y \le x+1$
$\qquad P_2:\quad p \le x$
$\qquad P_3:\quad q \le y$
$\qquad ?\;P_4:\quad x \le q$
$\qquad ?\;P_5:\quad y \le p+1$

Version 1

Note that the queried assertions in A and B are the strongest possible post-assertions for the guarded skips that one may come up with on account of the guards. Assertion $x=y$ in B and invariants P_0 and P_1 are inherited from Version 0.

As for expression $print(x)$ observe, that $P_0 \wedge P_2$ implies $p \le y$, so that, in B, assertion $y \le p$ can be strengthened to $y=p$. Because of co-assertion $x=y$, we also have $x=p$, so that $print(x)$ can now be replaced with $print(p)$.

As for the queried items we observe, that assertion $y \le p$ in B is a local loop invariant of B and that, thanks to P_2, it is globally correct as well: $p:=x$ in F is a widening. For assertion $x+1 \le q$ in B the argument is very similar. The invariance of P_4 and P_5 can now be left to the reader.

Finally, we deal with progress. If both A and B are stuck in their guarded skips, the rest of the system — F and G — will reach a state in which $p=x \wedge q=y$ stably holds. In that state, one of the guards — $x+1 \le q$

and $y \leq p -$ is stably true. So there is no deadlock, and since A and B are still coupled by their multibound $P_0 \wedge P_1$, individual progress is guaranteed as well.

Summarizing the above, retaining what will be needed later, we arrive at

Pre : $x = 0 \ \wedge \ y = 0 \ \wedge \ p = 0 \ \wedge \ q = 0$

A: $* \, [\ \mathbf{if} \ x + 1 \leq q \rightarrow skip \ \mathbf{fi}$
       $; \ \{ \ x + 1 \leq q \}$
       $x := x + 1$
       $]$

F: $* \, [\ p := x \ ]$

B: $* \, [\ \{ y = p \}$
       $print(p)$
       $; \ y := y + 1$
       $; \ \mathbf{if} \ y \leq p \rightarrow skip \ \mathbf{fi}$
       $]$

G: $* \, [\ q := y \ ]$
Inv : $p \leq x \leq q \leq y \leq p + 1$

Version 2

Remark Let us, just for a moment, entirely forget about our problem and carry out a syntactic comparison between Version 0 and Version 2. The only difference is that in B all occurrences of x are replaced by p, and similarly in A all y's by q. From F and G we see that p is a potentially old value of x, and q for y. Apparently, in this example such delays in the arrival of information are harmless.

We ourselves have been searching for simple theorems providing circumstances under which such delays are permissible, but we have not even been able to find a single one, let alone useful ones. On the contrary, in many examples delays have a disastrous effect. Many multiprograms lack such monotonicity properties and exhibit a capricious behaviour under seemingly harmless modifications.

End of Remark.

The Alternating Bit Protocol

For the final transformation we observe, that the "control" of the program only depends on the differences $x-q$ — in A's guard — and $y-p$ — in B's guard. Invariant Inv shows that these differences are only two-valued, which means that by a suitable coordinate transformation we can achieve that the program runs under control of boolean variables only. For this coordinate transformation we propose coupling invariants

Q_0: $c \equiv g \equiv x+1 \leq q$ and

Q_1: $d \equiv f \equiv y \leq p$,

with c — like x — private to A,
    d — like y — private to B,
    f — like p — private to F, and
    g — like q — private to G.

For the invariance of Q_0 and Q_1, we have to investigate — and possibly adjust — all assignments to x, y, p, and q. (Note that each assignment affects only one of them.)

Re   "$\{x+1 \leq q\}\ x := x+1$"   in A

For the invariance of Q_0, we propose to replace $x := x+1$ by $c, x := C, x+1$ and we calculate a suitable expression C:

$$(c, x := C, x+1).Q_0$$

$\equiv$ {substitution}

    $C \equiv g \equiv x+2 \leq q$

$\equiv$ {from Inv: $q \leq x+1$}

    $C \equiv g \equiv false$

$\equiv$ {Q_0}

    $C \equiv c \equiv x+1 \leq q \equiv false$

$\equiv$ {pre-assertion $x+1 \leq q$ of $x := x+1$}

    $C \equiv \neg c$.

Hence — not too amazingly — a flipping of c along with the increment of x does the job.

Re   "$\{y=p\}\ y := y+1$"   in B

Very similarly, $y := y+1$ is replaced by $d, y := \neg d, y+1$.

Re "$p := x$" in F

The invariance of Q_1 under $p := x$ may require an adjustment of f. Just like p takes over the value of x, we try to let f take over the value of x's "ally" c. So we try

$$(f, p := c, x). Q_1$$

$\equiv$ {substitution}

$d \equiv c \equiv y \leq x$

$\equiv$ {invariant Q_2, introduced below}

true   .

Invariant Q_2, given by

Q_2: $d \equiv c \equiv y \leq x$,

will be dealt with shortly.

Re "$q := y$" in G

Very similarly, Q_0 is maintained by $g, q := \neg d, y$, since $(g, q := \neg d, y). Q_0$ equivales Q_2 as well.

End of Re's.

Remark When we ourselves first encountered Q_2, we did not think of it being an invariant. In our first efforts we tried to derive it from Q_0 and Q_1, but that soon turned out to be undoable: there was no way to eliminate the channel variables p, f, q, and g from Q_0 and Q_1, which would be necessary because they don't occur in Q_2. So, it was the shape of these formulae that told us that we had better hope that Q_2 would be an "independent" invariant as well.
End of Remark.

Finally, we show the invariance of Q_2.
We need only consider $c, x := \neg c, x + 1$ in A and $d, y := \neg d, y + 1$ in B. As for the former, we calculate

$$(c, x := \neg c, x + 1). Q_2$$

$\equiv$ {substitution}

$d \equiv \neg c \equiv y \leq x + 1$

$\equiv$ {from Inv: $y \leq x + 1$}

$$\neg(d \equiv c)$$

$\equiv$ $\{Q_2\}$

$$x < y$$

$\equiv$ {from Inv and pre-assertion $x+1 \leq q$ of $c, x := \neg c, x+1$:

$x+1 \leq q \leq y$}

true   .

Likewise, statement $d, y := \neg d, y+1$ maintains Q_2.

In summary, we have arrived at

Pre :	$x=0 \wedge y=0 \wedge p=0 \wedge q=0$
	$\wedge\ c \wedge \neg g \wedge d \wedge f$
A:	$*[$ **if** $c \equiv g \rightarrow$ *skip* **fi**
	$;\ c, x := \neg c,\ x+1$
	$]$
F:	$*[\ f, p := c, x\ ]$
B:	$*[$ *print*(p)
	$;\ d, y := \neg d,\ y+1$
	$;\ $ **if** $d \equiv f \rightarrow$ *skip* **fi**
	$]$
G:	$*[\ g, q := \neg d, y\ ]$

Version 3: The (Concurrent) Alternating Bit Protocol

Finally, we can eliminate the (clairvoyance) variable y and its offspring q from the program text, since they no longer contribute to the computation. The resulting algorithm is known as the (Concurrent) Alternating Bit Protocol — see e.g. [BSW69, CM88, Mil89, Bro92, Sne95, Lyn96].

Final Remarks

The above treatment of the Alternating Bit Protocol is very similar to the one in [FvGS98] (not surprisingly so). There we experienced that the most tricky, debatable and debated part of this treatment concentrated on our model of faulty channels, not on the program derivation itself. In our first draft, we just had

$$* [\, p := x \,]$$

as our model for a faulty channel, and we would argue why. Some people around fully accepted it, but quite some others opposed it, even vehemently so. Then it was our colleague Johan Lukkien who spotted the source of the opposition and told us that what these people wanted to see was an *apparatus* — i.e. an implementation! — with which they could identify a faulty channel. This gave rise to our adoption of the more specific model

$$* [\, af?p \,], \quad * [\, fb!p \,]$$

which we learned from [Sne95]. We then could have gone further down the line by proposing potential strategies for component A to perform operations $af!x$ with positive frequency, but we refrained from doing so, because we felt that the more *logically* irrelevant detail we would bring in, the more we would obfuscate the essence of the Alternating Bit Protocol.

In fact, all the above simplifications have taught us that the Alternating Bit Protocol is not a tricky algorithm at all, but just a simple adaptation of the two-phase handshake protocol (i.e. of the simplest protocol for data transmission available): the adaptation consists in inserting faulty channels between the sending and receiving component, and in equipping these components with facilities to regularly deposit data items into those channels. We hope that we have given, to at least some of our readers, a different view on this beautiful and fundamental algorithm.

31

Peterson's Mutual Exclusion Algorithm Revisited

This last technical chapter is not really about Peterson's algorithm, although it may reinforce the beauty of that design. What this chapter really is about, is a serious and fundamental criticism that one may have of the method of multiprogramming proposed in this book. The method is invariably driven by the requirement of partial correctness, thereby largely neglecting the aspect of individual progress, or "liveness". Of course, we do have some rules of thumb that prevent us from excluding progress beforehand, the most notable one being to choose the annotation and the induced guards as weak as possible. But how good is this? Is there a mathematical underpinning? The answer is simple: there isn't!

The problem is this. First of all, guarded skips (or statements) are an essential and indispensable construct in multiprogramming. Then there is the Guard Strengthening Lemma, which says that partial correctness is preserved under guard strengthening. So this is a nice monotonicity property. Unfortunately, there is no such thing as a Guard Weakening Lemma telling us that progress is preserved under guard weakening. In fact, progress can be endangered (and also achieved) both by guard strengthening and ... by guard weakening — see e.g. the very final observation of Chapter 21. So there is no clear-cut monotonicity with regard to progress properties. This may offer yet another explanation why individual progress is such a nasty aspect. The entire literature on multiprogramming, both formal and informal, witnesses this.

*   *
*

In sequential programming we encounter the two aspects of partial correctness and progress as well. In that area, the latter is called termination. The sequential programmer, however, does not deal with termination as a mere afterthought. On the contrary: he guarantees termination right at the beginning of the design, by choosing a variant or bound function on a well-founded set (e.g. the naturals) together with operations that decrease it. Only then will he be bothered by partial correctness. The question is whether the multiprogrammer should not follow the same strategy.

In this chapter we carry out an (encouraging) experiment along these lines, viz. we construct a two-component mutual exclusion algorithm by a derivation that is entirely driven by formally stated progress requirements. It is a pleasant surprise that, along these lines also, Peterson's algorithm emerges again, and this indeed once more explains the beauty of that design.

The problem of mutual exclusion

We briefly recall the problem statement, for reasons of completeness and as a stepping stone towards what follows.

We are given two components, Comp.p and Comp.q. They are engaged in a computation proper given by

Comp.p: $*[\,ncs.p\,;cs.p\,]$

Comp.q: $*[\,ncs.q\,;cs.q\,]$.

The two fragments $cs.p$ and $cs.q$ are given to always terminate; the two fragments $ncs.p$ and $ncs.q$ may or may not terminate.

Now the problem is to superimpose, on the computation proper, an additional algorithm — phrased in terms of fresh variables — with the effect that

ME: $cs.p$ and $cs.q$ are never executed simultaneously,   and

IP: a component that has terminated its ncs will start the execution of its cs within a finite number of steps of the system, and vice versa with the rôles of ncs and cs interchanged.

Requirement ME — which is the requirement of Mutual Exclusion — potentially hampers the computation proper, in that a component's transition from its *ncs* to its *cs* is not unconditional. Requirement IP , however, — which is the requirement of Individual Progress — states that the computation proper should not be hampered indefinitely.

Thus, after the superposition, the components may take the form

Comp.*p*: * [*ncs.p*	Comp.*q*: * [*ncs.q*
; *entry.p*	; *entry.q*
; **if** $\alpha \rightarrow$ *skip* **fi**	; **if** $\beta \rightarrow$ *skip* **fi**
; *cs.p*	; *cs.q*
; *exit.p*	; *exit.q*
]	]

Statement **if** $\alpha \rightarrow$ *skip* **fi** captures the potential blocking of Comp.*p* necessitated by ME . Fragments *entry* and *exit* are placeholders for additional code. We emphasize that all the code added to the computation proper operates on a completely fresh state space. In particular, guards α and β *cannot* be influenced by *ncs* or *cs* .

Modeling Individual Progress

This time we largely ignore the Mutual Exclusion requirement to begin with and focus on Individual Progress instead. We try to formalize, from our operational understanding, what Individual Progress means for the multiprogram given above.

In order to keep the design as simple as possible, we will strive for a solution in which the *entry-* and *exit-* fragments terminate by construction. (They will, indeed, turn out to consist of a number of assignment statements only.) As a result, the only way in which Comp.*p* can then fail to make progress in its computation proper is by getting stuck in its guarded skip **if** $\alpha \rightarrow$ *skip* **fi** .

We now identify the (three) possible scenarios for which **if** $\alpha \rightarrow$ *skip* **fi** can fail to terminate.

Remark Recall that termination of a guarded skip is only guaranteed if the rest of the system converges to a state in which the corresponding guard is *stably true*.
End of Remark.

The three possible scenarios are

- Comp.q is also engaged in the execution of its guarded skip, while both α and β are false. This is a situation of total deadlock. Using an ad-hoc notation, we preclude this danger by requiring that our solution satisfy

(0) $inif.p \wedge inif.q \;\Rightarrow\; \alpha \vee \beta$.

(Here, $inif.p$ stands for a state of the system where Comp.p is executing or about to execute its guarded skip.)

- Comp.q is engaged in a nonterminating execution of its ncs while α has value *false*. (Recall that the value of α cannot be changed by the computation proper.) We preclude this danger by requiring

(1a) $inif.p \wedge inncs.q \;\Rightarrow\; \alpha$.

(Here, $inncs.q$ stands for a state of the system where Comp.q is executing or about to execute its ncs .) For reasons of symmetry between the components, we also require

(1b) $inif.q \wedge inncs.p \;\Rightarrow\; \beta$.

- The remaining situation is that each of Comp.q's executions of $ncs.q$ and if $\beta \rightarrow skip$ fi does terminate, but Comp.q does not converge to a state in which α is stably *true*. This we preclude through the introduction of a natural-valued variable t, operated upon by the components as follows

Comp.p :	Comp.q :
$*\,[\,ncs.p$	$*\,[\,ncs.q$
$;\, t := 0$	$;\, t := t+1$
$;\,$ if $\alpha \rightarrow skip$ fi	$;\,$ if $\beta \rightarrow skip$ fi
$;\, cs.p$	$;\, cs.q$
$\,]$	$\,]$,

and by requiring that for some natural N

(2a) $inif.p \wedge N < t \;\Rightarrow\; \alpha$.

Then, oscillations on α are only possible as long as *bound function* t is not large enough, and when it is large enough, α is stably *true*. Note that, thanks to the introduction of bound function t, we can now completely forget about the phenomenon of an oscillating guard, a phenomenon that makes classic progress arguments so cumbersome. For reasons of symmetry, we also introduce variable s and natural M, which are required to satisfy

(2b) $inif.q \wedge M < s \;\Rightarrow\; \beta$,

and we choose our components to have the form

Comp.p:	Comp.q:
* [*ncs.p*	* [*ncs.q*
; $s,t := s+1,0$	; $t,s := t+1,0$
; if $\alpha \rightarrow$ *skip* fi	; if $\beta \rightarrow$ *skip* fi
; *cs.p*	; *cs.q*
]	]

$$ *\quad\quad * $$
$$ * $$

And here, our operational reasoning comes to an end. Its only purpose was to get across that (0), (1), and (2) are sweetly reasonable conditions for guaranteeing Individual Progress. They will now serve as the starting point for a formal derivation of an algorithm satisfying ME and IP.

Of course, (0) through (2) are vacuously satisfied by taking α and β both equal to *true*, but we have to bear in mind that Mutual Exclusion requirement ME demands strong values for α and β (e.g. choosing both of them equal to *false* would be fine). So we have to be a little bit careful and find out a permissible spectrum for the guards α and β.

Towards an implementation

Finding a permissible spectrum for α and β means solving (0) through (2) for α and β. We repeat these equations, combining (1a) and (2a) into (3a), and (1b) and (2b) into (3b):

(0)   *inif.p* $\wedge$ *inif.q* $\Rightarrow$ $\alpha \vee \beta$

(3a)   *inif.p* $\wedge$ (*inncs.q* $\vee$ $N < t$) $\Rightarrow$ α

(3b)   *inif.q* $\wedge$ (*inncs.p* $\vee$ $M < s$) $\Rightarrow$ β .

As we already alluded to before, the requirement of Mutual Exclusion is best served with strong guards α and β. Equation (3a) tells us what α can be at strongest, and (3b) does the same for β. But what about (0)?

We now try to prove (0) using (3), with the purpose of finding out what else might be needed:

$\alpha \lor \beta$

$\Leftarrow \qquad \{(3a) \text{ and } (3b)\}$

$(inif.p \land (inncs.q \lor N < t))$
$\lor$
$(inif.q \land (inncs.p \lor M < s))$

$\equiv \qquad \{\text{from the antecedent of } (0): \quad inif.p \land inif.q\}$

$inncs.q \lor N < t \lor inncs.p \lor M < s$

$\equiv \qquad \{\text{from the antecedent of } (0): \quad inif.p \quad, \text{ and}$
$\qquad\qquad \text{from the structure of } Comp.p, \text{ therefore}, \neg inncs.p;$
$\qquad\qquad \text{by symmetry, also } \neg inncs.q \}$

$N < t \lor M < s \qquad .$

So, if in addition to (3), we can guarantee the invariance of

$N < t \lor M < s \quad,$

then (0) is implied. And here is the place to remember that we are still free to choose values for the natural parameters M and N, and for reasons of simplicity we shall use that freedom. The multiprogram as is grants us, for suitable initial values of s and t, the invariance of

$P_0: \qquad 0 \leq s \land 0 \leq t$

and of

$P_1: \qquad 0 < s \not\equiv 0 < t \qquad,$

and, therefore, also of

$0 < s \lor 0 < t \qquad .$

So with choice $M, N := 0, 0$ we have (the invariance of)

$M < s \lor N < t \qquad,$

so that, indeed, (0) is implied, and we are left with just (3).

Equations (3) give us the spectra for α and β that we were after. Now, if the current design is to lead to a correct solution of our mutual exclusion problem at all, we *must* investigate the strongest possible choices for α and β.

Remark This "must" is a direct consequence of the Guard Strengthening Lemma: if ME cannot be guaranteed for the strongest α and β satisfying (3), the same will hold for all other solutions of (3).
End of Remark.

For α, the strongest possible choice is — see (3a) for $N = 0$ —

$$inif.p \wedge (inncs.q \vee 0 < t) \quad ,$$

but because, by definition, $inif.p$ is a correct precondition of **if** $\alpha \rightarrow$ **skip fi**, we can omit this conjunct. Thus we arrive at

$$\alpha \equiv inncs.q \vee 0 < t \quad ,$$

and, symmetrically,

$$\beta \equiv inncs.p \vee 0 < s \quad .$$

And now the only task left is to investigate whether this choice indeed guarantees Mutual Exclusion.

Peterson's Algorithm emerges

First, we introduce variables $x.p$ and $x.q$ so as to eliminate the auxiliary expressions $inncs.p$ and $inncs.q$. We do so in the usual way by adopting the encodings

$$x.p \equiv inncs.p \quad \text{and} \quad x.q \equiv inncs.q \quad ,$$

and adjusting the components accordingly.

Second, we observe that, as far as control is concerned, the interest in the integers s and t is just binary — viz. we are only interested in their being positive or not. By $P1$, they are not positive simultaneously. Therefore, we can replace the pair of them by a single two-valued variable v. We propose coordinate transformation

$$v = p \equiv 0 < s \quad \text{and} \quad v = q \equiv 0 < t \quad .$$

And thus our final version of the multiprogram becomes

Pre : $\quad x.p \ \wedge \ x.q \ \wedge \ (v=p \ \vee \ v=q)$
Comp.p: $\quad * [\ ncs.p$
$\quad\quad ; \ x.p := false$
$\quad\quad ; \ v := p$
$\quad\quad ; \ \text{if } x.q \ \vee \ v=q \rightarrow skip \ \text{fi}$
$\quad\quad ; \ cs.p$
$\quad\quad ; \ x.p := true$
$\quad\quad]$
Comp.q: $\quad * [\ ncs.q$
$\quad\quad ; \ x.q := false$
$\quad\quad ; \ v := q$
$\quad\quad ; \ \text{if } x.p \ \vee \ v=p \rightarrow skip \ \text{fi}$
$\quad\quad ; \ cs.q$
$\quad\quad ; \ x.q := true$
$\quad\quad]$

Peterson's Mutual Exclusion Algorithm

And ... this *is* Peterson's algorithm, and it is well-known that it correctly implements Mutual Exclusion — see Chapter 14 and an abundance of a-posteriori proofs in the established literature.

In conclusion

By definition, showing Individual Progress requires showing for each guard that, due to the rest of the system, its value does not oscillate forever and eventually becomes stably *true*. Temporal logics describe progress issues by means of temporal operators, but they tend to remain rather descriptive. An alternative and more constructive approach towards progress is the introduction of variant functions on well-founded sets. They can serve to a-priori specify an upperbound on the number of oscillations, and when designing programs in adherence to these specifications, the need to care for progress vanishes as snow before the sun: progress is built into the design. In this chapter, we have seen a small example of this approach, the example we promised at the end of Chapter 8. At this moment, not many experiments of this kind have been carried out yet, but we very much hope they will be. And we hope they will be successful, because then the harshest problem of multiprogramming, viz. the care for progress, might reduce to essentially smaller proportions.

A second observation with regard to the foregoing derivation is that it makes crystal clear that the method of multiprogramming that we explained in this book is — to put it mildly — not free from optimism or even opportunism. It is the absence of something like a Guard Weakening Lemma that accounts for it. The above derivation, which was guided by progress requirements in the first place, left us no choice in how to investigate partial correctness. All through the rest of this book, however, we designed our programs guided by the requirement of partial correctness, and in the end we could only hope that progress would be catered for as well. So, our design method is principally "flawed". Yet, in spite of this, we have managed to travel a long way and we have ample evidence to believe that, even with this "flawed" method, the end of this road is still far beyond the horizon.

*   *
*

All in all, the firm methodological conclusion is that the design of multiprograms is to be guided by progress requirements in the first place, and that the incorporation of variant functions may make this practically doable. We gently leave this line of investigation as an exercise to the next generation.

32

Epilogue

Now that all the work has been done, in particular by the reader who traveled this far, we may start pondering on what has been achieved and what has not, and on what we explored and on what we ignored. Let us first discuss two technical subjects that are intrinsically related to concurrency, but that we decided to leave alone. They pertain to speeding up computations and to aspects of communication.

Indeed, one important incentive for considering concurrency is to speed up vast data processing jobs. Application areas for these abound. In modern image processing, the amount of data to be manipulated is so huge that not a single computer — not even the fastest one available — can cope with this task within reasonable time limits. If in axial tomography, the (long) span of time in which a patient is not allowed to move is to be shortened, the introduction of more computing machinery for processing the information collected during the scan is most welcome. The amount of data involved in reliable weather prediction is so gigantic that parallel processing is indispensable. Etcetera. In these application areas one of the problems is how to divide the data and the computational tasks over the various computers, so as to obtain optimal performance. Viable and important as this type of problem is, we decided not to address it. It forms a subject of study in its own right.

The other important aspect we ignored is the issue of communication and its implementation. We can safely state that in this book we addressed just *one* type of problem, viz. given a computation proper in terms of a number of independent components, synchronize these components in such a way that their composite behaviour will be as specified. In achieving such a synchronization, (fresh) variables to record the state of the system invariably see the light. These variables carry information to be changed and inspected by the components in the system. The question then is how this information is communicated and accessed. The simplest physical realization is, of course, a directly accessible common store, but this is only one possibility. Our abstract universe of variables can be implemented in a variety of ways, depending on the application. The home pages on the Internet can be accessed from all over the world and changed by all authorized people. These variables are definitely not stored in a single physical memory device. The same holds for the amount of money on our bank accounts, which can be increased and decreased from almost any place on earth. And in electronic circuitry, the state is held by transistors, C-elements and similar devices, and it is changed by controlled flow of current. In short, how to communicate is very dependent on the technology used. So no matter how important (and intriguing) an aspect of concurrency this is, we decided to leave it alone. It is a separate and separable issue, and a subject of study in its own right.

*   *

*

Now, let us focus on what we explored and on what we think we achieved. For a better understanding of this, let us go back in time to trace the circumstances that gave rise to the work described in this monograph.

When we started our explorations, there was an enormous gap between programmers' mastery of sequential programming and that of parallel programming. Whereas, thanks to the emergence of Hoare's Axiomatic Basis [Hoa69], sequential programming had matured to a well-understood formal discipline, parallel programming had largely remained a trial-and-error activity, carried out in inadequate operational parlance and in quite misleading anthropomorphic terminology:

> when guy_1 wants to enter his critical section, he first does guy_2 the courtesy of setting turn to 2 letting him through if he wants, and only then raises his own flag to indicate his own desire to enter.

Where did this discrepancy come from?

In the 1960s, it dawned upon academia that the main source of trouble in coming to grips with (sequential) programming, was the prevalent attitude to think of programs in terms of what happens during execution.

Hoare's insight was that, if operational reasoning was to be abandoned, one should concentrate on the *static* program text instead and treat it as a mathematical formula with its own algebraic or logical laws. And this is precisely what Hoare's triples did: they did away with operational interpretation of programs in one fell swoop. As time went by, it became clear that Hoare's semantics could be used for more than just verification — for which it seemed originally intended [Hoa71]. Indeed, it soon formed the basis for program specification and program derivation [Dij76, Gri81]. Thus an entire discipline of sequential programming developed, and nowadays each professional programmer using this discipline will agree that he can construct his programs with an effectiveness, confidence and precision that outperforms the traditional approach by several orders of magnitude.

The above development took place in the 1970s, when also the theory of Owicki and Gries saw the light [OG76]. But didn't that theory do for concurrent programming exactly what the Hoare-triples had done for sequential programming? Apparently, it was not felt that way. After all, concurrency had brought about far more complicated problems with all its ill-understood, outlandish phenomena as, for instance, deadlock, liveness, fairness, and starvation, whereas the Owicki/Gries theory could deal with a-posteriori verification of partial correctness only. Thus, the theory got stigmatized for over ten years, and this in spite of its conceptual and technical simplicity.

When due to local circumstances, we ourselves became actively involved in concurrency, we had to decide on a formalism. Knowing that simplicity is not to be ignored lightly, we ventured[†] a leap in the dark and decided on the theory of Owicki and Gries. And then the unexpected happened. Our first experiments, described in Chapter 13, gave rise to results exceeding our wildest expectations: derivation of multiprograms actually seemed to be within reach. This was the beginning of a long series of experiments, which have ultimately led to the publication of this book. Gathering from our experiences, we can now safely state that, in principle, the design of multiprograms can, just like the design of sequential programs, be considered a largely understood and technically feasible process, to be carried out along a number of well-defined design principles. Nevertheless, we may ask ourselves what remains to be done in order to further our abilities.

*   *
*

First of all, we have ample reason to believe that the limited number of examples that we dealt with is just the tip of an iceberg, and that many

---

[†]Nothing ventured, nothing gained.

more (existing) synchronization algorithms can be derived and presented along the lines we sketched. And we know from experience that tackling more case studies is an appropriate way to mature a subject, because it may reveal oversights and disclose new design patterns.

Second, there is the problem of individual progress that we touched and discussed all the time. As we expressed before, we hope and believe that the overall application of variant functions, in one form or another, will in the end prove to be the simplest and most effective technique for handling individual progress. But we have not been able to explore this in full generality. The incorporation of multibounds was merely an (encouraging) step in this direction. As far as progress is concerned, the experiments in Chapter 31 and at the end of Chapter 18 may serve as food for further thought.

Third, one may ask whether our method scales up. We think that the answer is affirmative. The patterns of reasoning and the design principles that we laid down through our relatively small programming problems don't lose their validity when applied on a more intricate or grandiose scale. But in scaling up, a couple of intimately related higher-order considerations will be nearly inevitable, viz. the conception and installation of a body of simple and useful theorems, and the incorporation of abstraction and abstract thought. The body of theorems may comprise theorems for composition and decomposition of parallel systems, including superposition of protocols, and theorems about valid program transformations — of which our Guard Conjunction Lemma is just one of the few specimens. The incorporation of abstraction means that we must be willing and able to grasp the behaviour of a system in terms of its specification. For multiprograms, system invariants and compositionality theorems are likely to play an important rôle in this. But all in all, the conclusion is that we must learn how to specify crisply and precisely, which — alas — is a quite underdeveloped, though highly important field of interest to all of modern computing science.

*   *

*

And here we have reached the end of this book. We take our leave with one sincere request to the reader who feels like expanding this method of multiprogramming or filling in the gaps. May he be guided by the adagium:

> Simplicity is a major scientific concern

References

[AO91]   Krzysztof R. Apt and Ernst-Rüdiger Olderog. *Verification of Sequential and Concurrent Programs*. Springer-Verlag, Berlin, 1991.

[BF96]   D.S. Buhăceanu and W.H.J. Feijen. Formal Derivation of an Algorithm for Distributed Phase Synchronization. *Information Processing Letters*, 60: 207–213, 1996.

[BH72]   Per Brinch Hansen. A Comparison of Two Synchronizing Concepts. *Acta Informatica*, 1(3): 190–199, 1972.

[BH73]   Per Brinch Hansen. *Operating Systems Principles*. Prentice-Hall, Englewood Cliffs, N.J., 1973.

[Bro92]   M. Broy. Functional Specification of Time Sensitive Communicating Systems. In Manfred Broy, editor, *Proceedings of the NATO Advanced Study Institute on Programming and Mathematical Method*, pages 325–367, Berlin Heidelberg, 1992. Springer-Verlag. held at Marktoberdorf 1990.

[BSW69]   K.A. Bartlett, R.A. Scantlebury, and P.T. Wilkinson. A Note on Reliable Full-Duplex Transmission over Half-Duplex Links. *Communications of the ACM*, 12(5): 260–261, 1969.

[CL85]   K.M. Chandy and L. Lamport. Distributed snapshots: Determining global states of distributed systems. *ACM TOCS*, 3(1): 63–75, 1985.

[CM88]   K. Mani Chandy and Jayadev Misra. *Parallel Program Design: A Foundation*. Addison-Wesley, Amsterdam, 1988.

[DFvG83] Edsger W. Dijkstra, W.H.J. Feijen, and A.J.M. van Gasteren. Derivation of a termination detection algorithm for distributed computations. *Information Processing Letters*, 16(5): 217–219, 1983.

[Dij59]   Edsger W. Dijkstra. A Note on Two Problems in Connexion with Graphs. *Numerische Mathematik*, 1: 269–271, 1959.

[Dij65]   Edsger W. Dijkstra. Solution of a Problem in Concurrent Programming Control. *Communications of the ACM*, 8(9): 569, September 1965.

[Dij68]   Edsger W. Dijkstra. Co-operating Sequential Processes. In F. Genuys, editor, *Programming Languages*. Academic Press, New York, 1968.

[Dij71]   Edsger W. Dijkstra. A class of allocation strategies inducing bounded delays only. Technical Note EWD319, 1971.

[Dij76]   Edsger W. Dijkstra. *A Discipline of Programming*. Prentice-Hall, Englewood Cliffs, 1976.

[Dij79]   Edsger W. Dijkstra. On not duplicating volatile information. Technical Note EWD719, 1979.

[Dij82]   Edsger W. Dijkstra. A Personal Summary of the Gries-Owicki Theory. In *Selected Writings on Computing: A Personal Perspective*. Springer-Verlag, New York, 1982.

[Dij86]   Edsger W. Dijkstra. A belated proof of self-stabilization. *Distributed Computing*, 1: 5–6, 1986.

[Dij87]   Edsger W. Dijkstra. Shmuel Safra's version of termination detection. Technical Note EWD998, 1987.

[DS80]   E.W. Dijkstra and C.S. Scholten. Termination detection for diffusing computations. *Information Processing Letters*, 11(1): 1–4, 1980.

[DS90]   Edsger W. Dijkstra and Carel S. Scholten. *Predicate Calculus and Program Semantics*. Springer-Verlag, New York, 1990.

[EM72]   Murray A. Eisenberg and Michael R. McGuire. Further Comments on Dijkstra's Concurrent Programming Control Problem. *Communications of the ACM*, 15(11):999, 1972.

[Fei87]   W.H.J. Feijen. Some correctness proofs for the Safe Sluice. Internal Memorandum WF87, Department of Mathematics and Computing Science, Eindhoven University of Technology, September 1987.

[Fei90]   W.H.J. Feijen. Exercises in Formula Manipulation. In Edsger W. Dijkstra, editor, *Formal Development of Programs and Proofs*, pages 139–158. Addison Wesley, Amsterdam, 1990.

[Fra80]   N. Francez. Distributed termination. *ACM Toplas*, 2(1): 42–55, January 1980.

[Fra86]   N. Francez. *Fairness*. Springer-Verlag, New York, 1986.

[FvG97]   W.H.J. Feijen and A.J.M. van Gasteren. On a Method for the Formal Design of Multiprograms. In Manfred Broy and Birgit Schieder, editors, *Proceedings of the NATO Advanced Study Institute on Mathematical Methods in Program Development, held at Marktoberdorf 1996*, pages 53–82. Springer-Verlag, Berlin Heidelberg, 1997.

[FvGS98]   W.H.J. Feijen, A.J.M. van Gasteren, and Birgit Schieder. An elementary derivation of the alternating bit protocol. In Johan Jeuring, editor, *Mathematics of Program Construction*, volume 1422 of *Lecture Notes in Computer Science*, Berlin Heidelberg, 1998. Springer-Verlag. 4th International Conference, MPC'98, Marstrand, Sweden, June 1998.

[Gri81]   David Gries. *The Science of Programming*. Springer-Verlag, New York, 1981.

[Hoa69]   C.A.R. Hoare. An Axiomatic Basis for Computer Programming. *Communications of the ACM*, 12(10): 576–580 and 583, October 1969.

[Hoa71]   C.A.R. Hoare. Proof of a Program: FIND. *Communications of the ACM*, 14(1): 39–45, January 1971.

[Hoa72]   C.A.R. Hoare. Towards a Theory of Parallel Programming. In C.A.R. Hoare and Ron H. Perrot, editors, *Operating Systems Techniques, proceedings of an International seminar, held at the Queen's University, Belfast, Aug-Sep 1971*. Academic Press, London, 1972.

[Hoa74]   C.A.R. Hoare. Monitors: An Operating System Structuring Concept. *Communications of the ACM*, 17(10): 549–557, October 1974.

[Hoa78]   C.A.R. Hoare. Communicating Sequential Processes. *Communications of the ACM*, 21(8): 666–677, 1978.

[Hoa85]   C.A.R. Hoare. *Communicating Sequential Processes*. Prentice-Hall International, UK, 1985.

[Hof94]   H. Peter Hofstee. Distributing a class of sequential programs. *Science of Computer Programming*, 22(1-2): 45–65, 1994. Mathematics of Program Construction, Oxford 1992.

[Hoo93]   J. Hooman. Properties of Program Transformations. Technical Note, Department of Mathematics and Computing Science, Eindhoven University of Technology, 1993.

[Kna92]   Edgar Knapp. Derivation of concurrent programs: two examples. *Science of Computer Programming*, 19: 1–23, 1992.

[KR93]   Hermann Kopetz and Johannes Reisinger. The Non-Blocking Write Protocol NBW: A Solution to a Real-Time Synchronization Problem. In *Real-Time Systems Symposium*. IEEE Computer Society Press, 1993.

[Lam74]   Leslie Lamport. A New Solution of Dijkstra's Concurrent Programming Problem. *Communications of the ACM*, 17(8): 453–455, August 1974.

[Lam77]   Leslie Lamport. Concurrent Reading and Writing. *Communications of the ACM*, 20(11): 806–811, November 1977.

[Lam88]   Leslie Lamport. Control Predicates are Better than Dummy Variables for Reasoning about Program Control. *ACM Transactions on Programming Languages and Systems*, 10(2): 267–281, April 1988.

[Luk98]   Johan J. Lukkien, 1998. Private communication.

[Lyn96]   Nancy A. Lynch. *Distributed algorithms*. Morgan Kaufmann, San Francisco, 1996.

[Mar81]   A.J. Martin. An Axiomatic Definition of Synchronization Primitives. *Acta Informatica*, 16: 219–235, 1981.

[Mar85]   A.J. Martin. Distributed mutual exclusion on a ring of processes. *Science of Computer Programming*, 5(3): 265–276, 1985.

[Mar96]   A.J. Martin. A Program Transformation Approach to Asynchronous VLSI Design. In Manfred Broy, editor, *Proceedings of the NATO Advanced Study Institute on Deductive Program Design, held at Marktoberdorf 1994*, pages 441–467. Springer, Berlin Heidelberg, 1996.

[MB85]   Alain J. Martin and Jerry R. Burch. Fair mutual exclusion with unfair P and V operations. *Information Processing Letters*, 21(2): 97–100, 1985.

[Mil89]   Robin Milner. *Communication and Concurrency*. Prentice-Hall International, UK, 1989.

[Mis91]   Jayadev Misra. Phase Synchronization. *Information Processing Letters*, 38(2): 101–105, 1991.

[Moe93]   Perry D. Moerland. Exercises in Multiprogramming. Computing Science Notes 93/07, Department of Computing Science, Eindhoven University of Technology, 1993.

[OG76]   S. Owicki and D. Gries. An Axiomatic Proof Technique for Parallel Programs I. *Acta Informatica*, 6: 319–340, 1976.

[Pet81]   G.L. Peterson. Myths about the mutual exclusion problem. *Information Processing Letters*, 12: 115–116, 1981.

[Pnu77]   A. Pnueli. The temporal logic of programs. In *Eighteenth Annual Symposium on Foundations of Computer Science*, pages 46–57, Providence, R.I., November 1977. ACM.

[Ray86]   Michel Raynal. *Algorithms for Mutual Exclusion*. North Oxford Academic, London, 1986.

[Sch97]   F.B. Schneider. *On Concurrent Programming*. Graduate Texts in Computer Science. Springer-Verlag, New York, 1997.

[Sne90]   Jan L.A. van de Snepscheut. A Distributed Algorithm for Mutual Exclusion. An Experiment in Presentation. In Edsger W. Dijkstra, editor, *Formal Development of Programs and Proofs*, pages 195–200. Addison Wesley, Amsterdam, 1990.

[Sne93]   Jan L.A. van de Snepscheut. *What Computing is All About*. Springer-Verlag, New York, 1993.

[Sne95]   Jan L.A. van de Snepscheut. The Sliding-Window Protocol Revisited. *Formal Aspects of Computing*, 7: 3–17, 1–2, 1995.

[Som94]   F.W. van der Sommen. Multiprogram Derivations. Master's Thesis, Department of Mathematics and Computing Science, Eindhoven University of Technology, 1994.

[Tel94]   Gerard Tel. *Introduction to distributed algorithms*. Cambridge University Press, Cambridge, 1994.

Index